PRESENT DANGERS

PRESENT DANGERS

Rediscovering the First Amendment

DAVID LOWENTHAL

foreword by Harvey C. Mansfield

SPENCE PUBLISHING COMPANY • DALLAS

2002

Published in the United States by
Spence Publishing Company
111 Cole Street
Dallas, Texas 75207

Library of Congress Control Number: 2002111335

Printed in the United States of America

To old friends, some departed,

who brought new life to American studies

and America itself.

It is rather for us to be here dedicated to the great task remaining before us—that from these honored dead we take increased devotion to that cause for which they gave the last full measure of devotion—that we here highly resolve that these dead shall not have died in vain—that this nation, under God, shall have a new birth of freedom—and that government of the people, by the people, for the people, shall not perish from the earth.

Abraham Lincoln
Gettysburg Address (1863)

If in the long run the beliefs expressed in proletarian dictatorship are destined to be accepted by the dominant forces of the community, the only meaning of free speech is that they should be given their chance and have their way.

Oliver Wendell Holmes Jr.
Gitlow v. New York (1925)

THE FIRST AMENDMENT (1791)

Congress shall make no law respecting an establishment of religion, or prohibiting the free exercise thereof; or abridging the freedom of speech, or of the press; or the right of the people peaceably to assemble, and to petition the Government for a redress of grievances.

Applicable Portions of
THE FOURTEENTH AMENDMENT (1868)

SECTION 1: All persons born or naturalized in the United States, and subject to the jurisdiction thereof, are citizens of the United States and of the State wherein they reside. No State shall make or enforce any law which shall abridge the privileges or immunities of citizens of the United States; nor shall any State deprive any person of life, liberty, or property, without due process of law; nor deny to any person within its jurisdiction the equal protection of the laws.

SECTION 5: The Congress shall have power to enforce, by appropriate legislation, the provisions of this article.

Contents

PART II

DOES THE FIRST AMENDMENT PROTECT OBSCENITY?

PART III

DOES THE FIRST AMENDMENT ERECT A WALL OF SEPARATION BETWEEN CHURCH AND STATE?

CONCLUSION

Regaining the Past for the Present

266

9-11

HARD AS IT IS TO SAY, the catastrophe of September 11 could have been worse, much worse. It was probably intended to be worse. For the terrorists, the damage in New York City to those soaring symbols of American enterprise and power was complete and the mission successful, perhaps beyond their wildest dreams. But, as we can guess, the insidious plot failed completely in Washington, D.C. Picture such enemies planning not a symbolic blow, a glancing blow, but a heavy if not mortal blow there. They would hardly aim at the Pentagon, which by its very shape could not be destroyed. No, their most important target, more important even than the Twin Towers, would be the government of the United States itself, and our government has its home in two places: the White House and Capitol Hill. One smashing blow at each with a fully fueled jet liner and the great nerve centers, the historic symbols, the concentrated pride of American democracy would be laid waste. The terrorists failed of both, just missing in one case, and meeting with heroic on-board resistance in the other. Thank God they failed. Had they succeeded, their victory and our plight would have been far greater.

It took months of planning, training, and rehearsal to organize this carefully conceived—this brilliantly conceived—blow against our country. Somewhere in the caves of Afghanistan, the first idea for it was kindled in the twisted minds of bin Laden and his most intimate circle, no doubt thrilling them with its audacity and with the economy of effort by which it could bring their great enemy to its knees. Once the main participants were chosen, most of the immediate preparation took place here on our shores, including lessons courtesy of one of our best flight schools. That innocent and unsuspecting civilians—men, women, and children—should be the victims was taken for granted and very possibly welcomed by these self-appointed directors of death and their self-immolating followers in the holy war against America. And so fastidiously did these dark spirits work that they aroused no apprehensions, and the concerted doings of a few individuals succeeded in frustrating the advanced detection technology and far-flung spy network of the most powerful nation on earth. There was no warning, and within a few hours the devastation was done. No one will ever forget the sight of two rigid perpendicular structures, two man-made rivals to great mountain peaks, collapsing like sacks of sand, and people everywhere fleeing in terror.

Almost immediately afterward the FBI began a massive round-up of suspects, mostly non-U. S. citizens, while the country was left wondering how the authorities already knew enough to identify these suspects and whether the authorities could have taken any preventive measures. And how could there be so many such suspects in our country? Where did they come from? Why were they here? What happened to our immigration laws and rules? And of course, why would anyone want to do this to us? Our home-grown "extremist" organizations had wanted to hurt us for some time, and sure enough, they exulted in the tragedy of September 11 as they called upon their followers to lash out further against our stricken government.

One by one the terrorists on board the planes were identified and their footsteps traced. But Americans can no longer view the world in the same way. We have learned—if we did not already know—that part of the world is out to get us, and that our openness as a society permitted an enemy to enter our ports and make its preparations almost under our noses. Within our own borders we aren't exactly surrounded by enemies, but there are enough here to be worrisome, and to do great damage only a few are needed. We have always known that the world is unsafe for many others; now our own country is unsafe for us.

We find ourselves in a peculiar war. Osama bin Laden and Al Qaida have declared against us a "jihad" or holy war to the death. We are repelled by the inhumanity, the fanaticism of it all. We do not understand such people, or the Islam they claim to serve, and we hardly know how to cope with them. Can we preserve our constitutional guarantees, our First Amendment freedoms, and at the same time act with the speed and severity required for our safety? This book will throw more light on this subject than the Supreme Court opinions and leading texts of the last half-century. The interpretation of the First Amendment presented here is the original one and constitutes the soundest approach to such problems.

We need not require government to wait for a "clear and present danger" before acting against mortal threats to itself. Had we had reason to suspect, before the 9-11 attack, that it was being planned—*even if the planners had been United States citizens*—our government could have acted against such conspirators without violating the First Amendment, properly interpreted. Getting that interpretation straight, and showing why the current alternative must be rejected, is the purpose of this book.

And yet the experience of the country with this kind of danger, with an enemy similar in many ways, is not as novel as at first appears. Think of the communist threat here, especially in the forty-year period just after World War II. In Europe and in world affairs generally, communism had become a powerful force. The Soviet Union was one of two superpowers possessing the atomic bomb, and its hegemony seemed secure. In the immediate aftermath of the war, Stalin had strengthened his despotism at home as his armies helped establish communist regimes in eastern Europe. In the republics of western Europe there were large communist parties, always working to weaken their own democracies and strengthen the Soviet Union. So while the American Communist Party remained small, there were influences connected with it that both visibly and invisibly tried to sway us toward actions favorable to the Soviet Union. Zealots trained in the camps or school of the enemy (I say "enemy" because it is folly to deny being an enemy of somebody who says he's yours), zealots who infiltrated the various ruling structures of the country, zealots who often made no bones about their ultimate loyalties and were animated by a hatred of the capitalistic system and all who supported it, zealots who spread Marxist doctrines in the colleges and universities—these were common phenomena of that time, and as difficult for the ordinary American to understand as today's member of Al Qaida. There we had enemies as fanatical, as dedicated to our destruction, and in some ways much more difficult to cope with because, like us, they spoke the language of liberty and equality, and were citizens distributed throughout the society.

Read on to see the difficulties the country encountered in dealing with this dangerous threat to itself. Meanwhile, our weakness in dealing with real threats apart from the attack of September 11 continues unabated. We have grown used to groups calling for violence against the government, against other groups, or even against individuals—as if calls for damaging property or assaulting or killing fellow citizens were an intrinsic and cherished part of American freedom. The Oklahoma City bombing was done by someone whose hatred of the government had been cultivated by certain groups over many years, but nothing has ever been done to stop that teaching. This abuse of the press—this license—is not what the framers of the First Amendment had in mind. It weakens, fragments and demeans our society, and soils the fair name of liberty. I argue against this dangerous permissiveness, as also against other forms it has taken with respect to the mass media and religion that are eroding our strength and diminishing our dignity as a nation.

Foreword

THE AUTHOR OF THIS BOOK is a professor, but his book is not academic in the usual sense. It deals with questions having practical import for us here and now. The limits of free speech and the place of religion in civil society are matters of the moment, and hardly trivial, for they concern the essentials of how we order our lives together. Readers will be invited to enter controversies they know are important, and they will not be discouraged from pursuing aspects of the topics that do not fit into some arbitrary academic system. They will also be led to consider new questions, mostly by way of reopening old questions now held by most academic authorities to be closed.

Although David Lowenthal consults the enormous scholarly literature on the First Amendment, the path he takes is not determined by what has been said by others. He recognizes that the authority of scholarship is the authority of the present, the authority of scholars who happen to be dominant now, whereas the authority of the Constitution arises from its power to stand for enduring principles and to meet recurring necessities. Nor does Professor Lowenthal engage in polemics with other professors. As a rule he goes to the sources, in the belief that the best and most sovereign expression of an opinion, even of an erroneous opinion, is the one to tackle. So he reserves his severities for those responsible for our difficulties, such as Justices Holmes and Brandeis in the *Gitlow* case, and leaves their small-fry followers untouched save for depriving them of any ground to stand on. To be sure, on one or two occasions perhaps, succumbing to superhuman temptation, Professor Lowenthal has a go at such as the Reverend John R. Graham, but only as a mouthpiece of Justice Douglas.

In a further sense Professor Lowenthal's book is unacademic, for it is written in simple, powerful prose that is easy to understand, or better to say, hard to mistake. He says what he means, and when he qualifies a point, it is done for a reason and not out of habit. He is neither stodgy nor strident but rather steady, insistent, and when he needs to be, devastating. His learning is for use and not for show, but though his resort to the grand liberal philosophers Milton, Locke, and Mill always responds to a necessity and seeks to clarify a practical issue, his insight is not prejudiced by a desire for relevance. He knows that theory and practice overlap but do not coincide.

In sum, the book is not academic in the pejorative sense. Nonetheless, as it were without meaning to, it takes up an academic controversy in political philosophy today between defenders of liberalism and their critics, proposing a communitarian or republican alternative. Perhaps it is unclear whether communitarianism is an "alternative" to liberalism, since on practical matters the two parties often agree, and their disagreement may seem only to concern the theoretical foundation for the same, often-misguided, policy. But in theory at least, a grand divide has been discovered between the philosophy of rights in liberalism and the community of a self-governing, republican people. The first is said to be based on the conception of an abstract self that in practice becomes a selfish individual, and the second, on the contrary conception of a common good that demands the sacrifice of individual rights.

Professor Lowenthal's book does not accept that dichotomy. His whole effort is inspired by the desire to defend both liberalism and republicanism. Instead of trying to answer an abstract problem abstractly, Professor Lowenthal brings it to life and shows in practice how "liberal" First Amendment rights must be understood in a manner compatible with a "republican" community. The result is a much sharper posing of theoretical issues and much sounder resolution of them than if they were considered theoretically. In addition to using political philosophy practically, Professor Lowenthal shows by example how it arises from practical disputes.

Above all, Professor Lowenthal does not theorize on his own or merely with the help, sometimes substantial but always inadequate, of his colleagues. For both authority and wisdom, he returns to the American founders. It was they who recognized the problem and produced a solution. They saw that John Locke's liberalism needed to be made republican and that the republican tradition could be revived with the rights of man. Their political wisdom had an introspective quality rarely seen. Rather than spend their time denouncing the enemies of the form of government that they, together with the American people, had chosen, they devoted themselves to the study of its defects. That self-awareness—which may seem easy to achieve but is not—is responsible for the peculiar features and unprecedented success of the American Constitution. Although the Constitution is not a mixed regime in Aristotle's sense, it was made in the self-distrusting spirit he recommends: partisan to be sure, but not blindly so.

I would be a fool to try to hold the reader's attention when something better awaits him. But to conclude, I must express my pleasure—it is no surprise—that so excellent a book should have been written by one of my oldest friends.

HARVEY C. MANSFIELD

WILLIAM R. KENAN PROFESSOR OF GOVERNMENT

HARVARD UNIVERSITY

Preface

THIS BOOK IS AN INQUIRY into the meaning of the First Amendment—its meaning when it was framed and ratified, its meaning now. It examines the Amendment as a whole and considers First Amendment freedoms in the context of the protections the body of the Constitution itself gives freedom. It shows that the words, the ideas, and the political logic of the founders and framers reveal an understanding of freedom very different from—and much sounder than—the one to which we have grown accustomed in the past thirty years. The founders and framers understood freedom to require limits that would prevent harm to others and to the republic. They did not include the abuse of freedom, or license, in the notion of freedom itself.

Created by popular demand, so to speak, the First Amendment guaranteed the freedoms that serve as a bulwark of republican government at the national level—a means of keeping a new and in some ways awesome government responsible to the people. First Amendment freedoms are therefore primarily political in purpose and call for an interpretation consonant with, and not antipathetic to, the end of preserving republican government. Today we tend to begin from the contrary assumption that the focus of the First Amendment is the individual and his rights rather than the needs of the republic or the common good. This understanding of the Amendment has led to a vast overexpansion of individual liberty dangerous to the moral and political health of the republic—and ultimately to liberty itself.

So misinterpreted, the First Amendment, intended as a bulwark of the republic, has become a prime agent of its destruction. For the past four decades and more the Supreme Court itself has led the nation away from the moderate freedom that the common good requires and generations of liberals have advocated. Although the Court took its earliest steps in this direction as far back as the end of World War I, it was in the aftermath of World War II that it began to exercise its vast powers for radical change. Ceasing to be the conservative guardian of the Constitution that the founders expected it to be, often thwarting the will of large popular majorities in the national and state legislatures, the Court made individual freedom its god—at the expense of the moral, social, and political needs of ordered society. Thus, the First Amendment has become a vehicle for degrading and destabilizing the republic it was meant to strengthen and preserve.

What are we to think of a Supreme Court's holding that the freedom of speech and press protects the advocacy of violence and lawbreaking, that it even protects the incitement to imminent lawless action, that it ceases to protect only when such action becomes likely? Calling for the assassination of a public official is protected, even urging it on an angry crowd—until, that is, the crowd is likely to start assassinating. Then and only then may the police intervene. What potential victim of violence believes his safety guaranteed by such a rule? Yet in *Brandenburg v. Ohio* (1969), the Court unanimously struck down an Ohio statute that outlawed the advocacy of violence without attaching the other conditions, in the process freeing a leader of the Ku Klux Klan accused under an Ohio statute that outlawed the advocacy of violence.

Or think of the five to four decision in *Lee v. Weisman* (1992) striking down the practice in Providence, Rhode Island, of inviting a mem-

ber of the clergy (in this case a rabbi) to deliver nonsectarian prayers of
invocation and benediction at a middle school graduation. The Court
found the school system in violation of the establishment clause of the
First Amendment, as if there were no essential difference between
Providence's practice and the creation of a national church. It is indeed
ironic that one of the things for which the "God of the free" was thanked
in the rabbi's invocation is an America "where diversity is celebrated and
the rights of minorities are protected."

Consider, finally, the Court's five to four ruling in *Texas v. Johnson*
(1989) that the burning of the American flag is a form of political expression protected by the First and Fourteenth Amendments. Does the
First Amendment mention a "freedom of expression"? No, it protects
the freedom of speech, press, assembly, and petition. Did Johnson not
have a mouth with which to complain of his country? Could he not have
had recourse to the printed word, and then peaceably assembled and
petitioned with others to redress his grievances? In all these he would
have been protected by the First Amendment—but burning the American flag? Why did the Court assume that the word "expression" could
be substituted for "speech and press"? Why should Johnson's right to
express himself through flag burning take precedence over the country's
interest in dignifying the symbol it has chosen to represent itself? Was
the issue so clear to the majority as to warrant its risking popular op-
probrium and anger in Johnson's behalf? And—almost as an anticli-
max—why is it taken for granted by the Court that the Fourteenth
Amendment incorporates the First Amendment among its guarantees,
thereby transferring the case from the jurisdiction of the Texas courts
to its own?

While the courts have permitted Congress to ban dialed telephone
messages that are obscene, they have forbidden the banning of those
that are merely "indecent," suggesting something like a constitutional
right to indecency. In 1992 Congress and the Federal Communications
Commission were forbidden by the courts to require (even for the sake

of children) a twenty-four-hour-a-day ban on indecency on radio and television. The court of appeals ruled that there must be some allowance in the evening for adult fare—again suggesting something like a right to indecency (but not obscenity) under the First Amendment. Along similar lines, lower court juries in 1990 cleared from the charge of obscenity not only the photographs of Robert Mapplethorpe, but the violent rap lyrics of 2 Live Crew. A 1973 ruling by the Supreme Court has made it possible for the material in question to be found legally not obscene if any "serious" value can be attributed to it. In both cases a parade of "expert" witnesses overawed the jurors, convinced them of the "serious" value of the materials involved, and persuaded them to extend the mantle of First Amendment protection to what was certainly obscene and indecent in the first case, and dangerous as well in the second. Again, the interest of art, if that is the proper word for what Mapplethorpe and 2 Live Crew produce, was permitted to outweigh society's interest in morality and public safety.

From the beginning, a small vanguard of the American people has applauded this apparent emancipation of the individual, and since then the incessant blandishments of the mass media have persuaded many others to revel in it even to the point of regarding our growing decadence as a form of superlative health. But much of America remains uneasy about this liberation—about a sexual freedom that is destroying both love and marriage, about the loosening of moral and religious ties, about the decline of authority of every kind. We have become a nation badly divided between traditionalists and innovators. And how has it happened that the Supreme Court has played so large a part in this development, straying so far from the thought of the founders, our constitutional traditions, and political common sense? One cannot read many of the Court's landmark decisions without wondering how any political system could be drawn into such errors, let alone one founded, as ours was, on a philosophy of political realism. Would men like

Hamilton and Jefferson, Madison and Marshall, nurtured on the thought of Locke, Montesquieu, and Blackstone, have cheered the modern Court's general expansion of liberty? Would they have given First Amendment protection, as the modern Court has, to groups dedicated to overthrowing the republic or to stripping other citizens of life, liberty, or property? Would they have been willing to threaten the foundations of moral and social life by drastically narrowing the legal definition of obscenity? Would they have interpreted the First Amendment as requiring the absolute separation of religion and government at all levels—a notion which still informs the Court's theory, if not its practice?

THESE THREE QUESTIONS of First Amendment interpretation and application are the basis for the tripartite organization of this book. In each part I try to pursue an independent inquiry into the Amendment's original meaning, asking questions that seem natural, and hoping that both questions and answers prove useful to those willing to look afresh at issues that have been examined a thousand times before.

All too often scholars have approached the Amendment as if it were a chaotic jumble of parts that could have been put together in any order whatsoever. Refusing to credit eighteenth-century gentlemen with the rational and rhetorical powers they are confident of possessing themselves, scholars generally underestimate the Amendment's internal coherence. There is, in fact, a basic philosophical and practical logic to it—a good reason why it begins with religious and then goes on to political considerations; a good reason why it links the freedom of speech and press to the freedoms of petition and peaceable assembly. The Amendment states the fundamental requirements of republican government in America. Properly interpreted, therefore, the First Amendment is wholly consistent with the republican framework established in the body of the Constitution. For the founders had already made liberty—a novel and most extensive form of liberty—the heart and soul of the nation they wished to form through the new Constitution.

We will find ourselves pursuing many lines of inquiry to reach our end. Does the First Amendment or the Constitution generally require the toleration of anti-democratic parties? Adopting the reasoning of Justices Holmes and Brandeis, the Supreme Court has in recent decades answered in the affirmative. A more accurate answer requires an analysis not only of these texts, but of the political distinctions and principles the founders absorbed from the writings of John Locke and Sir William Blackstone. And to this analysis, of course, we must add some knowledge of twentieth-century totalitarian revolutions. It should come as no surprise to so historically conscious an age as ours that the word "freedom" in the First Amendment did not originally have the wide-open connotation it has today, when freedom and license have been so completely confounded. Nor should it come as a surprise that, at the time of the Amendment's ratification, the use of speech or press to encourage crimes of any sort, and especially such serious crimes as murder, sedition, treason, and revolution, was hardly considered part of the freedom of the press. The Holmes-Brandeis "clear and present danger" rule for determining just when government may act against conspiracies to overthrow it would have been regarded by the founding generation as both a constitutional and a prudential monstrosity. And it is not difficult to show as a general matter that constitutional democracy is incompatible with the right, as claimed under the First Amendment, to encourage disobedience to duly enacted laws. Even sedition laws, much maligned and misunderstood as they have been, may in certain situations prove necessary to preserve the republic. On the other hand, not even vast majorities of citizens may constitutionally organize for the purpose of consigning some minority to servitude or destruction, despite the open-ended amending power formally granted the people. These are some of the issues dealt with in the first part of this work.

Underlying the political reasoning of the founding fathers was a systematic philosophy of government drawn primarily from the writings of John Locke. Most fully and explicitly expressed in the Declaration of Independence, this philosophy inspired the Constitution and the Bill of Rights as well. Its basic premise is that all men are born free and equal, possessing the same God-given rights, yet incapable of protecting these rights without the institution of government. Government is based on the interest all men have in their own life, liberty, and happiness—an interest which leads them to surrender or limit some rights for the sake of securing the rest. It follows that freedoms consistent with men living securely together in society are tolerable, and freedoms inconsistent with it intolerable: this is the principle which determines the permissible scope of freedom. Above all, those mortal divisions that preceded government, and first required its establishment, must be prevented from recurring within political society itself. The founders seem to have concluded that the very division of individual from individual might to some extent have to be transcended in the direction of forming one people of which all were parts—the famous "We the People," rather than we the individuals, of the Preamble.

Because this philosophy of government does in fact give a novel emphasis to the rights of men, it seems to lay insufficient emphasis on their duties. It even seems to imply that their duties derive from their rights, and hence are less manifest as moral directives. Nevertheless, our government does not merely rely on a low form of selfishness, and its goals are far from vulgar or mean—otherwise, how could it have fired the idealism of men like Washington, Jefferson and the rest of that extraordinary generation? The American Republic calls upon men to reduce their subservience to others, to make themselves independent, to take care of themselves soberly and well, to be subject to no government other than their own. It asks them to live in peace with each other, respecting the differences that remain among them. It summons them to exertions for the liberty of all, even at the cost of life, and makes them the champions of liberty not only in America but all over the globe. While stopping far short of demanding full moral or political virtue, it does require a certain public morality essential to freedom itself. Wholly apart from Christianity, therefore, Locke and his followers, both English and American, were so concerned about the elementary conditions of moral and social life that they were willing to suppress opinions that might destroy the moral rules necessary to maintain civil society. In Sir William Blackstone's *Commentaries on the Laws of England*—the most authoritative book of jurisprudence of the founding generation—this moral concern took the form of excluding immoral or obscene "libels," as they were then called, from the freedom of the press.

On our shores this philosophy of government was reinforced by the moral sobriety of a Christian people. Such a powerful combination of reason and faith may account for the extraordinary fact that neither the Supreme Court nor the American people has ever wavered in excluding obscenity from the freedom of the press. Even to the present they have sensed in obscenity an irredeemable attack on moral responsibility and the family. On the other hand, in the name of freedom of thought, the modern Court, by reducing drastically the scope of what can be prosecuted as obscenity, has helped to inundate American life with obscene spectacles, printed materials, and music. So low have we sunk that we often hear these wretched products celebrated as the finest emblems of a free society. The Court has forgotten why it was that obscenity was excepted from First Amendment protection throughout our history—that is, why the emancipation of sex must mean the end of the family and of love as well. It has forgotten that liberalism originally acknowledged that at some point the claims of public morality rise superior to the claims of individual freedom. This, at least, is my argument in the second part of this work, which along the way discusses some of the controls a free society must exercise over the mass media if it is to avoid being ruled or destroyed by them.

The third and final part turns to the explicit wording of the First Amendment dealing with religion. It shows, among other things, that the Amendment was meant to let state establishments of religion stand, even while banning such establishments nationally; that the framers understood a religious establishment to entail, necessarily, some form of exclusive religious preference; that the protection of the "free exercise of religion" did not involve making court-ordered exceptions to secular laws for religions; and finally, that the Court has erred badly in extending to irreligion or "belief" as such the protections provided in the First Amendment for religion alone. Beyond addressing such constitutional questions, I make an effort to restate the grounds for believing, with both Washington and Tocqueville, that constitutional democracy requires the support of religion.

IN LAYING OUT the understanding of the First Amendment to which I have been led in these investigations, I have not tried to convey all the points of view to be found in the immense literature on the subject. The various positions of today or yesterday will not all, or even for the most part, be expressed and considered. I have made every effort to examine with scrupulous care what I take to be the major alternatives, and at all costs to avoid mere partisanship—otherwise the demonstrative value of the book would be nil. But a compendium of authors and alternative points of view is to be sought elsewhere. Nor have I tried to cover all or even most of the relevant Supreme Court cases, choosing instead to concentrate on only a few of the most instructive ones—those which best illustrate differing interpretations and applications of the Constitution or are most conducive to reflection on them.

Nor, again, have I believed that erroneous but long-held positions on this or that vital subject foreclose a return to the understandings and practical applications for which I argue. If the Court has made major errors, it is important for the nation to know it and take whatever wise corrective action it can. Many of the Court's most fundamental errors go back only thirty or forty years—far short of the fifty-eight years needed to correct the *Plessy v. Ferguson* decision of 1896. Even the far-reaching error of incorporating First Amendment freedoms into the Fourteenth Amendment is capable of correction. But far more important than correcting any given error or set of errors is correcting the reigning constitutional theory, and its implied political philosophy, that to the public detriment has replaced the constitutionalism of the founders and framers. Above all, we must realize that no thinker who has come after them—whether John Stuart Mill, Herbert Spencer, Alexis de Tocqueville, Alexander Meiklejohn, or any other—and certainly no popular opinions of the age, can legitimately or wisely be substituted for them: they and they alone are our founders. It follows that recovering the original meaning of the texts they composed is the first task of constitutional scholarship. The reverence in which we naturally hold the founders will be further enhanced if it can be shown that their ideas remain constitutionally, politically, and morally superior to those that have displaced them. Or where the founders were themselves divided, as sometimes happened, it will be necessary to consider the source of their differences and determine which of the alternatives was most solidly based. I will also attempt to understand the innovations and underlying ideas that have led the Supreme Court—and the nation—to its present pass.

In all three parts I discuss (1) the current constitutional situation and its baneful practical effects; (2) the earlier constitutional view, traceable to the original meaning of the First Amendment, and why it better suits the needs of a free society; (3) the course of constitutional development—the new jurisprudence—leading to our present situation, with special attention to errors in pivotal cases; (4) the intellectual sources of the new jurisprudence and its defects; and finally (5) what to do now. Although I do not follow this order strictly in each part of the book, one general conclusion is inevitable: the new jurisprudence has produced bad constitutional law with extremely worrisome effects on the polity.

A few terms require definition. Generally I reserve the term "founders" for those who helped write the Constitution and "framers" for those who helped write the First Amendment. I call "libertarian" those who favor the overextension of liberty effected by the Court in recent decades, whether their ideas about other aspects of political life may be called liberal or conservative. That over-extension began, as far as I can discern, with Holmes and Brandeis toward the end of World War I. It gained momentum after World War II, and by the 1950s and 1960s began an almost unchallenged domination of the Court. This is what I call the "new jurisprudence."

I should also explain why the religious part of the First Amendment, which opens it, is made the third topic instead of the first here. This is because the harm done by constitutional misinterpretation regarding revolutionary groups and obscenity is even more extensive and urgently dangerous than the harm done in the area of religion. But the overall logic of the Amendment must certainly be understood through the order in which the parts are presented, and then it is vital that we understand why the religious parts come first.

In writing I have had in mind not only politicians, lawyers, judges, and teachers of constitutional law, whose business it is to follow the law, but intelligent, decently educated, and public-spirited citizens concerned about the direction Court and country have taken in recent decades. I have assumed that in a democracy reasoning about the Constitution and its applications should not and need not be a recondite skill available only to an elite of trained specialists. For the sake of specialists and non-specialists alike, I have tried to provide a fresh look at old issues—a fair-minded non-technical search for solutions. To assist those unfamiliar with the field, I have provided a glossary of cases—some more recent than those discussed in the text—before the notes at the end of the book.

Like the work itself, it includes descriptions of a relatively small number of key cases. Armed with a good grasp of such cases and the fundamental issues, thoughtful readers should have little difficulty understanding more recent cases. Throughout I have sought to revive the kind of political understanding and reasoning common in the founding generation but scarce in our own. Once again I learned how important it is to be suspicious of prevailing opinion and to be confident one can make progress on one's own, no matter how many have gone before. If I have faltered or fallen in seeking and presenting the truth, I hope some kind reader will lose no time in setting me right.

I know it is too much to hope for in our ideologically supercharged age, but I beg to be judged on the merits of my arguments taken together, rather than cast into the inferno at the first sign of a disliked idea. The errors for which I criticize the Court usually transcend the "conservative" and "liberal" labels of which we are so fond today. In fact, these errors are common to both groups who, with insufficient understanding and little historical perspective, have adopted a post-Holmesian Mill-derived mode of thought and read it back into the Constitution. Nevertheless, I realize that by attacking the status quo so severely (I hope not unfairly), the natural tendency on the part of its defenders will be to set out against me in ships. Among those who have defended the new jurisprudence, however, are some who have minds that may be swayed by evidence rather than shibboleths. They may be moved, if not utterly convinced, by the older mode of reasoning, better historical inquiry, and more complete understanding of philosophical foundations, all of which I have tried to supply.

I must also presume in my readers a common assessment of our present condition. Unless we share those perceptions and concerns, the need for change will hardly be felt urgent or even important. But if I am right about our condition's being dangerous, and the danger's increasing, our country may have difficulty sustaining national concord and republican government itself unless changes are made soon. There are rough times ahead—times that may prove more difficult than the challenges of war and depression met so successfully in the first half of the last century. One sign of our condition is the noticeable decline in civility, in the capacity to listen respectfully to each other and reason together, that besets us. Itself a by-product of the spreading notion that we are not rational beings, it causes us to fall into snarling hostile groups that have no common measure for deciding differences. I would like to think I have made some contribution to buoying up our confidence in reason and with it our capacity for living and acting together.

In this spirit I say to those whose views I have censured: We have a common cause, the good of the country we love. We all seek the truth in its behalf. That good and that truth must be what we treasure most. Much is at stake, and neither you nor I wish in the slightest to add to our country's burdens. Applying a care befitting the gravity of our subject, let us concede where the evidence says we must, and resist where it does not, letting no personal or party feeling stand in the way.

THE GERM OF THE IDEAS expressed here on obscenity and the religion clauses of the First Amendment first appeared in *The Political Science Reviewer* of 1972 and the *American Spectator* of 1977, respectively. More recently, I contributed a chapter on Holmes's "clear and present danger" rule to *The Public Interest Law Review* of 1991. In pursuing the fundamental issues I have been helped by the keen mind and wit of my Boston College colleague David Manwaring, with whom I argued First Amendment problems for several years running in a course called "Debates on Civil Liberties." I appreciate the favorable judgment Robert K. Faulkner and Mary Ann Glendon expressed along the way, and no less the extensive critique offered by another friend, Edward Lev. I am indebted to both Boston College and the Earhart Foundation for their generosity in affording me the time to complete this project, the former through a sabbatical leave, the latter through a supporting grant. I should add how much I have valued over the years the encouragement given to serious thought and teaching by my department and the administration at Boston College. I must also say how grateful I am to Harvey Mansfield for writing a foreword to this book in which he speaks so well of it—and so touchingly to me—as it launches onto troubled seas.

Finally, I owe much to my publisher, Thomas Spence, and his editor in chief, Mitchell Muncy, for their willingness to court controversy on important matters; to Mitchell also for perceptive analyses and suggestions that have improved the work; to my friend Mrs. Paula Nedved for helpful as well as enthusiastic support, and the final transcription of the text. The original text was transcribed onto the computer by my wife, Sandra Steeves Lowenthal.

To all these my heartfelt thanks.

PART I

DOES THE FIRST AMENDMENT

PROTECT REVOLUTIONARY GROUPS?

Enemies Within

I N RECENT HISTORY, democracies have been overthrown from within by legalized revolutionary parties: the Weimar Republic in Germany by the Nazis in 1933 and the Czechoslovakian republic by
the Communists in 1948. Short of revolution, other problems besetting
democracies are more severe in those countries that tolerate large, active anti-democratic political groups: witness Italy and France after
World War II. In the United States there is the danger, present and potential, posed by armed paramilitary organizations that despise the government and various classes of citizens, and who have to the present
day been perfectly free to organize and train their members and spread
their pernicious teachings.

Liberal democracies have not responded well, or in the same way,
to this predicament born of their dedication to liberty. And their responses have grown weaker, not stronger, with time.[1] Increasingly, their
leaders have come to accept that the nature of freedom is such that it
protects, until the very last minute, the freedom to destroy freedom. In
the United States, leader of the free world and an example to nations
everywhere struggling to become or remain free, developments on this
front since World War II are cause for grave alarm.

Shortly after 1945, the Soviet Union revealed its contempt for the Yalta Agreement by subverting the governments of Eastern Europe. The West responded to the threat of aggression from the East by forming NATO. The United States responded to the threat of domestic communist subversion by supplementing existing legislation, state as well as national, such as the Smith Act of 1940. Organizations devoted to advocating the overthrow of the government had to be placed under appropriate restraints, for they were in fact conspiratorial ideological armies in the guise of ordinary political parties.

Culminating in the Communist Control Act of 1954, this legislative network was not always aimed exclusively at the Communist Party, but it did particularly seek to render that party impotent. Not only was the Communist Party prohibited from participating in ordinary elections, but an effort was also made to control its "front" organizations and its influence in high places inside and outside government, as well as the entrance of communists into this country. The fears which brought about this legislation had to some extent been irresponsibly fanned by Senator Joe McCarthy of Wisconsin, but they were not created by him or by the various investigative committees of Congress. They derived from a genuine threat: The American Communist Party was in fact attempting to undermine the United States government through espionage, influence in high positions in government, universities, and the unions, and various "front" organizations which denigrated the government and supported the Soviet cause. And all this while Stalin was overseeing the most powerful and ruthless despotism in the world and Soviet imperialism was taking hold in Eastern Europe.

For a while it looked as if these healthy and necessary legislative responses by the American people, acting through their elected representatives, would be supported by the Supreme Court. And so they were as late as the celebrated case of *Dennis v. United States* in 1951. With the accession of Earl Warren as Chief Justice in 1953, however, the Court shifted sharply in favor of individual liberty, and hence the claims of

Communist and other revolutionary parties against such legislation. Either striking statutes down or investing them with an interpretation contrary to that obviously intended by Congress or the states, the Court created both confusion and despair in the other branches of government. Prosecutions under the Smith Act for advocating revolution and conspiring to advocate revolution became much more difficult and then practically impossible. It became practically impossible as well for states to require loyalty oaths of teachers and other state employees and to keep those advocating the violent overthrow of the government out of public education and public employment. Past or even present membership in revolutionary organizations could not be made a bar to the practice of law, so far did the Court go.[2]

The impression the Court conveyed was that First Amendment freedoms protect all varieties of opinion and all parties until they directly and immediately threaten to break ordinary laws. In 1969 the Court made itself plain. An Ohio criminal syndicalism statute had declared it a crime to advocate "the duty, necessity or propriety of crime, sabotage, violence, or unlawful methods of terrorism as a means of accomplishing industrial or political reform." Not so, said the Court: "The constitutional guarantees of free speech and free press do not permit a State to forbid or proscribe advocacy of the use of force or law violation except where such advocacy is directed to inciting or producing imminent lawless action and is likely to incite or produce such action."[3]

With one stroke of the judicial pen, the First Amendment was made to require the toleration of organized threats to freedom. To transgress, not only must revolutionaries incite to lawless action by their advocacy, but such action must be the *likely outcome* of such advocacy. Law enforcement must become prophetic. In Ohio the immediate effect of this ruling was to overturn the conviction of a leader not of the Communist Party, but of the Ku Klux Klan. A few years later, in 1974, the Court all on its own completed the legalization of the Communist Party in Indiana. No longer could that state require every electoral party to file an affidavit that "it does not advocate the overthrow of local, state or national government by force or violence."[4] Within twenty-five years of the *Dennis* decision of 1951, the Court had completely emasculated national and state legislation attempting to deal with the threat of parties advocating violence or revolution.

From the middle 1960s through the early 1970s, the country found itself in an state of prolonged political turmoil. The Court's stripping away of legal restrictions on revolutionary groups combined with repeated assaults on the law by irresponsible opponents of the government and the war in Vietnam. In those turbulent days, organized groups on college campuses and in the streets almost daily called for obstructing the war through draft evasion, desertion, tax evasion, bombings, and direct physical interference; for violent Marxist revolution; for assaulting and killing whites or blacks; and for killing police or other public officials. Nor were these calls without actual effect. On the contrary, they led to increased lawbreaking, daily, widespread, and often lethal. Individuals were kidnapped, tortured, and murdered; private and public property damaged and destroyed; institutions (such as universities) held for ransom; and the nation dangerously torn.

Here were calls for violence that resulted in violence, calls for killing police that resulted in the death of police officers, calls for harassing teachers and deans that resulted in such harassment, calls for vandalizing and looting stores or college property that resulted in these very acts. Often the organizations or individuals issuing the calls were easily identified prior to the commission of the action called for. Often such action was the very thing for which the groups were established in the first place. Yet, significantly, in the midst of dangers not merely "incited" and "imminent" but constantly and actually occurring, there was little effort made by the government to prevent verbal catalysts to serious lawbreaking. Nor, even more significantly, was there ever a call for action from the supporters of the "clear and present danger" test—the test supposedly designed to justify government intervention under precisely such circumstances. Those who had devoted their careers to arguing the sufficiency of this principle—required, so they claimed, by the First Amendment—to save democracy from internal subversion, themselves abandoned the principle at the very moment when recourse to it was most needed.

The most recent threats to ordered liberty come less from communists than from the Nazis, Aryan Nation, "militias," and the Klan, freed by the Court to mount efforts at dismantling our constitutional system. Today the public as a whole, and blacks and Jews in particular, seem shorn of legal protection prior to the commission of crimes against them. For it has become clear from the events of the late sixties and early seventies that the "clear and present danger" rule is in fact no rule at all, no protection against groups that seek to strip others of their rights. Government inaction during that violent decade reveals that under the "clear and present danger" rule it will refrain from taking preventive measures and will deal with acts of lawbreaking only *after* they occur. Citizens may therefore find themselves asking whether our founding fathers, known for their prescience and realism, meant the First Amendment to protect those who would use freedom for the destruction of freedom. Was this keystone of the Bill of Rights really intended to guarantee freedom of expression and organization to the enemies of freedom? If not, what view of the Amendment did the framers hold, and at what point, and why, did the Supreme Court substitute for their understanding an interpretation so antipathetic to republican self-government?

2

Interpreting the First Amendment

WHAT DOES THE FIRST AMENDMENT MEAN when it states that Congress shall make no law abridging the freedom of speech and press? From the way we ordinarily read this prohibition today, it would seem that all words spoken, written, or printed are simply beyond Congress's control. Yet it might surprise us to learn that no Supreme Court opinion, let alone ruling, has ever held so without qualification. Even the one or two justices who have at times supported an "absolute" interpretation of this part of the First Amendment have conceded that speech inciting immediately to illegal actions may be restricted by the government.[1]

This point cannot be made too emphatically: Never has the Court or any of its members contended that the First Amendment strips Congress of *all* power over speech and press, and almost all members of the Court have *always* contended that Congress retains more than negligible powers over speech and press. In view of the apparent clarity and precision of the First Amendment's language, how can this be?

One reason is simply that almost all justices have realized that a national government stripped entirely of such power would be seriously, if not mortally, weakened. For those justices who are tempted to read the Amendment simply and absolutely, this presents a great problem and leads to much confusion—perhaps to much hypocrisy. They wish to claim the text is simple and absolute even while insisting on the less-than-absolute interpretation they themselves place on it for purposes of adjudication. This inconsistency in logic they may justify by thinking the spirit of the text requires that they approach as closely as possible to an absolute reading of the Amendment: at the very least government will be kept from claiming even greater powers over speech and press. They may take some comfort in the thought that they allow far less governmental power in this area than the Court itself granted in earlier, less enlightened days.

We should note that both the new libertarians and their traditionalist opponents often agree on one fundamental premise. While some libertarians think of the Constitution as requiring interpretations that change with the times, others agree with traditionalists in taking it for granted that to interpret a law is to reveal the meaning it had to those who made it when they made it. They would not dispute the approach so fully described by Sir William Blackstone back in 1765: "The fairest and most rational method to interpret the will of the legislator is by exploring his intentions at the time when the law was made, by *signs* the most natural and probable. And these signs are either the words, the context, the subject matter, the effects and consequence, or the spirit and reason of the law."[2]

Disagreement arises because each of the two schools looks back to different legislators as the true authors of the First Amendment. Most libertarians regard James Madison as its author and find the key to understanding it in ideas shared by Madison and Thomas Jefferson—ideas later (they claim) rediscovered by Justices Oliver Wendell Holmes Jr. and Louis Brandeis and given expression in the "clear and present danger" rule. The traditionalists, for their part, trace the meaning of the First Amendment back to the Blackstonian philosophy shared by the founders generally. To establish the truth, it would suffice to show that either

Jeffersonianism, on the one hand, or Blackstonianism, on the other, does not lie behind the Amendment's language.

THE ORIGINAL MEANING

The intended meaning of the First Amendment can be ascertained with great probability, and it is the meaning claimed not by the libertarians or absolutists but by the traditionalists. The framers of the First Amendment drew their understanding of it from Blackstone—the greatest jurist and legal scholar of their day, the first to make the study of the common law a university subject, and author of *Commentaries on the Laws of England*, the renowned work on which American lawyers of the founding generation had been nourished. With Blackstone the framers held that the word "freedom," or "liberty," was a term of distinction, to be contrasted with "license," or the abuse of liberty. This view Blackstone held not in order to defend censorship, but as a means of justifying its abolition. Granting that the press could do harm, such harm was to be prevented, or punished, by laws that held authors responsible for the effects of their words. In this way, Blackstone could celebrate the abolition of press censorship in 1694 as the beginning of freedom of the press in England. Though authors were no longer subject to censorship (that is, restraint *prior* to publication), they were not free to print anything they wished. The abolition of censorship was justified precisely on the grounds that authors would be made responsible for the harm their writings might cause. As Blackstone himself put it,

> To subject the press to the restrictive power of a licenser, as was formerly done, both before and since the revolution, is to subject all freedom of sentiment to the prejudices of one man, and make him the arbitrary and infallible judge of all controverted points in learning, religion and government. But to punish (as the law does at present) any dangerous or offensive writings, which, when published, shall on a fair and impartial trial be adjudged of a perni-

cious tendency, is necessary for the preservation of peace and good order, of government and religion, the only solid foundations of civil liberty. [3]

The common law of England did not leave the meaning of "pernicious tendency" to the imagination. It carefully distinguished six categories of "libel," or misuse of words: blasphemous, immoral, treasonable, schismatical, seditious, and scandalous. The first and fourth arose from the existence of an established church in England. Immoral libel involved, for the most part, what we now call obscenity, and scandalous libel seems the same as what we call ordinary libel. This leaves seditious and treasonable libel—the two preeminently political forms of the abuse of speech and press. Seditious libel was the political counterpart of scandalous libel. In fact, the word "libel" was often used to denote what was common to both, signifying "malicious defamations of any person, and especially a magistrate, made public by either printing, writing, signs or pictures in order to provoke him to wrath or expose him to public hatred, contempt and ridicule." In this country the idea of "seditious libel" was given a republican extension through the Alien and Sedition Acts of 1798 and included defaming the most prominent parts of government—the Congress and President. Even so, sedition was not understood as an attempt at revolutionary overthrow: its object was to cause disaffection, disobedience, and even resistance, but not revolution. In England, verbal attacks on the government or its major parts for the purpose of overthrow would have involved treasonable libel or treason itself—crimes by their nature much more serious than seditious libel. In this country these two kinds of libel have been much too readily confused, despite inherent differences that require that they be conceived and treated differently.[4]

At the time of the passage of the First Amendment and the whole Bill of Rights in 1791, not only was discourse about the freedom of speech and press overwhelmingly Blackstonian, but the guarantees written into state constitutions of the day were either stated in explicitly Blackstonian terms or understood in that way. Abuses of the press or libels were not part of the freedom of the press, and were therefore subject to prosecution. The Blackstonian background of the First Amendment has often been adduced by such traditionalist justices and commentators as Edward Corwin. In the comprehensive summary of the Court's interpretation of the Constitution, which he was asked to prepare for the Library of Congress, Corwin quotes Justice Frankfurter's 1951 excerpt from the Court's earlier decision in *Robertson v. Baldwin* (1897):

> The law is perfectly settled that the first ten amendments to the Constitution, commonly known as the Bill of Rights, were not intended to lay down any novel principles of government, but simply to embody certain guarantees and immunities which we had inherited from our English ancestors, and which had from time immemorial been subject to certain well-recognized exceptions arising from the necessities of the case. In incorporating these principles into the fundamental law there was no intention of disregarding the exceptions, which continued to be recognized as if they had been formally expressed. [5]

The exceptions (such as those to the freedom of speech and press) continued to be recognized, said Frankfurter, reaffirming what the Court had held fifty years before. More recently, the Blackstonianism of the First Amendment received unexpected confirmation in the investigations of libertarian historian Leonard Levy, when he unhappily discovered that to those who framed and ratified it the First Amendment meant Blackstone and not libertarianism:

> Freedom of speech and press, as all the scattered evidence suggests, was not understood to include a right to broadcast sedition by words. The security of the state against libelous advocacy or attack was always regarded as outweighing any social interest in open expression, at least though the period of the adoption of the First

Amendment. . . . [If] a choice must be made between two propositions, first, that the clause [in the First Amendment] substantially embodied the Blackstonian definition and left the law of
seditious libel in force, or second, that it repudiated Blackstone and
superseded the common law, the known evidence points strongly
in support of the former proposition. Contrary to Justice Holmes,
history favors the notion.[6]

Levy mentions Holmes because of Holmes's claim, which we will
examine later, that the First Amendment was anti-Blackstonian. But
Frankfurter had already made the basic point. The Bill of Rights, rather
than expressing new principles of government, intended to guarantee
to the anxious citizens of the various states the same protections against
the new national government to which they were accustomed in their
own states. And Frankfurter makes the further point that exceptions to
the general principles stated in those amendments were understood as
continuing to qualify those principles even if the exceptions were left
unstated. Frankfurter's claim was true even of many state constitutions
at the time the Bill of Rights was adopted. In the Massachusetts Constitution of 1779-80 there is a plain statement that the liberty of the press
ought not to be restrained. The New Hampshire Constitution of 1792
says the liberty of the press ought to be inviolably preserved—again
without adding any exceptions. Yet in the Pennsylvania Constitution
of 1790, responsibility for abusing the press is mentioned along with the
liberty itself, and prosecutions are spoken of explicitly. Does this mean
these states understood that freedom differently? Not at all: the exceptions were understood as obtaining without having to be stated. In the
North Carolina Constitution of 1776, section xv states that the freedom
of the press ought never to be restrained, but section xxxiv provides for
trying and punishing "preachers of treasonable or seditious discourses."
These provisions were not viewed as inconsistent, but rather as comple-
mentary parts of the Blackstonian doctrine that the liberty of the press
deserves protection but licentiousness of the press punishment.

After 1800 it seems to have become customary in state constitutions to state the liberty of the press and the legal responsibility for abusing the press together, but in the 1790s the practice still varied, with South Carolina (1790), Vermont (1793) and Georgia (1798) all omitting the qualification, while Pennsylvania (1790), Delaware (1792) and Kentucky (1799) all included it. [7] Madison himself, when he introduced his original version of the Bill of Rights in 1789, put the matter this way: "The people shall not be deprived or abridged of their right to speak, to write, or to publish their sentiments; and the freedom of the press, as one of the great bulwarks of liberty, shall be inviolable." His listeners would hardly have recognized in this statement anything other than the Blackstonian doctrine that protected the press in their own states and would now protect it from the national government. Madison's version is much less specific than the final version, which singles out Congress in its prohibition. But nothing essential is changed by Madison's omission, for the abuses of the press were traditionally punished by the common law, thus obviating the necessity for Congress to make such laws. Even if it did prove necessary for Congress to do so, the prevailing Blackstonian view would not have seen punishing abuses of the press as abridging the freedom of the press.

MADISON VERSUS MARSHALL

The common law tradition, therefore, and not merely partisan zeal, accounts for the confidence with which President Adams and the Federalists passed the Alien and Sedition Acts in 1798. These Acts limited the influence of dangerous aliens and outlawed false and malicious attacks on the government intended to stimulate disaffection, disobedience, and resistance. The Virginia and Kentucky Resolutions, authored by Madison and Jefferson respectively, were passed in fierce reaction to these laws. Both claimed that the First Amendment from the outset had utterly deprived the national government of control over speech and press, rendering the Sedition Act unconstitutional. In Virginia's Resolution, supported by a majority of the legislature, Madison argued that the national government had neither delegated nor implied (instrumental) power to pass such a law, that a press free and unfettered even by punishment subsequent to publication was essential to republican government, and that insuring such complete freedom from the national legislature was the purpose of the First Amendment.[8]

A much less well-known report denying each of these claims was issued by the minority in Virginia's legislature and is usually attributed to none other than John Marshall, whom President Adams appointed a year later as chief justice of the Supreme Court.[9] The disagreement between the great Madison's Virginia Resolutions and the great Marshall's Minority Report represents perhaps the first deep constitutional split among the founding fathers. Marshall begins by raising the prospect of an approaching war with France, for which President Adams had to prepare. The Acts were measures to protect the nation and the public peace against the "intrigues and conspiracies of dangerous aliens," *and* the calumnies of "wicked citizens." If the problems requiring the suppression of libels against the government afflict all government as such, and if the states all claim and exercise such a right, the right cannot be withheld from the national government without a mortally debilitating effect. Obedience to government, Marshall argues, requires that citizens have a good opinion of their government, which will be difficult or impossible to sustain if slanderous attacks on the government cannot be prevented. If the national government has the constitutional authority to punish actual resistance to its laws, as the Constitution's "necessary and proper" clause certainly implies, it also has the authority to punish libelous speech and writing that "obviously lead[s] to and prepare[s] resistance." Such libels are not protected by the First Amendment, since they constitute a serious, legally defined abuse of the press: "It is in vain to urge that truth will prevail, and that slander, when detected, recoils on the calumniator. The experience of the world, and our own experience, prove that a continued course of defamation will at length sully the fairest reputation, and will throw suspicion on the purest conduct. Although the calumnies of the factious and discontented may not poison the minds of a majority of the citizens, yet they will infect a very considerable number, and prompt them to deeds destructive of the public peace, and dangerous to the general safety." [10]

In his rebuttal of Madison's interpretation of the First Amendment, Marshall observes that the wording of the First Amendment varies among its parts, and that while Congress is forbidden to make any law respecting an establishment of religion, it is not forbidden to make any law with respect to the freedom of the press. It is only forbidden there to make laws that *abridge* the freedom of the press, the implication being that laws that do not abridge this freedom are perfectly constitutional. Since seditious libel was not at that time considered part of the freedom of the press, Congress's outlawing seditious libel would not fall within the ban of the First Amendment.

The Federalist minority did not flinch at acknowledging, consistent with this view, that the precise language of the First Amendment would forbid Congress to make laws *prohibiting* the free exercise of religion, but would not forbid laws *abridging* the free exercise of religion. And certainly, we may add, such laws have since proved necessary. But Madison took this as a profound threat to religion and the press alike, insisting that the authors of the First Amendment did not intend to imply such distinctions. In evidence he cited the fact that many state ratifying conventions (back in 1788-89), including Virginia's, sought to protect both religion and speech-press equally and absolutely against the national government. The First Amendment, he contended, was later designed for just such a purpose. [11]

Madison's reasoning is open to several objections. First, it still falls short of showing that the words "freedom of speech and press" in the

First Amendment were expected to have any other meaning than the Blackstonian meaning they demonstrably had in state constitutions. His argument that republican government requires a press free even of subsequent punishment is surely disingenuous, since another part of the same Resolution maintains that federal officials suffering defamation could seek protection for the "injured reputations" in the very tribunals which protected their lives, liberties, and property, meaning the state courts.[12] While this suggests recourse to civil suits by the officials involved rather than criminal prosecutions undertaken by the states themselves, Madison undoubtedly knew that provisions in various state constitutions allowed just such prosecutions. Jefferson certainly knew this, and later called for the vigorous prosecution of certain Federalist opponents. In both his Second Inaugural (1805) and a letter to Abigail Adams (1804), he denounces the outpouring of political slander with which he had to contend and plainly acknowledges the power of the state legislatures to outlaw "falsehood and defamation." As he wrote to Mrs. Adams, "While we deny that Congress have a right to control the freedom of the press, we *have ever asserted the right of the States, and their exclusive right, to do so.*"[13]

Both Madison and Jefferson acknowledged that federal officials must be protected against defamatory libel, but insisted that the First Amendment requires this to occur in state courts—that is, in the states where the libels take place. Such skilled politicians as they must have realized the unreliability of the protection thus afforded members of the federal government. The courts of a hostile state, or a state where hostile forces predominate, could hardly be expected to do justice in cases of defamatory libel against federal officials, and might not even be inclined to bring charges in the first place. If it is important to protect government officials against libel, the national government must have its own means of protecting its officials, just as state governments have the means of protecting their officials. The logic of the case is with the Federalists and undoubtedly gave additional force to the Blackstonian meaning they found in a First Amendment provision for freedom of the press not essentially different from similar provisions in state constitutions.

Nevertheless, we may wonder why the Federalists found it necessary to put in statute form a ban on seditious libel that could be presumed fully formed and available in the common law. The details of the Sedition Act suggest that it may have been not out of low anti-republican motives but high pro-republican ones. Evidently, they wanted to adapt common law principles to republican circumstances and to improve protection for citizens as well. Defaming the government of the United States, either house of Congress, or the president required specific mention in the statute, and the penalties (a maximum fine of two thousand dollars, and two years' imprisonment) were explicit. The Federalists went beyond even the trial improvements Charles Fox had recently introduced in England through the Libel Act of 1792. Not only were juries given much more authority to determine guilt and innocence than they previously had been, but truth was made a defense that could be used to clear the materials charged with being libelous. Thereafter, in fact, it was again the Federalists, in the person of Alexander Hamilton, who further refined the law of libel. Hamilton's defense of Croswell, charged in 1803 with criminally libeling President Jefferson in the state of New York, did not succeed. Yet Hamilton offered a republican definition of the "liberty of the press" so sound that the states proceeded to adopt it as the standard for revising their libel laws. The liberty of the press, Hamilton maintained, consists in "publishing with impunity, truth with good motives, and for justifiable ends, whether it related to men or to measures." [14]

Notice that this splendid and long enduring formulation allowed no right to publish what is false, out of bad motives, or for unjustifiable ends. To keep the right to publish from causing untold harm, it was forced to operate within the framework of moral and civic duty. Notice also the decidedly political bent of Hamilton's formulation, by which he relates the right to the criticism of "men and measures"—that is, to the functioning of republican government.

The controversy surrounding the Sedition Act in 1798 should call into question our contemporary prejudice against the kinds of restrictions it imposed on speech and press—a prejudice settled in our historical consciousness by Jefferson's great electoral victory, and the Federalists' defeat, in 1800. Such is our respect for John Marshall that the mere thought of his having authored the Minority Report is enough to make us take its arguments seriously. Nevertheless, the constitutional argument for federal powers to prevent abuses of the press can be made even more comprehensively and compellingly. We must take an unusually broad look at the First Amendment to see whether we may discover aspects of its intended meaning taken for granted by its framers, but since overlooked or forgotten.

BULWARK OF LIBERTY

A glance at the text of the First Amendment shows that it has two main parts of unequal length. The first half restricts Congress's authority in the area of religion. The second half prevents Congress from undertaking what follows the word "abridging," that is, from "abridging the freedom of speech or of the press; or the right of the people peaceably to assemble, and to petition the government for a redress of grievances."

From the structure of this second half, we can see that the framers wanted to keep Congress from abridging two linked freedoms—of speech and of the press, and two linked rights—of assembly and petition. Why are these two freedoms and two rights joined as the objects of the verb "abridging?" They have in common their joint role as necessary instruments and safeguards of republican government. In a word, they are the means by which the people are able to communicate with each other and with the government about public affairs. The first half of the Amendment as a whole may be said to protect religion from the national government, while the second half guarantees to citizens the means of keeping that new government subservient to the Constitution and the needs of the people. In words the founders (or Abraham Lincoln nearly a century later) would have used, the two halves of the First Amendment together protect "religious and civil liberty." That is the only way they can be understood as composing a single whole, one coherent amendment, rather than a collection of disparate prohibitions. When we understand the Amendment in this way, moreover, our esteem for those who drafted it must increase appreciably: it is the work of men who chose their words carefully, knew what they wanted to say, and in what order.

Put simply, what the First Amendment tries to secure above all is republican government at the national level—a government detached from religious preference and responsive to the people. It is perfectly consistent with the form of government established in the body of the Constitution—a republican union of republics, dedicated, as its highest aim, to securing "the blessings of liberty for ourselves and our posterity." It follows that the First Amendment cannot possibly have been intended to protect political movements dedicated to the overthrow of republican government, as Justice Holmes would later claim in *Gitlow v. New York* (1925), or to grant immunity to speech or press likely to cause harm to persons and property, as his colleague Justice Brandeis would later claim in *Whitney v. California* (1927). The First Amendment is an instrument devised to assure the people of the various states that the new government would be kept republican and prevented from becoming despotic. It was certainly not meant to assure movements bent on despotic rule of the freedom needed to gather strength for overthrowing republican government. If we look again at the second half of the Amendment, which follows the word "abridging," we find a clear indication of what the framers understood to be the only acceptable means of correcting republican government, which they were both limiting and affirming with this Amendment. The people are guaranteed a right to speak, write, assemble peaceably, and petition—all essential means of correcting the national government. Criticism of the government, to keep it republican and working properly, begins with speaking and writing—the work of individuals—and culminates in *peaceable* assemblies and petitions—the work of groups. But here protected freedom ends. By the clearest implication, the First Amendment entitles no one, individual or group, to disobey, assemble riotously or violently, rebel, or replace republican government with some non-republican form of government. It throws no mantle of protection whatsoever over the enemies of freedom. This fundamental political connection between rights guaranteed and republican government upheld was already present in Madison's 1789 formulation of the First Amendment, in which the right of the people to express their sentiments, culminating in the freedom of the press, was called "one of the greatest bulwarks of liberty."

Granting that the First Amendment does not protect anti-republican uses of its freedoms and rights, let us turn back to the body of the Constitution to see whether the powers duly granted the national government might at times require restrictions on speech or press. Clearly Congress and the national government as a whole have no direct delegated authority in this area, but would they be constitutionally entitled to take such authority upon themselves in order to perform the functions with which they are entrusted? Madison believed not, but Marshall disagreed. Both acknowledge that Congress has the authority to make all laws "necessary and proper" to accomplishing the ends entrusted to it, but Madison gives these words the narrowest possible construction and Marshall the much more commodious one that has since been universally accepted (with the help of his opinion in *McCulloch v. Maryland* in 1819). A law is a means of compelling obedience to a specified command, and must be accompanied by penalties for disobedience. Now it is obviously possible, using speech and the press, to counsel, urge, or incite people to defy and disobey duly enacted laws. Does Congress—under the "necessary and proper" clause—have the right to make it a federal crime to promote the commission of federal crimes?

To show the necessity of answering this question in the affirmative, let us consider what would follow if the answer were in the negative. Congress passes a law on some important subject—say on taxes, conscription, or civil rights. The law may have been opposed, unsuccessfully, by energetic minorities, over whose opposition it has been passed. Do these minorities now have an obligation to obey it, or may they work to frustrate its execution by persuading people to disobey it? It is clear that allowing such persuasion-to-disobey spells the end of republican government. To pass a law constitutionally entails the expectation that it will be obeyed. Without such an assurance, every disputed act of legislation enters a continued battlefield after its passage, with no one able to tell how much of the country will comply with it, or what magnitude of force will be needed to compel compliance. Who does not see, therefore, that the Congress that has a right to pass a law also has a right to make it a crime to encourage disobedience to that law?

Government as such—all government—requires a widely shared sense of duty among its people to obey even laws they strongly dislike. This is particularly true in a democracy, where the laws derive their authority from the consent of the people and are passed by majority vote of their representatives. But even a widespread sense of duty to obey the law will be effective only if it is supported by the government's ability to punish those who urge lawbreaking. Without the combination of a sense of duty and the occasional punishment of those who preach defiance, democracy must constantly be on the point of degenerating into civil war or anarchy. For this reason it was long acknowledged—until the advent of Justices Holmes and Brandeis—that both levels of republican government, national and state, may make urging defiance of their laws a crime.[15] Judge Learned Hand, in 1917, put it well: "One may not counsel or advise others to violate the law as it stands. Words are not only the keys to persuasion but the triggers of action, and those which have no purport but to counsel the violation of law cannot *by any latitude of interpretation* be a part of that public opinion which is the final source of government in a democratic state." [16]

Without arguing further, it is clear that Madison erred in the Virginia Resolution when he denied to the national government all powers over speech and press. Marshall's assertion of such powers, in the Minority Report, was correct, for without such powers, ordinarily latent perhaps, given a well disposed people, but inevitably necessary at some point, democratic government is itself impossible.

PROTECTING FEDERAL LAW

Our case to this point may be reinforced by examining other parts of the Constitution. Congress has the explicit right to "suppress insurrections," and it is charged with the duty of guaranteeing to every state "a republican form of government"—a duty that certainly implies at least a coeval right to guarantee republican government to the nation as a whole. In the same spirit, the Constitution defines the crime of treason as "levying war" against the United States and provides for its punishment. But if, in all these cases, Congress has a right to accomplish republican ends and prevent the overthrow of the republic, it must have the means of frustrating efforts on the part of some citizens to cause insurrections, to overthrow republican government in state or nation, and to commit treason—and without any need whatsoever to wait until such efforts are on the point of bearing fruit.[17] In fact, as with all efforts to encourage the violation of law or the defiance of the legislature, the earlier they are forestalled, the better.

The Constitution is the supreme law of the land, and public officials are compelled to support it (or in the president's case, to take a specific oath to "preserve, protect and defend the Constitution"). Does this not imply that all officials are especially bound to do all their offices permit to provide this very support—and to oppose those who would deny or threaten this support? Striking out, then, at the enemies of the republic, and at those who would destroy it by counseling disobedience to duly enacted laws, is plainly enjoined on all public officials, state and national, and not on Congress alone. Some will protest that the First Amendment guarantees freedom even to those who would destroy freedom, that it guarantees freedom to those who would counsel, urge, or even incite to the violation of the law.[18] Such cannot be the case if the First Amendment is intended, above all, as an instrument of republican government, a way of insuring that the national government is responsive to citizens, so that their rights may be kept secure. Only if it can be shown that a Nazi or Communist or Black Panther Party or Ku Klux Klan contributes to republican ends can a case be made through the First Amendment for permitting it legal status. Otherwise, such groups are all legally and prudently shorn of this status from the outset, and not only without violating any part of the Constitution, but in keeping with its positive injunctions.

If Congress may make it a crime to overthrow the government, it may make it a crime to counsel or incite to that crime (as the Supreme Court agreed in *Gitlow* on the state level and *Dennis* on the national). If Congress may declare war and raise armed forces to fight, it may make it a crime to give verbal support to the enemy and counsel draft evasion, desertion, or strikes in munitions factories (as in *Schenck v. United States*, *Frohwerk v. United States*, and *Abrams v. United States*). Congress may make it a crime to assassinate federal officials, and may therefore also—as it did in the case of the President some years ago—prohibit the call for such assassinations. It may protect all its officials from verbal threat or intimidation and its property and operations from verbal menace as well. It may protect all citizens, including especially targeted groups like blacks or Jews, against those who threaten their civil rights or foment hatred against them.[19] Finally, Congress may take all "necessary and proper" steps toward limiting or eliminating the influence of groups hostile to republican constitutional order by outlawing them, keeping their members out of government and other positions of possibly dangerous consequence, requiring oaths to support the Constitution, and so on. Congress has, in short, no constitutional duty to cooperate in a struggle against itself. On the contrary, its highest constitutional duty is to frustrate, by all necessary legal means, those who would overthrow or seriously weaken free society.

A republican objection to this argument might be that it presumes the national government will never grow corrupt and that its laws will always merit obedience. The founding fathers bent all their efforts toward establishing a government so designed internally and so subject to public scrutiny, criticism, and review as to reduce the possibility of its corruption far beyond that of any preceding government. With so many legal means of redress available to the people, there would be little need for rebellion. Moreover, the founders did not think popular revolutions necessarily just simply because the people approve them (a point we will discuss separately below). The people must be imbued with, and follow, the just principles of the Declaration of Independence. Even so, why not for safety's sake incorporate a right to revolution in the Constitution itself, making it legal to disobey and resist unjust laws, and if ultimately necessary, to overthrow the government?

It is clear that governments which permit internal resistance will from the outset be unable to govern. What the fledgling American Republic—the first to be constructed by human reason and ratified by popular consent—needed most, after the addition of the Bill of Rights, was to prove it could sustain a responsible, effective, and stable government. If it could not govern, if it could not lay down laws and have them obeyed, the whole structure would prove no more durable than the Articles of Confederation or the small republics of the ancient world.[20] By pressing freedom too far the cause of human freedom itself could be irretrievably lost. As no one knew better than James Madison, and as we witness with increasing frequency in our own day, popular government is prone to factious divisions, instability, and weakness that must be checked by constitutional and other means if the republic is to survive and prosper.[21] No better way can be found to discredit modern republicanism—and make way for despotism—than so to enlarge the scope of freedom as to make effective governance impossible. This disposition to anarchy, attractive to febrile minds, has proved a much more dangerous problem for America than corrupt or overbearing government. The founding fathers did not propose to add still another popular government to the scrapheap of history.[22] They knew they had to grant sufficient power to their elected representatives for laws to be obeyed, internal enemies frustrated, and foreign foes vanquished. These greatest of political necessities call for effective legislative and executive action, and it is a tribute to the founding fathers and the character of the American people that such action has been regularly, and for the most part soberly, forthcoming.

Fundamentally, only three alternatives to this understanding of the Constitution have arisen in our history. One is the view Madison expressed in the Virginia Resolution, that republican government as such requires a press free from all restraint, not only prior but subsequent to publication. Yet Madison contradicts himself by what he says elsewhere in the same document concerning the way in which federal officials may protect their reputations. He is certainly contradicted by Jefferson's position, which denies to the federal government, but leaves with the states, a power to control abuses of the press. This second position had far more support in 1798 than Madison's absolute view, which in such an extreme form had very few supporters.[23] Madison's view had no supporters on the Supreme Court until, well into the twentieth century, Justices Black and Douglas asserted their "absolute" reading of the First Amendment and applied it equally to the states. Yet Black and Douglas were able to proclaim such a view without being ridiculed only because Holmes's and

Brandeis's revolutionary "clear and present danger" rule had already had such great success. This rule grants free speech and press to all, including groups dedicated to overthrowing republican institutions, until the clear danger of serious lawbreaking becomes imminent. The "clear and present danger" rule is the third alternative and, in one form or another, has dominated the Court in recent decades, leaving aside the uneasy compromise that called for "balancing" the interest in freedom of speech and press against the harm threatened by particular groups.

Since *Gitlow* in 1925 almost all on the Supreme Court have understood the First Amendment to bind the states as well, requiring the same constitutional rule for both levels of government. In this way they have surrendered the Jeffersonian-Madisonian effort to read the First Amendment absolutely against the national government, while leaving authority over press abuses to the states. We must remember that Jefferson agreed with Marshall about the danger of seditious libel to republican government, disagreeing only as to the level of government which should address it. Moreover, the founding generation would have considered direct calls for the revolutionary overthrow of the republic, because of their treasonous intent, much more seriously criminal than the seditious libel of their time. It is fair to say, therefore, that the new Holmes-Brandeis regime constitutes a radical departure from what the founding generation, Jeffersonians and Federalists alike, thought necessary to preserve republican institutions. And this at a time when organized ideological threats to the American Republic have become much more dangerous than anything known in its early years.

Over recent decades, then, the national judiciary, in an unjustified rupture of its own long tradition, has intervened to restrict our constitutional ability to cope with urgent political problems. At the expense of the other two branches, it has made itself the arbiter of precisely what action may be taken against those striving to overthrow the government or violate its laws. Why has it thus intruded itself? Is it aware of the dangers to its own status in our constitutional scheme, to the rule of law, and to the Republic? What novel view of political life, supposedly drawn from the Constitution and missed by earlier generations, did Holmes, Brandeis, and their followers adopt, abandoning the Blackstonian tradition and bringing the Court into almost constant conflict with the elected representatives of the people, state and national? These are the questions we must now address.

3

The Constitutional Revolution
of Holmes and Brandeis

D ESPITE THE ELECTORAL VICTORIES OF THE JEFFERSONIANS in
and after 1800, the constitutional view of the freedom of the
press that established itself in both court and country was
thoroughly Blackstonian. This is clear not only from the provisions that
remained part of old state constitutions and were written into new ones
throughout the nineteenth century, but from the most respected interpretations of the Constitution. Foremost by far among these was Joseph Story's *Commentaries on the Constitution of the United States* (1833).
Story was a member of the Supreme Court and a friend and associate
of John Marshall despite having been appointed by James Madison. His
work remained the standard treatise on the Constitution well into the
twentieth century. While arguing powerfully in favor of the Bill of
Rights, Story considered it obvious that the First Amendment was
meant to protect the freedom, not the abuses, of the press:

> That this amendment was intended to secure to every citizen an
> absolute right to speak, or write, or print whatever he might please,
> without any responsibility, public or private, therefor, is a suppo-
> sition too wild to be indulged by any rational man. This would be
> to allow to every citizen a right to destroy at his pleasure the repu-

tation, the peace, the property, and even the personal safety of every other citizen. A man might, out of mere malice and revenge, accuse another of the most infamous crimes. . . ; might inflict the most distressing punishments upon the weak, the timid and the innocent; might prejudice all a man's civil, and political, and private rights; and might stir up sedition, rebellion and treason even against the government itself. . . . It is plain, then, that the language of this amendment imports no more than that every man shall have a right to speak, write and print his opinions upon any subject whatsoever, without any prior restraint, so always that he does not injure any other person in his rights, person, property or reputation; and so always that he does not thereby disturb the public peace, or attempt to subvert the government. It is neither more nor less than an expression of the great doctrine recently brought into operation in the law of libel, *that every man shall be at liberty to publish what is true, with good motives and for justifiable ends.* And with this reasonable limitation it is not only right in itself, but it is an inestimable privilege in a free government. . . .[1]

This is purest Blackstone, perfected in the emphasized phrase by the definition of libel Hamilton had proposed in the Croswell case. It was the view of the First Amendment (and of the freedom of speech and press within the states) universally accepted throughout the rest of the nineteenth and well into the twentieth century and was articulated in a number of cases which came before the Court near the end of the century. In *Davis v. Beason* (1890), a unanimous Court upheld an Idaho territory statute making it illegal to encourage bigamy or polygamy. Given that these are crimes, said the Court, "to teach, advise and counsel their practice is to aid in their commission, and such teaching and counseling are themselves criminal and proper subjects of punishment, as aiding and abetting crime are in all other cases."[2] We recognize in this passage the same principle Judge Learned Hand restated so pointedly in the Masses Publishing Company case of 1917.[3] Some twenty-five years after *Davis*, it was still the guiding principle in *Fox v. Washington* (1915), in which the Court upheld the constitutionality of a Washington statute outlawing "the wilful printing, circulation, etc., of matter advocating or encouraging the commission of any crime or breach of the peace or which shall tend to encourage or advocate disrespect for law or any court or courts of justice." [4] Again the Court agreed it may constitutionally be made a statutory crime to advocate a crime, and the courts themselves may be protected from defamation.

CLEAR AND PRESENT DANGER

This is the constitutional tradition that continued to guide the Court in cases associated with World War I, in the *Gitlow* case of 1925, and even as late as the *Dennis* case of 1951. It was the tradition Justice Holmes found securely in place when he joined the Court in 1902. Nevertheless, Holmes began in 1919 to challenge the tradition with his "clear and present danger" test, but so powerful was the tradition that he himself accepted it between 1907 and 1919, as the following excerpts from his opinions reveal. First, we have a statement in *Patterson v. Colorado* (1907) directly interpreting the meaning of the freedom of the press in a manner highly reminiscent of Blackstone: "[T]he main purpose of such constitutional provisions is 'to prevent all such previous restraints upon publications as had been practiced by other governments,' and they do not prevent the subsequent punishment of such as may be deemed contrary to the public welfare. . . . The preliminary freedom extends as well to the false as to the true; the subsequent punishment may extend as well to the true as to the false." [5] And in *Frohwerk v. United States* (1919): "[T]he First Amendment while prohibiting legislation against free speech as such cannot have been and obviously was not, intended to give immunity for every possible use of language. . . . We venture to believe that neither Hamilton nor Madison, nor any other competent person then or later, ever supposed that to make criminal the counseling of a murder within the jurisdiction of Congress would be an unconstitutional interference with free speech."[6]

It is difficult to believe that the author of these concise and entirely sympathetic renditions of earlier constitutional doctrine—of the Blackstonianism that despite the controversy of the Alien and Sedition Acts reigned uninterrupted in all courts of the nation—should at almost the same moment as *Frohwerk* devise the wording that would undermine that doctrine. For in neither of the above two cases did Holmes suggest that Congress or a state could find words encouraging crimes illegal only when such words would immediately precipitate criminal activity or that judges and juries were ultimately to decide just when a "clear and present danger" entitled government to intervene against speech or press.

Holmes first employed the idea of "clear and present danger" when he spoke for the Court in *Schenck* (decided a week before *Frohwerk*), but its potential for undermining statutes and convictions was not immediately obvious. Schenck and other leaders of the Socialist Party had been found guilty of violating the Espionage Act Congress had passed two years before in 1917, during World War I. They had published, and mailed to draftees, a leaflet attacking the draft as a form of despotism and the war against Germany as a capitalist war. Holmes was willing to find that "in many places and in ordinary times the defendants in saying all that was said in the circular would have been within their constitutional rights." But a war was on, the words were being addressed to draftees, and "The question in every case is whether the words used are used in such circumstances and are of such a nature as to create a clear and present danger that they will bring about the substantive evils that Congress has a right to prevent."[7]

Holmes provides no direct interpretation of the First Amendment in support of this new understanding of its requirements, simply quoting as a precedent an earlier and very general finding that "the character of every act depends on the circumstances in which it is done." He does indicate that a similar attack on the draft in peacetime might well be constitutional. But if the draft is legally adopted, need Congress tolerate writings that counsel draft evasion or desertion? Under the old Blackstonian rule, and within its power of making and enforcing all legislation, it need not. The government is not compelled to show a "clear and present danger" that draftees might be affected—with a danger arising only if the nation is at war. Even if the advocacy occurred in peacetime, it could affect one potential or actual soldier, which would constitute an interference with Congress's power to raise armed forces.

That same year, in *Abrams*, Holmes, joined by Brandeis, issued a dissent that has been highly lauded and provides a somewhat fuller exposition of their argument. They assert the authority of something they call "the theory of our Constitution" and hold that the logical consequence of believing one's own opinions infallible is the desire to persecute others should their opinions differ. But once Americans realize that

> time has upset many fighting faiths, they may come to believe even more than they believe the very foundations of their own conduct that the ultimate good desired is better reached by free trade in ideas—that the best test of truth is the power of the thought to get itself accepted in the competition of the market, and that truth is the only ground upon which their wishes safely can be carried out. That at any rate is the theory of our Constitution. It is an experiment, as all life is an experiment. . . . While that experiment is part of our system I think that we should be eternally vigilant against attempts to check the expression of opinions that we loathe and believe to be fraught with death, unless they so imminently threaten immediate interference with the lawful and pressing purposes of the law that an immediate check is required to save the country. I wholly disagree with the argument of the Government

that the First Amendment left the common law as to seditious libel in force. History seems to me against the notion. I have conceived that the United States through many years had shown its repentance for the Sedition Act of 1798 by repaying the fine that it imposed. [8]

Only dangerous emergencies, Holmes and Brandeis conclude, warrant making any exceptions to the "sweeping command" of the First Amendment. We have already seen many reasons why Holmes's statement about seditious libel is mistaken. Leonard Levy, turning Holmes's own phrase against him, feels compelled to maintain, despite his own inclinations, that "contrary to Justice Holmes history favors the notion" that such exceptions are appropriate.[9] As for the country's repenting of the Sedition Act, this repentance, begun under Jefferson, is hardly a constitutional argument. For even some Federalists felt that the Act, while constitutional, was divisive and unwise. Nor does Holmes consider that his "clear and present danger" rule is not what Jefferson and Madison thought the First Amendment required, which was no *national* authority over speech and press. Holmes and Brandeis have many more historical obstacles to overcome than they admit in their dissent, including evidence from state constitutions of the day. But their greatest innovation, so far, lies in their offhand way of referring to "fighting faiths," clearly intending the term to apply not only to actual religious beliefs but to secular political faiths as well. In fact, it seems in particular they mean to include beliefs such as those on which the American system of government is founded. American political beliefs are "fighting faiths" like all the others.

For the founding generation, the principles which guided them were not matters merely of faith, even "fighting" faith. In the Declaration, Jefferson and the unanimous Continental Congress speak of them as "self-evident truths"—truths *infallibly* known to be true. Holmes and Brandeis appear to have lost contact with the political philosophy that underlies the Declaration and the Constitution and was shared by Jeffersonians and Hamiltonians alike.

The two justices insist that the "theory of our Constitution" requires that we allow the expression of opinions that "we loathe and believe fraught with death." They mean we must allow the "fighting faith" original to our system of government to be confronted by opposing "fighting faiths" we loathe and believe destructive of republican government. They would leave it to the marketplace of ideas to determine whether the "fighting faith" of our system is to be replaced by some form of monarchy, despotism, oligarchy, or caste system. They seem to have forgotten that our system of government is based on an original agreement (implemented by popular ratification) to unite in accepting only a form of government specifically designed to protect the inalienable rights of every citizen. Every system of government opposed to such an end is considered fundamentally illegitimate and inherently antagonistic to our own. To escape a condition—it was called the "state of nature"—in which their rights were insecure, individuals submitted to government. Uniting with like-minded people who shared the same purpose, they determined to establish a government that would secure the inalienable and equal rights of all. Those who do not share this purpose, who favor inequality or despotism, are from the outset excluded from the union. They constitute its first enemies, since what they desire will return the other members of society to the insecurity of the state of nature. Those of the same stamp who later arise within the society are enemies for precisely the same reason, and have no just claim to use the freedoms secured and maintained by others for the sake of destroying those freedoms or depriving any or all citizens of their rights.

Holmes and Brandeis make a further error in supposing that belief in the infallibility of our ideas necessarily leads us to persecute those who differ with us, and as a corollary, that the sense of our own fallibility is the foundation of toleration and free expression. On the contrary, it is the belief in fixed standards of justice that gives unbending support to the principle of toleration. This, in fact, is how the founders conceived an idea of religious, philosophical, and even political toleration so broad as to encompass all but outright enemies of toleration itself. Certainly it does not follow from Holmes's and Brandeis's philosophy, which denies such fixed standards, that we should adopt and preserve as infallible the fixed standard of toleration. Toleration as a "fighting faith" will not only disappear when the opposing forces of intolerance overpower it, but its erstwhile defenders will be among the first to surrender, since it has no status whatsoever as a fixed standard deserving of their allegiance. Toleration will have succumbed to the struggle for existence, in which not the just but the strong survive. And one of the forces contributing to its downfall will be the legal opinions of Supreme Court justices.

SERIOUS INJURY

If the foregoing appears an unwarranted distortion of Holmes's and Brandeis's opinions, we need only to turn to their famous dissent in *Gitlow* to be persuaded otherwise. In 1925 the Supreme Court confirmed Gitlow's conviction for engaging in what a New York statute defined as criminal anarchy. Gitlow was a member of the Left Wing Section of the Socialist Party and had cooperated in publishing the "Manifesto and Program of the Left Wing," calling for the violent overthrow of the government and its replacement by the dictatorship of the proletariat. Applying traditional constitutional doctrine, the majority of the Court had no difficulty finding that the First Amendment did not protect Gitlow's call for revolution. Dissenting, Holmes and Brandeis claimed there was clearly no imminent danger of an attempt to overthrow the government by Gitlow's tiny band, and hence no constitutional ground for preventing them from publishing their revolutionary tracts until such time as they presented such a danger. This innovation would have had the effect of legalizing the Communist Party and exposing the country much more extensively to the manifold evils of communist subversion. As if this were not enough, the two justices saw fit to add what may be the single most disgraceful sentence in our jurisprudence: "If in the long run the beliefs expressed in proletarian dictatorship are destined to be accepted by the dominant forces of the community, the only meaning of free speech is that they should be given their chance and have their way."[10]

Holmes and Brandeis did not stop to wonder at the tragic irony of free speech leading to the end of free speech, of the marketplace of ideas undoing itself, of democracy clearing the way for dictatorship. They did not even qualify their opinion by insisting that the "dominant forces" consist of a majority of the people and "have their way" democratically rather than through the brute seizure of power. Nor did they speak of the duty to resist proletarian dictatorship, nor of the likelihood that it would entail a dictatorship *over* the proletariat, as was already apparent from the example of Bolshevik Russia. Nevertheless, the real surprise in this statement is their failure to invoke their own "clear and present danger" rule, which would supposedly protect the republic against those who would overthrow it through "dominant forces." The failure of the authors of this rule even to mention its application at the very juncture at which they claimed it would be useful betrays its utter hollowness and casts a morbid light on their novel approach to the Constitution.

Holmes and Brandeis perpetuated this absurdity in their concurrence (written by Brandeis) in *Whitney v. California* (1927). Applying the First Amendment to the state of California as well as the federal government, Brandeis claims that the Amendment forbids the states to prohibit the dissemination of doctrines even the vast majority of its citizens believe to be "false and fraught with evil consequences."[11] Even directly advocating the violation of law is protected by the First Amendment "where the advocacy falls short of incitement and there is nothing to indicate the advocacy would immediately be acted on." Then, in a sentence which must surely qualify as the second most disgraceful in our jurisprudence, Brandeis adds that "the fact that speech is likely to result in some violence or in destruction of property is not enough to justify its suppression. There must be the probability of serious injury to the state." [12]

Here, Brandeis presents us with another reversal of the principles held by the founding generation and a contradiction with himself as well. Has he not just implied that an incitement to the violation of law would be *unprotected* by the Constitution if there were evidence it would immediately be acted on? Now he adds that the evil which speech tries to bring about must be "serious" to warrant its suppression. Yet contrary to his own previous formulation, even *likely* injury to individuals (what he calls "some violence") or to property does not qualify as sufficiently serious. Counseling the murder of an individual, on this account, is protected by the First Amendment. Inciting a murder is protected by the First Amendment. Inciting a murder *with a likelihood of its occurring* is protected by the First Amendment. All these cases fall short of "serious injury to the state," and speech is otherwise too important to restrict, as "those who won our independence" knew.

One would expect such a questionable reading of the constitution to have bedeviling conceptual offspring. We should comment briefly on two of these. First, Brandeis maintains that the freedom of speech and press even protects assembling a political party "advocating the desirability of a proletarian revolution by mass action," at least so long as it is to take place "far in the future." Brandeis's failure here to distinguish "assembling a political party" to overthrow the government from the advocacy of such overthrow by individuals is certainly surprising, for he believes the freedom to organize such a conspiracy follows directly from the freedom of speech and press itself. A century earlier Tocqueville had insisted on the distinction between the freedom of individuals and the much more limited freedom of associations. Two decades after *Whitney*, in *Dennis*, Justice Jackson would still insist on the special dangers presented by organized political conspiracies.

Second is the dichotomy between advocacy and incitement, which leaped from Brandeis's pen in *Whitney*. In its original form, the "clear and present danger" rule did not incorporate this dichotomy. The central question was whether there was an imminent criminal effect rather than whether the use of speech or press sought to produce such an effect immediately (incitement) or only express support for it (advocacy). In fact, Holmes's and Brandeis's insistence in their *Gitlow* dissent, two years before *Whitney*, that "every idea is an incitement" would obviously, if maintained, make this dichotomy impossible. Yet in their *Whitney* concurrence they do not maintain it. They make the requirement of incitement (and not just advocacy) a necessary component of the "clear and present danger" test, permitting a leading constitutional authority to declare in 1941 that "the real issue in every free speech controversy is this: whether the state can punish all words which have some tendency, however remote, to bring about acts in violation of law, or only words which directly incite to acts in violation of law." [13]

At precisely what point does advocating violent revolution become an incitement? Is it, as sometimes contended later by Justices Black and Douglas and constitutional lawyers like Thomas Emerson, when speech is part of a criminal action already under way—that is, closely "brigaded" with action? Often this would be much too late to save democracy from its revolutionary opponents. Apart from considerations of prudence, what about clarity of definitions? Is it possible to advocate in highly charged language a crime two years hence, but incite in quiet, rational tones to one now? Must advocacy always be general rather than specific? May one advocate the assassination of the President at the earliest possible moment? When a man says to a mob, "You have a right to kill your opponents," or "Your opponents deserve to die," but does not urge the mob toward any action, is he advocating or inciting? When a man says to his co-conspirators, "We must work our way into the unions and then commit sabotage for the communist cause," should this be any the less illegal because he is not calling for sabotage right now?

Our constitutional tradition, seeking to remain consistent with the operation and preservation of a strong democracy, did not concern itself with such hair-splitting. It did not seek to protect the individual regardless of his intention of doing harm, but thought the clearly demonstrable effort to do harm of any kind made him undeserving of protection. It held that the man who might say, "The President deserves to be shot, but wait until next year, when the time will be riper," is only slightly less criminal than one who urges it now, whether or not it is likely to occur, for such a person is calling for an action destructive of republican self-government. To such a person, or to those who heed him, only the opportunity, not the incentive, is lacking. Government, of course, will find incitements to immediate crime more urgently dangerous, but incitements shade off into advocacy (though Holmes's "every idea is an incitement" goes too far), and it is impossible, and undesirable, to try to distinguish in law where one begins and the other ends. Together they share a criminal intent that the law need not and should not tolerate.[14]

DID THE FOUNDERS AGREE?

Brandeis's appeal to "those who won our independence" for this novel understanding of the scope of our liberty would be merely ridiculous or contemptible had it not been made venerable by his reputation. Even a cursory reading of Justice Story's interpretation of the liberty of the press, expressing the basic Blackstonian view that prevailed for so long, brings us much closer to the understanding of the founding fathers. The founding generation would have been aghast at a so-called "theory of our Constitution" that might require us to accept subjection to something called "proletarian dictatorship" without resistance or objection. This, they would rightly conclude, is what comes from abandoning the principles of the Declaration of Independence and especially the truth that all men are endowed with equal and inalienable rights. This loss of fixed standards of justice made Holmes and Brandeis, the judicial caretakers of the republic, willing to expose men to the domination of sheer power. Among the founders, Jeffersonians and Hamiltonians alike would have refused to accept this as "the command of the Constitution." For, unlike Holmes and Brandeis, the founders did not take so casual a view of violence to persons or property, or of organized efforts to overthrow the republic. They regarded the freedom of speech and press primarily as bulwarks of republican government, and republican government as aimed at securing inalienable rights, including the rights to life and property.[15] They did not seek to protect political change in the abstract, and certainly none that would result in the destruction of democracy and the end of the freedoms of speech and press themselves. Nor would they have been inclined to allow, as Brandeis does, a general right to advocate the violation of law, since they would have wondered whether the rule of law could long be sustained on such a basis.

To fix this point firmly in the mind, compare Holmes's and Brandeis's servile yielding to the "dominant forces" of proletarian dictatorship with the cry of the young Abraham Lincoln—nourished on the principles of the Declaration of Independence—when he was forced to consider that his country might find its freedom overwhelmed from within: "If ever I feel the soul within me elevate and expand to those dimensions not wholly unworthy of its almighty Architect, it is when I contemplate the cause of my country deserted by all the world beside, and I standing boldly and alone, and hurling defiance at her victorious oppressors. . . . But if, after all, we shall fail, be it so. We still shall have the proud consolation of saying to our consciences, and to the departed shade of our country's freedom, that the cause approved of our judgment, and adored of our hearts, in disaster, in chains, in torture, in death, we never faltered in defending."[16]

Holmes, Brandeis, and their libertarian followers frequently cite two members of the founding generation—Madison and Jefferson—in favor of the "clear and present danger" rule. One would think the First Amendment had flowed directly from their joint pen, and was of a piece with all they wrote elsewhere. The case of Jefferson has special interest for us. Jefferson was neither a member of the constitutional convention nor a framer of the First Amendment. His views, strictly speaking, are extraneous to the Constitution, and may or may not be those of the founders and framers. In *Whitney*, Brandeis quotes two passages from Jefferson in support of his view of the First Amendment. One he presents without reference; the other comes from Jefferson's First Inaugural as president in 1801. In both, Jefferson maintains that reason may be safely left to combat false or subversive opinions, so long as the law stands ready to punish any criminal acts they may produce. Similar statements can be found in his Bill for Religious Freedom in Virginia (1779) and his *Notes on Virginia* (1785). In the former, Jefferson asserts that "the opinions of men are not the object of civil government," and that "it is time enough for the rightful purposes of civil government to interfere when principles break out into overt acts against peace and order."[17] In the latter, we find the following often-quoted passage: "The legitimate powers of government extend to such acts only as are injurious to others. But it does me no injury for my neighbor to say there are twenty gods, or no God. It neither picks my pocket nor breaks my leg."[18]

Leaving aside the fact that Jefferson seems to have been arguing in these passages more for freedom of religion than for freedom of speech and press, he does express himself with perfect generality, and makes only "overt acts" rather than opinions subject to government control. Now if this were Jefferson's last word on the subject, and if he had been the principal author of the First Amendment and in a position to write only his own opinions into the Amendment, then we would be forced to conclude that no government power over speech and press is permitted. But Jefferson had other, more mature thoughts on these mat-

ters, and of course did not author the Amendment. Regardless, his position here is clearly of no avail to those who favor the "clear and present
danger" rule, since that rule does permit government control of speech
and press at some point.

We have fallen under the influence of an illusion concerning
Jefferson and Madison that constantly impedes historical accuracy. This
illusion makes us suppose that they won every constitutional battle they
fought, and speak more authoritatively about the Constitution than anyone else. They are taken to be constitutional oracles without peer. But
the truth is that Jefferson's opinions were in his own day often regarded
as extreme, and even had at times to be moderated by his friend Madison. We should also consider the possibility that in later years Jefferson
changed his mind about the scope of governmental authority and that
the most spectacular quotations from his earlier writings may not be
typical of his mature thought. Admittedly, his First Inaugural—the one
generally quoted—seems to appeal to his own earlier idea that all opinions deserve to be let alone by government: "If there be any among us
who would wish to dissolve this Union or to change its republican form,
let them stand undisturbed as monuments of the safety with which error of opinion may be tolerated where reason is left free to combat it."
Yet if we read his Second Inaugural, four years later (paragraphs 11 to
13), we see how seriously he has come to take the torrent of slander
against him. The states, he insists, should undertake to prosecute "false
and defamatory" publications, not for their opinions but for their malicious falsification of facts. This, at least, can be a basis for criminal libel
in a republic, "and no other definite line can be drawn between the inestimable liberty of the press and its demoralizing licentiousness." His
tone could not be more Blackstonian.

Jefferson's views of the relation between opinion and republican government are much more diverse and complex than excerpts from certain of his writings indicate. We have already seen his clear statement
to Abigail Adams affirming the authority of the states over speech and

press. He also came to believe, as his exchange of letters with Madison in 1825 reveals, that public education had to make the formation of sound republican opinion one of its primary objectives. To this end, Jefferson wanted to prescribe the political works to be studied by all students at the University of Virginia.[19] But if in 1825 he still held his opinion of 1779 that "the opinions of men are not the object of civil government," would this make sense? Commentators often treat such changes in Jefferson's thought as lapses and take his earlier thoughts on the subject (which they find more appealing) as a more accurate expression of his position. Instead, they should wonder whether experience might not have taught Jefferson that his earlier understanding was simplistic and inconsistent with the real needs of republican government.

~ 4 ~

The New Founding Father

I T IS GENERALLY ACKNOWLEDGED that the founders grounded their political philosophy in the thought of the English philosopher John Locke, whose *Letter on Toleration* and *Treatises of Civil Government* had achieved wide popularity and influence in the eighteenth century. The language employed by Holmes and Brandeis, on the other hand, suggests different philosophical sources, and it is not difficult to identify the thinkers whose ideas they absorbed from their intellectual milieu: John Stuart Mill and Charles Darwin. (Holmes had actually met Mill in 1865.) Of course, the term "liberty" that Holmes and Brandeis use is the same the founders used, but its frame of reference has changed. Their "theory of our Constitution," with its "fighting faiths" engaged in "the competition of the market," owes much more to the general view of liberty of thought and discussion found in Mill's *On Liberty* than it does to Locke's *Treatises*. From Mill they took their criticism of infallibility, their insistence that an open exchange of ideas on all subjects represents the apex of human freedom, and the "clear and present danger test" itself (though not by that name), along with a zealous suspicion of legislative or popular majorities for their potential persecution of the new and the few.[1]

Yet the "theory" is a rather wayward presentation of Mill. For in Mill's thought not all opinions are "faiths." Mill was never so vulgar as to think that the truth of an idea depended on its marketability or that it could be identified, at any given time, with what prevails in some so-called "marketplace of ideas." For Mill, freedom of discussion was the best way of permitting truth to emerge and spread, but it carried with it no assurance that the ideas (not "faiths") that prevailed would neces-sarily be the truest. Holmes and Brandeis enunciated their "clear and present danger" rule some sixty years after *On Liberty* was published, and during this time evolutionary and historicist ideas had become dominant in intellectual circles. From social Darwinism, they took the idea of truth determined not by its intrinsic merit but by the approval of the marketplace, of "fighting faiths," changing with time, seeking to dominate each other, and actually doing so by sheer force from which there is no appeal. This is the world not of the Declaration of Indepen-dence, with its inalienable rights of man, but of the survival of the fittest. What was at first the vigorous protection of unpopular minorities against the pressure of legislative majorities ends up being the domination of weak minorities by strong majorities, or simply the rule of the strong.[2]

No complicated inquiry is needed, therefore, to demonstrate that Holmes and Brandeis do not derive their new "clear and present dan-ger" test from the Constitution, laying out precedents and alternative interpretations, then drawing a reasoned conclusion.[3] Nor do they ad-mit that they have taken some of their legal principles from views of human affairs essentially different from, and antipathetic to, that of the founders. Their appeal to the authority of the founding generation, and to Jefferson and Madison in particular, for what the founders would have regarded as a pernicious absurdity seems all the more perverse. In fact, Jefferson and Madison serve these innovators as nothing more than stand-ins for Mill. In this role they are simply useful totems—especially when selectively cited—rather than men whose whole thought must be studied before it can be understood and applied.

Only the Declaration of Independence contains the definitive statement of American political principles, and it was the single greatest force inspiring the Constitution, just as it was the philosopher Montesquieu upon whom the founders most drew for constitutional structures. Only the Declaration can explain the full meaning of the Preamble to the Constitution, which enumerates its various purposes, culminating in the highest aim of "securing the blessings of liberty for ourselves and our posterity." And few who have studied the matter will deny that the philosopher from whom the Declaration drew virtually all of its principles was John Locke.[4] Therefore, if one were to seek a fuller explanation of the Declaration's principles than it could itself supply within so brief a compass, one might well find that explanation either in other statements by the founders themselves, or perhaps more systematically in Locke's writings, but hardly in Mill's.

MILL ON LIBERTY

What departures from the Declaration and Locke did Mill introduce into political theory that render him an unreliable guide for liberal society? Mill, it is fair to say, wanted to extend liberty even further than Locke and the Declaration. By Mill's day, Enlightenment rationalism, combined with political liberalism, had made great strides in Europe and America. Everywhere the *ancien regime* was in retreat; everywhere the forces of philosophy, science, and liberty were advancing. Locke's philosophy of the rights of man was sweeping the world toward liberal representative democracy. Soon, Mill feared, the enemies of liberty would be not kings, nobles, or priests but the people themselves, oppressing minorities in both social and political life. The rule of the people seemed inexorably on its way to a secure dominion, but what effect would it have on individual liberty?

Mill's fears were not wholly abstract in nature, for he had been impressed by Tocqueville's study of American democracy and shaken by

its description of the tyranny of the majority, of the awesome uniformity of opinion popular rule had produced, and of democracy's inevitable movement in the direction of a welfare state (as we would call it),
minutely regulating daily life in the name of security and equality, but
extinguishing individual liberty.[5] Mill was determined to introduce a
new principle of liberty—a simple and absolute principle—which if
adopted would forestall the liberty-crushing effect of democracy. This
principle could only obtain in states mature enough to conduct their
affairs on the basis of rational thought and discussion—but he was sure
all the nations of Europe and America that he need concern himself
with had already achieved that level of rational maturity.[6] The simple
and absolute principle which Mill formulated states that the only ground
for interfering by coercion with the words or deeds of another is to prevent or punish harm-doing by that person.[7] It follows from this principle that no one may be compelled either to help himself or others, or
not to hurt himself. Efforts may be made to persuade, but neither legal
nor social coercion is permissible since the presumption is that people
are mature enough to think for themselves.

It is not long before Mill abandons or qualifies this simple principle,
often without acknowledging as much. He admits people may sometimes be compelled to help others. He admits they may be prevented
from hurting themselves, but only if self-harm causes them to violate a
definite obligation they have assumed—that is, causes calculable harm
to others. And he admits, of course, that every new generation must receive a most demanding intellectual and moral education (which will
be compulsory—for their own good and the good of others) in order to
be brought to the level of rational maturity required for responsible individual freedom.[8] Now the object of all this freedom is individual happiness, and human happiness consists mainly (as we learn from his essay
Utilitarianism) of the higher pleasures—intellectual, moral, and aesthetic
pleasures.[9] The freedom of thought and discussion is both an end and
a means: it facilitates intellectual cultivation for its own sake and also

serves as the individual's means of discovering the best or happiest way of life for himself. Mill is the first philosopher of standing to make "individuality" one of his most important themes: our natures are essentially individual; life is a quest for that which suits our individuality best, perfects our individual nature, and makes us happiest as individuals.

Throughout *On Liberty*, Mill presumes the increasing rationality of civilized men and the existence of other vital social prerequisites. These include the reduction of warfare among civilized nations and a lack of serious internal threats either now or in the all-democratic future.[10] To Mill, the prime danger to be avoided is the attempt of majorities to press their moral and religious opinions upon others: he has absolutely nothing to say about organized attempts by minorities to overthrow a regime of liberty itself. Yet by 1859, revolutionary efforts against existing regimes were a fact of life—including threats from the new communist parties operating according to the principles of Marx's and Engel's *Manifesto* of 1848. Nor were counterrevolutionary groups inactive and harmless in the various European countries. Mill never considers these obvious political problems or directly argues—like his latter-day followers—that his equivalent of the "clear and present danger" rule would suffice to hold dangerous groups in check. He begins his crucial chapter, "Liberty of Thought and Discussion," by mentioning some prosecutions in England the year before for circulating through the press the doctrine of tyrannicide. But his response is simple: "If the arguments of the present chapter are of any validity, there ought to exist the fullest liberty of professing and discussing, as a matter of ethical conviction, any doctrine, however immoral it may be considered."[11]

Mill goes on to add that actual instigation to tyrannicide "may be a proper subject of punishment, but only if an overt act has followed, and at least a probable connection can be established between the act and the instigation." Let us apply this principle to the idea not of killing tyrants but of killing the leading officials of democracy, or killing Jews or blacks. On Mill's argument, such actions may freely be discussed "as matters of ethical conviction," but no prosecution may be undertaken until such an official, or a Jew or black, *has actually been killed* and it can be shown with probability that the person discussing such murders instigated the killing. Apart from the difficulty of tracing this kind of causation, it is remarkable that Mill should not apply to such cases the "clear and present danger" principle he develops at the beginning of the following chapter of *On Liberty*. Mill allows that speech or writings calling for an immediate crime in threatening circumstances may be restricted, but he permits no action against the stimulation of crime by any doctrine (this sounds like what we have called "advocacy" rather than "incitement") *before* the crime has occurred. Apply this now to revolutionary forces favoring not tyrannicide but the destruction of democracy—a case he never considers—and it would follow that Mill's doctrine completely disarms the republic and does not allow action until *after* the republic has been overthrown.

It cannot be said that man's rationality generally, or the conditions of peace among civilized countries, or the internal impregnability of liberal democracy has improved in the twentieth century. On the contrary, Mill in his optimism could not have predicted the outbreak of war on a global scale and of fierce and relentless political fanaticisms and tyrannies exceeding the worst barbarism of past ages. About such possibilities Mill's philosophy is almost completely silent, and this makes applying his libertarian views in a changed context even more foolish and irresponsible than it would otherwise have been. But Mill does more than leave liberal society defenseless against fanatical internal enemies, even when they are linked with aggressive foreign powers. In many ways he actually gives encouragement to such enemies. For Mill makes the acquisition of knowledge rather than security the chief object of liberal society. He tells us all our own ideas are fallible, and that regarding them as infallible makes us into persecutors. [12] He asks us to entertain all minority views, to treat all attacks on our own ideas as possible contributions to knowledge, and worthy of a hearing, almost regardless of their content.[13] He thereby elevates to respectability even the most absurd and extreme views, permits them legal expression and organization, however threatening to the state or other citizens, and forces democracy to expend valuable resources guarding against them, preventing government from undertaking a more patient consideration of its affairs. In addition, by stimulating as much non-conformity in thinking and style of life as possible, Mill undermines the consensus necessary to the governance of any society, and especially of a liberal democracy, where the ties among individuals are looser to begin with. In fact, to protect minorities against the legislative process itself, Mill advocated proportional representation. Scholars generally agree that the Weimar Republic's adoption of this baneful principle, which we will discuss later, made it much more difficult to govern Germany by republican means.

Although Mill's liberalism views the purpose of a free society as the diffusion of knowledge rather than security—on the premise that security is no longer a worry—Mill's most significant departure from the liberalism of Locke is his abandonment of the doctrine of natural rights. This doctrine, in the Declaration of Independence as in Locke, originally established a fixed principle defining the legitimate purposes and limits of government. It anchored government in an immovable claim of justice that individuals, by an endowment from their Creator, could make in their own behalf, conferring on individual rights a solidity and dignity they could have in no other system. The purposes of government then centered around the protection of these rights, which in the absence of government were very insecure. Nor could they be made secure without the people's uniting for the sake of these rights and forming a responsible representative democracy. In Mill's utilitarian thought, individuals have no relation to a Creator, no inalienable rights, no clear reason for wanting government in the first place, and no fixed principles for the formation of governments.

This philosophy may appeal to intellectuals, but its principles are much less memorable, much less anchored in claims of justice, and hence less susceptible of political application than the "self-evident truths" of Locke and Jefferson. The remaining strength of the idea of "human rights" today—a pale shadow of the rights earlier generations of liberals believed natural and inalienable—proves how intrinsically powerful was the original form of that idea. The liberty of thought and discussion, which Mill made primary, has no intrinsic appeal to the common man. This has always been its greatest shortcoming and the reason why its statement and application have in our country come more from a Mill-dominated federal judiciary and like-minded intellectuals than from the representatives of the people themselves. To put this another way, Locke allied the intellectuals and the leaders of the people with the people by finding a common ground in their interests in life, liberty, property, and the pursuit of happiness; Mill sought to assimilate the people and their leaders to the interests of the intellectuals.

These defects in Mill's philosophy of government, as compared with the Declaration of Independence, are relevant here only to dispel the claim, explicit or implicit, that his views constitute a better philosophy for liberal democracy. Much more could be said on the subject, but for present purposes we need only add that Mill's libertarian followers in this country hardly ever adopt his whole philosophy, or understand with any thoroughness how it differs from that of the Declaration or John Locke. Their enthusiasm for individual liberty is the passion which sustains them, and in Mill they find this liberty extended fully. They are, of course, much less solicitous of the cohesiveness and durability of society as a whole, even though without these qualities individual liberty must itself be short-lived. Yet, like Holmes and Brandeis, they are not interested in Mill's fixed notion of the good life, and generally find themselves either subjectivizing or relativizing his fundamental principles. They no longer presume qualitative differences among the pleasures, and hence among ways of life, and from this denial comes the current conception of equal and changeable "lifestyles," based on ultimately arbitrary and non-rational individual choices. They cannot any longer take seriously Mill's expansive view of education, higher and lower.

These libertarians are also unwilling to grant that any final knowledge of principles can be achieved, turning Mill's attack on infallibility against his own "simple and absolute principle" of liberty. They reject the absoluteness of all such principles on other grounds as well, most of them either historical-evolutionary or positivistic. But without his fixed principle of liberty and the objective character of his conception of the good life for men, Mill's philosophy loses whatever strength it might have originally possessed. It is in this eviscerated form that it has entered and taken hold in American jurisprudence.

A peculiarity of Mill's career is that he seems to have been wiser when he was younger, for there is no more penetrating critic of *On Liberty* than the Mill of two decades before. In his essay on Coleridge (1840), he has occasion to criticize French philosophers at the end of the previous century for assuming that humanity would flourish spontaneously once the religious and political despotisms of the old regime were destroyed. Observing the obedience regularly given in the large European nations to both law and morality, they did not realize "by what a host of civilizing and restraining influences a state of things so repugnant to man's self-will and love of independence has been brought about, and how imperatively it demands the continuance of those influences as the condition of its own existence." [14]

Mill enumerates three conditions that must be met in such nations. The first is a "system of *education*, beginning with infancy and continued through life, of which, whatever else it might include, one main and incessant ingredient was *restraining discipline*, to train the human being in the habit, and thence the power, of subordinating his personal impulses and aims, to what were considered the ends of society . . . . And whenever and in proportion as the strictness of this discipline was relaxed, the natural tendency of mankind to anarchy reasserted itself." [15]

In *On Liberty*, education takes the form of training the reason of individuals only when they are young so they can make good use of their freedom as adults.

The second condition of "permanent political society" is the feeling of allegiance or loyalty, directed at "*something* which is settled, something permanent, and not to be called in question." The "something" may vary, "but in all political societies which have had a durable existence, there has been some fixed point; something which men agreed in holding sacred . . . which, in short (except perhaps during temporary crisis), was in the common estimation placed *above* discussion." Mill believes he can easily show why this is so:

> A state never is, nor, until mankind are vastly improved, can hope to be, for any long time exempt from internal dissension; for there neither is now nor has ever been any state of society in which collisions did not occur between the immediate interests and passions of powerful sections of the people. What, then, enables society to weather these storms, and pass through turbulent times without any permanent weakening of the ties which hold it together? Precisely this—that however important the interests about which men fall out, the conflict does not affect the fundamental principles of the system of social union which happens to exist; nor threaten large portions of the community with the subversion of that on which they have built their calculations, and with which their hopes and aims have become identified. *But when the questioning of these principles is (not an occasional disease, but) the habitual condition of the body politic; and when all the violent animosities are called forth, which spring naturally from such a situation, the state is virtually in a position of civil war; and can never long remain free from it in act and fact.*[16]

To this magnificent criticism, before the fact, of his own "absolute" principle of liberty must be added his consideration of the third condition of durable political societies: "a strong and active principle of nationality." By this principle Mill does not mean hostility toward other nations, but "a feeling of common interest among those who live under the same government, and are contained within the same natural or historical boundaries. We mean, that one part of the community shall not consider themselves as foreigners with regard to another part; that they shall cherish the tie which holds them together; shall feel that they are one people, that their lot is cast together, that evil to any of their fellow-countrymen is evil to themselves, and that they cannot selfishly free themselves from their share of any common inconvenience by severing the connexion."[17] How Mill, nineteen years later, could devise a philosophy of government that would, like those of the eighteenth-century *philosophes*, confine the force of education and discipline to the young, subject all points and principles to constant criticism (including the "absolute" principle of liberty itself), and dissolve the common bonds of society is a question that must be left to others.

ARE THE FOUNDERS REPLACEABLE?

It is not necessary, at this point, to discuss further how badly Holmes and Brandeis digested the intellectual fare of their day—how much of Mill, for example, they ignored despite its essential relation to what they had appropriated from him. Not being great thinkers themselves, they fabricated from diverse ingredients a veritable witch's brew of philosophical notions, and the mixture has not been rendered healthier by the passage of time. Is this mixture of incompatible ideas a better foundation for liberal democracy than the philosophy of the Declaration of Independence? How could Holmes and Brandeis have been so eager to replace the well-considered philosophy of the founders—of which they were themselves indisputably beneficiaries—with something that is not really a philosophy at all?

A vital issue of constitutional interpretation, involving the proper role of judges, is raised by their having adopted an interpretive framework different from that of the founders. The fact that the two justices

no longer held the intellectual views of the founding fathers would be
of little consequence had they believed their judicial function necessarily entailed explicating and applying the understanding of the founders.
As it happens, however, they felt bound to substitute the intellectually
more advanced (so they thought) philosophies of their own age for the
somewhat benighted views of the founders. They updated the Constitution by dipping into the current "marketplace of ideas" and read the
latest of these ideas back into the Constitution as though they had always been there. In the name of progress, the country, through the justices of the Supreme Court, received a new and presumably better
founding—except that this founding was never subject to popular debate and ratification. This second, hidden founding occurred because
these justices forsook their primary obligation to apply but not reshape
the law, even though it was precisely this traditional understanding of
the role of the judge which had permitted the judiciary, through judicial review, to become so powerful an element of republican government
in the first place.

For the question is whether any alien doctrines, any doctrines other
than those of the founders and framers, written into the language of
the Constitution, should be so employed. In a now-famous remark,
Holmes himself once said that he did not think the Fourteenth Amendment enacted Herbert Spencer's *Social Statics*.[18] Is it any less appropriate to suggest that the First Amendment did not enact John Stuart Mill's
On Liberty, or the philosophical notions of Oliver Wendell Holmes Jr.?
The alternatives in this issue are these, and only these: either the current intellectual predilections of justices will guide their interpretation
of the Constitution, or they must submit to the "dead hand," or "dead
mind," of the founders, kept alive only if we make the effort to do so.

Undoubtedly, what the American people assume they have is a fixed,
objective Constitution—apart from amendments, a fixed and reliable
supreme law, adopted once and for all from the beginning. Its parts, they
assume, have meanings intentionally devised that judges, seeking to in-

terpret it, are bound to look for, not create on their own. And these meanings are expected to be stable over time, built up and rendered continuous by the rule of precedent. Otherwise, the laws would change every time the Supreme Court changes, or whenever a justice reads a new book. In fact, since judges are almost always the servants rather than the masters of the intellectual world, the arbiters of constitutionality, at any given time, are the current crop of intellectuals or the most powerful intellectual fashion. In this way intellectuals would exercise a hidden dictatorship over the people, changing basic law without their consent through the process of judicial interpretation. We would then have a Constitution viewed not from the vantage point of those who wrote it or ratified it, but of Herbert Spencer, John Stuart Mill, Karl Marx, Sigmund Freud, Jean-Paul Sartre, or even the Book of Genesis. The Court itself would become something like a marketplace of ideas —or, more likely, a battleground of conflicting and irreconcilable worldviews, ideologies, or "faiths."

It is interesting to see how far we have departed from the older understanding of law still taken for granted by the American people. It could not have been stated more clearly than by Blackstone, who understood the connection between a judge's being bound by the law and the rule of precedent in judicial decisions:

> For it is an established rule to abide by former precedents, where the same points come again in litigation: as well to keep the scale of justice even and steady, and not liable to waver with every new judge's opinion; as also because the law in that case being solemnly declared and determined, what before was uncertain, and perhaps indifferent, is now become a permanent rule, which it is not in the breast of any subsequent judge to alter or vary according to his private sentiments: he being sworn to determine, not according to his own private judgment, but according to the known laws and customs of the land; not delegated to pronounce a new law, but to maintain and expound the old one. [19]

One would think this rule of law even more vital in a country with a written constitution like ours, where only a steady line of constitutional interpretation could keep the original document alive and bind generations to each other. Without it, in fact, Hamilton could not have defended the very idea of judicial review in *The Federalist,* Number 78, or Tocqueville have found lawyers and judges an important obstacle to the tyranny of majorities in *Democracy in America.*

In the twentieth century, nevertheless, American intellectuals and students of the law, under the influence of the new evolutionary science and the equally, if not more powerful surge of historical studies, began to promulgate another conception of constitutional interpretation. The key concept was "change": changed conditions of life required a changing constitution to cope with them—all through judicial interpretation rather than constitutional amendment. This superficially attractive view fed the ambition of the intellectuals and the judiciary, but once acted upon it could hardly be kept within bounds consistent with the public good. Carrying this infatuation with change to its logical conclusion, one scholar celebrates the new principle:

> As with all other constitutional provisions, it is not the founders' intentions but our intentions that count. It is, I think, a universally accepted truism that the glory of our Constitution is that it is a generally worded, and thus highly flexible, document that allows—indeed, requires—new interpretation to fit new situations. To say that the First Amendment contains no absolutely clear historical command, or that the command it contains has since been altered or even misunderstood, is simply to say that the First Amendment is like any other provision of the Constitution. It too requires that we decide what we want it to mean. [20]

The author sums it all up for us: "It is what we want, not what the founders wanted, that counts." Now the simplicity of this view is matched only by the simplicity of its presentation. After all, a "universally accepted truism" seems so self-evident as to require no argument. But the author neglects to tell us for whom it is a truism, or whether it has always been such. Does this truism about the need for altering the Constitution through judicial interpretation generally square with what the public expects of the judiciary? Does it square with what judges and justices say publicly about what they do in interpreting the Constitution? In fact it does not, for judges always claim to be bound by *its* letter, by *its* spirit, rather than by what *they* want. Is it not true that there have always been some justices who did not think the Constitution had to be, or should be, altered through judicial interpretation? And is it not also true that the view of constitutional interpretation on and off the bench throughout the nineteenth and through much of the twentieth century was precisely the opposite of this "truism"?

Often, for excellence of pedigree, this "truism" is traced to the great John Marshall, whose declaration (in *McCulloch v. Maryland*, 1819) that it is a Constitution we are expounding is taken to be the *Magna Carta* of judicial activism. But the merest inspection of that passage reveals something entirely different. To Marshall, the Constitution fixed the proper *ends* of the national legislature, but left the *means* to be pursued for their fulfillment discretionary with the legislature. And it is this discretion—not any discretionary power of interpretation in the judiciary—that Marshall considers the sole and solely necessary source of the flexibility needed to cope with changing situations.[21] General terms like "commerce" or "freedom" are not therefore expected to require constantly changing definitions, but fixed definitions appropriate to the intentions and meaning of the founders.

So what our author propounds is hardly the truism he takes it to be—but that is only the beginning of the difficulties his radical position must encounter. For who are the "we" he has in mind when he says that it is what *we* want, not what the founders wanted, that counts? Does he mean a majority of the American people at any given time? A majority of the judges? Of the constitutional lawyers? Of those who share a certain view of policy (like the "clear and present danger" rule this author also espouses)? Or does "we" break down into individuals who have nothing in common, but are expected to act solely on the basis of their own individual desires and wants? For it is what we *want*—not what reasoning from a common and objective constitutional document requires, that has become the new first principle of judicial interpretation. Are all "wants," or the "wants" of all judges equally valid in this new temple of justice? How far must a judge be bound by the text at all, since he is obviously not bound by the meaning those who composed the text thought they had placed in it?

The novel principle our author refers to as a "truism" is an invitation to chaos and the end of the American constitutional system. For if the judges, in the constitutional opinions they render, are merely stating what they think they themselves or the country *want*, they have become makers of policy and ought to be elected for limited terms, like all other policy-makers, to insure their accountability to the will of the people. The only alternative—and the one adhered to before the new "truism" was promulgated—held that a judge, by the very definition of his function, takes a law he did not make and applies it to particular situations in the manner the lawmaker intended and indicated by the wording of the law. This view holds forth the possibility of a rational agreement of judges with each other, and between themselves and the people—an agreement that the sovereignty accorded our "wants" (as judges interpret them) by the "truism" lacks completely. This view allows for reasoning about what the founders intended, about their meaning, about their political philosophy, about the intrinsic needs of republican government—with all the difficulties this often entails—but without ever surrendering the principle that it is *their* meaning, rather than our "wants," that must bind judges. In short, what judges ordinarily take for granted in interpreting *current* legislation they must apply to past legislation—and to the Constitution as well.

The judge is the intelligent mouthpiece of the original legislator, nothing more. Occasionally, he must try to settle disputes among the founders themselves—as in the case of the differences between Madison and Marshall about the constitutionality of the Sedition Act. Nevertheless, he is not the savior of society, armed with a discretionary prerogative, unbound by law, to alter even the supreme law of the land as he wishes. According to this understanding, the popular notion of the Constitution as a supreme, overarching, and fixed basic law may be preserved; interpretations of the law have a common objective ground that is in principle capable of being discovered; the rule of precedent may serve as a saving lifeline between the founders' intentions and all later generations.[22] Absent this understanding, the constitutional links binding the country together are bound to dissolve, with interpretations of law becoming variable, chaotic, idiosyncratic, overbearing, and tyrannical —or merely subject to fashion and temporary popular whim.[23]

The unspoken premise of the new libertarian philosophy is that it constitutes an intellectual underpinning for liberal democracy vastly superior to that of the founders and framers. This view is rarely stated by sitting judges in their written opinions: they know admitting publicly to changing the Constitution through interpretation would arouse a public furor. They realize that the public mind sharply distinguishes between judges who apply the law and legislators who make it. They realize that as practitioners of judicial review they must seem to be nothing but the mouthpiece of the founders and framers. And what better way is there of making a constitutional innovation acceptable than by claiming historical warrant for it? Whether we consider authors on or off the bench, it is remarkable how bereft of philosophical substance the new libertarianism is. Over many decades now it has produced not one great defense: nothing coming close to Locke's *Letter on Toleration* and *Second Treatise of Government*, from which the founding generation drew so much, or even Mill's *On Liberty*.

To make subservience to the founding fathers not only necessary but admirable, we must lose the sense of superiority to them that has been sedulously cultivated during more than a half-century of the nation's intellectual life. The fathers of the Constitution were not ordinary men. As a collection of forty, their equal has not been seen since, and certainly cannot be culled from the groves of academe today. Their practical political thought, as it entered the Constitution, was powerful, original, and far-sighted. They had studied law and political philosophy deeply, and knew how to reason and write. The reverence the people still feel we owe them is much closer to what they deserve than the vain sense of superiority the intellectuals are taught to feel toward them. Moreover, they sensed themselves in a position of responsibility for the formation and preservation of a new nation, and constantly acted with this responsibility in mind. We who come after them are their heirs and beneficiaries, and by not shouldering that same responsibility we are often led to propose rash changes that can only harm rather than improve the system they created. To be sure, it is impossible to expect men raised under their system not to embody some of the same independence of spirit they exemplified. But independence does not require superficiality, vanity, or folly, and is perfectly consistent with an admiration for the founders best described as "rational reverence"—that is, a reverence that grows deeper the more their work is studied.

THE MADE-OVER CONSTITUTION

We have established the original meaning of the First Amendment; reflected on its internal order and on the functions clearly delegated to the national government in the body of the Constitution, proving their mutual consistency; applied these conclusions to the status of the Communist Party and similar revolutionary groups; shown the "clear and present danger" rule to have no constitutional basis; and traced the rule instead to certain extra-constitutional ideas prevailing in Holmes's day.

We have concluded that nothing in the Constitution prevents the national or state governments from making laws against verbal incitement to lawbreaking, against the malicious defamation of the government and its officials, and against revolutionary groups, and indeed that much impels them to make such laws. The First Amendment—that great bulwark of republican government—was not intended to threaten republican government by protecting those who would abuse or overthrow it. Its citizens must be free to criticize strongly, even fiercely, but the Amendment requires "*peaceable* assembly." The process of speaking, writing, assembling, and petitioning is the peaceable way by which the republic corrects itself. On the basis of just such a distinction, Congress and the state legislatures have passed laws—and ought now to revive laws—defining and proscribing abuses of these fundamental rights, whether by individuals or by combinations of individuals formed into conspiracies.

The analysis to this point restores our understanding of and appreciation for the original constitutional tradition expressed in Story's *Commentaries* around 1840 and prevailing throughout the nineteenth and well into the twentieth century. For knowledge of that tradition and its basis has almost been completely expunged by the victory of the Holmes-Brandeis school of jurisprudence. But the success of this school is completely out of keeping with its intrinsic merits. It is surprising and illuminating to discover how weak was its challenge to traditional jurisprudence, how slight and tenuous its basis in the Constitution, how inadequate and tendentious its use of Jefferson and Madison, and how shallow and partial its historical understanding of the founders generally. It is hard to avoid the suspicion that Holmes, Brandeis, and their libertarian followers, having adopted a new intellectual framework, simply looked for ways of bringing the Constitution into line with it through constitutional interpretation.

This new use of judicial review is completely contrary to that for which Hamilton argued in *The Federalist*. He justified granting the

Court such extraordinary power by claiming that judicial review is the most important means of binding the country to a fixed Constitution, which otherwise might be bent to the will of legislative majorities. Under the new dispensation, however, the federal judiciary has abandoned its essentially conservative function and gone radical, using its constitutional independence to initiate fundamental changes in our political order that democratic majorities would oppose if they could. Drastic change is to be brought about, not by constitutional amendment, formally changing the Constitution through a democratic process, but by judicial review now understood in terms not essentially different from those of the older royal prerogative—that is, as a power to act for the public good beyond or even against the written law.

It is not that ever new national problems have required ever new constitutional interpretations, as we are often told. For the new libertarianism gives every appearance of wanting to be no less absolute and fixed than the Constitution was originally meant to be: its devotees can conceive of no new circumstances under which the libertarian interpretation ought to be modified or abandoned. Far from a response to changing national conditions, this refurbished Constitution, brought into harmony with the allegedly more advanced thought of the early twentieth century, was itself expected to alter the public's understanding of the problems that faced the country. Not the least of these alterations has been the loss of our perception of the particular dangers posed by organized anti-democratic conspiracies in the twentieth century. And to these dangers we now turn.

5

The Dangers of
Anti-Democratic Conspiracy

ONE OF THE MOST MISGUIDED FEATURES of the Holmes-Brandeis libertarianism was its framing of the challenge posed by revolutionary organizations in terms of individual liberty and individual freedom of speech and press. This became the general tendency of the Court even when the statutes under review made *conspiracy* a central element of the crime in question, and where the conduct of individuals *qua* members of organizations like the Communist Party was involved. The indictment in *Schenck* charged a conspiracy to violate the Espionage Act of 1917 by causing insubordination in the armed forces and obstructing recruiting. The indictment in *Dennis* charged conspiracy to teach the violent overthrow of the government, as forbidden by the Smith Act. Even where conspiracy was not specifically prohibited in the statutes, it is clear that the legislatures feared the establishment and growth of *organized groups* dedicated to the collapse or overthrow of American democracy.

WHAT IS SEDITION?

In the twentieth century the term "sedition" has been used for the crime of calling for, organizing for, and conspiring to violent overthrow of the government. Yet when Blackstone discusses sedition it is in terms of individuals sowing disaffection by defaming public officials or the general government. It does not ordinarily involve any organized or group effort, and certainly does not involve any call for revolution put forth by either individuals or groups. In this country, prosecutions for seditious libel under the Sedition Act of 1798 or in the states, whether at the hands of Federalists or Jeffersonians, were, like those in England, of individuals who were not acting as part of an organized group. And here, as in England, the spreading of disaffection through sedition fell far short of an outright call for revolution. This distinction between sedition and revolution is further supported in the definition of seditious offences given by the nineteenth-century historian of English law, Sir James Stephen. Whether done by words, libels, or conspiracies, he calls them offences against internal public tranquility "not accompanied by or leading to violence."[1] It is clear from Blackstone—and Stephen concurs—that direct verbal assaults on the king or government would have constituted crimes much more serious than seditious libel. They would have been considered treasonable libel or treason itself, all the more egregious when the result of an organized conspiracy.[2] Stephen seems to trace the problem of seditious *conspiracy* in England no farther back than the aftermath of the French Revolution, with the development of legal voluntary associations seeking to effect constitutional change via Acts of Parliament. He regarded it as an unsolved legal problem facing the English to determine how far such *reformist* criticisms of the government could go before they became seditious.[3] It is appropriate to infer that organized calls for revolution went far beyond the civic freedoms protected by English law.

No doubt republican government requires the greatest latitude for critical discourse, but stimulation to lawbreaking and defamation of public officials (untrue, ill-motivated, and ill-intentioned criticism) go beyond what is permissible and are destructive of republican government. This is so even when such criticism falls far short of avowing the purpose of destroying republican government. When it does avow such a purpose, and especially when it does so through an organized group, there is nothing in our legal tradition, or the English legal tradition, or in the philosophy of the Declaration of Independence or the Constitution, that calls for the toleration of such an appeal or such a group. This is not sedition but treasonable or revolutionary conspiracy, and the element of conspiracy makes it dangerous in the extreme. The use of speech and press involved is not a proper use of speech and press, but an improper use, made all the more dangerous by something that is not speech or press at all, namely, conspiratorial organization. To treat such a phenomenon as if it were only a question of granting freedom of speech and press to isolated individuals is to ignore the source of the greatest danger—the conspiracy.

Now this is precisely what Justice Jackson thought his colleagues had done in the *Dennis* case, where the fate of several leaders of California's Communist Party, under the Smith Act, was at stake. Jackson could not help being caustic in his own opinion: "What really is under review here is a conviction, after a trial for conspiracy, on an indictment charging conspiracy, brought under a statute outlawing conspiracy. With due respect to my colleagues, they seem to me to discuss anything under the sun except the law of conspiracy."[4] Proceeding with an elementary lesson in established law, Jackson explains to his colleagues that conspiring to commit an illegal action is a crime separate from the commission of it: "[A] combination of persons to commit a wrong, either as an end or a means to an end, is so much more dangerous, because of its increased power to do wrong, because it is more difficult to guard against and prevent the evil designs of a group of persons than of a single person, and because of the terror which fear of such a combination tends to create in the minds of people."[5] He sums up his justification of the Smith Act succinctly, restating the pre-Holmesian position of the Court: "But it is not forbidden to put down force or violence, it is not forbidden to punish its teaching or advocacy, and the end being punishable, there is no doubt of the power to punish conspiracy for the purpose."[6]

Justice Jackson has a great deal to say in *Dennis* about the peculiarly dangerous kind of conspiracy constituted by communist parties here and abroad. He graphically describes the various ways by which, in the guise of being ordinary legal parties, they wage war on the republic sheltering them, and await the opportunity to overthrow it.[7] Knowing how extensively the Court had long used the law of conspiracy in connection with antitrust prosecutions, Jackson does not hesitate to remind his colleagues, with some acerbity, that "It is not to be supposed that the power of Congress to protect the Nation's existence is more limited than its power to protect interstate commerce."[8] Nor did Jackson think American democracy obliged to grant legality to such internal conspiracies until the courts found them a "clear and present danger." In a posthumously published comment on *Dennis* he suggests that the framers had no experience of such internal conspiracies: "I find little indication that they [the framers of the Bill of Rights] foresaw a technique by which those liberties might be used to destroy themselves by immunizing a movement of a minority to impose upon the country an incompatible scheme of values which did not include political and civil liberties. The resort to that technique in this country, however fruitless, contemporaneously with the collapse or capture of free governments abroad, has stirred American anxieties deeply."[9]

Jackson plainly implies that had the framers foreseen such a technique, they would not have granted it constitutional protection. This is more than surmise on his part, for it would hardly have made sense to them to protect groups which, if successful, would by their unjust principles of government merit revolutionary overthrow themselves. And would the founders not have been especially fearful of groups likely to set up so ruthless and sweeping a despotism as to make resistance to it all but impossible? Would they not have regarded it as especially ominous that, until the general breakdown in Eastern Europe in 1989, no communist regime had ever been overthrown by opponents from within? Is it not the case that ruthless suppression of opposition characterize the communist regimes that remain?

It is true, as Jackson admits, that the framers and founders do not directly consider the case of revolutionary groups within the republic they were creating. But the Blackstonian principles which underlie the First Amendment and the clear implications of the powers granted the national government in the body of the Constitution lead ineluctably to Jackson's conclusion. The national government had to have all the power necessary for dealing with hostile forces, foreign and domestic. For this purpose it is indispensable that it have authority to deal with all efforts to encourage the violation of duly enacted laws, not excluding, of course, the greatest of all such efforts—the revolutionary overthrow of the republic itself. If the founders considered the dissemination of seditious libel by individuals a crime that either the national or state governments had a right to suppress, how much readier would they have been to suppress open and organized calls for the overthrow of the republic. We know that Jefferson himself wanted to see prosecuted those whose malicious defamations of himself and his government were motivated (as he thought) by an unavowed monarchism. How much more ready he would have been to prosecute those who might organize openly for the purpose of overthrowing the republic and returning the country to monarchy.

In *The First Amendment and the Future of American Democracy*, the most original and thought-provoking book ever written on the First Amendment, Walter Berns takes his cue on the problem of revolutionary groups from Tocqueville's analysis in *Democracy in America*. Following Tocqueville, Berns argues that the freedom of political speech and press (Tocqueville had actually spoken only of the press [10]) should be absolute for individuals but not for associations or groups, which pose a much greater threat to society and must therefore be placed under careful legal limits. Tocqueville made no effort to define these limits. Berns, fearing the executive and legislative branches more than the judiciary, follows Holmes and Brandeis in first allowing hostile associations to exist and then leaving it to the courts to decide when they have become dangerous enough to warrant suppression. Yet, paradoxically, he also admits that no legal formula—not even the "clear and present danger" rule—can adequately guide this determination by the courts.[11]

Whatever Tocqueville's wisdom, Berns makes a fundamental error in relying on Tocqueville no different in principle from those who rely on Spencer, Mill, Darwin, or any other non-founder. The task of constitutional interpretation is to discover what the Constitution itself means and demands rather than what commentators may recommend. This error is all the more surprising in Berns's case, since earlier in his book he demonstrates the Blackstonian character of the First Amendment and presents a summary of John Marshall's defense of the constitutionality of the Sedition Act which leaves the reader impressed with its impregnability.[12] Berns knows that Blackstone, the founders and framers, and Marshall all come to a conclusion very different from his own. They do not grant absolute freedom of speech and press to individuals, and they do not look to the courts for a final determination of danger (not even Tocqueville does this). Yet Berns never gives any constitutional reasons why we should abandon their position and adopt his.

Further, Berns's position is beset by insurmountable difficulties other than its complete lack of constitutional basis. For he would have to acknowledge, with the tradition, that there must be some instances in which an individual's words, advocating or inciting to some serious crime, cannot reasonably be protected. This, after all, was the kind of consideration that led Mill to formulate what later became known as the "clear and present danger" principle,[13] acknowledged today by all but the most extreme libertarians. This may even be the reason why Tocqueville himself speaks only of freedom of the press and not of speech: speech can have an immediacy of impact lacking in printed material as such. Furthermore, while Berns tells us he would not trust government (legislatures and executive departments) as far as Justice Sanford had in *Gitlow*, he does not tell us why. If the legal principles restricting speech and press are reasonable and clear (as his own case for Blackstone and Marshall gives good grounds for presuming), the government will be held by the courts to whatever laws are fashioned according to these principles. Why, then, the mistrust? And Berns destroys his own position by admitting that no legal formula can possibly be stated to guide the courts in judging whether a group presents "sufficient danger" to warrant losing its freedom. If there is no legal formula, there is no guide; and if no guide, no law; and if no law, the courts are left completely to their own subjective and idiosyncratic judgment. Is this position superior to that of Blackstone, Marshall, *Gitlow*, and *Dennis*? It would not seem so, and Berns has certainly not shown so—either constitutionally or prudentially.

CAN WE DISMANTLE DEMOCRACY?

Only the enemies of liberal society have tried to deny it the right to defend itself against direct, violent overthrow. The question dividing its friends is whether its internal enemies have the right to advocate, organize, and prepare an overthrow they have utterly no right to effect. We have considered the case of organized efforts at violent revolution. But what if the overthrow is to be accomplished not through force but through legal majorities? Do the people have the right, for instance, to strip Jews, blacks, or other minorities of their rights, abolish institutions of liberal society by democratic vote, or abandon republican government altogether in favor of some form of oligarchy or despotism? Such questions arise because the Declaration of Independence accords the people decisive political authority. In the Constitution this authority is manifest not only in the "We the People" of the Preamble but in the almost unlimited provision for constitutional amendment by extraordinary majorities of the people and their representatives. This provision would in principle allow the people constitutionally to repeal the Bill of Rights and dismantle their own democracy, either gradually or all at once. The only exception to the power of amendment stipulated by the Constitution is the provision that no state shall be deprived of equal voting in the Senate without its consent.

In Locke's political philosophy, as well as in the Declaration, the people are made the ultimate arbiter of whether a government has become despotic, whether revolution is necessary to reconstruct it, and what new political system would better conduce to their safety and happiness. Nevertheless, not everything that pleases the people is right or good—or even good for them. The people are expected to judge in political matters according to binding principles which are true independent of opinions about them. The people are expected to act upon a belief in the inalienable rights of all men, and the desire to overthrow or avert despotism, not seek it. Their power to judge their own "safety and happiness" is circumscribed by implied limitations. As Jefferson put it in his First Inaugural, "All, too, will bear in mind this sacred principle, that though the will of the majority is in all cases to prevail [within republican government], that will, to be rightful, must be reasonable; that the minority possess their equal rights, which equal laws must protect, and to violate which would be oppression." [14]

In short, the people to whom government is entrusted are a people enlightened by the philosophy of the rights of man. No other "people" will serve the needs of liberal philosophy and liberal society, and most peoples have hitherto been of another stamp. To wed the common people to a principle of individual liberty, very broadly conceived, may be said to be the great accomplishment of modern liberal philosophy. Locke, like Jefferson after him, knew full well that in earlier times, under the influence of old habits and bad opinions, the people had often served as the mainstays of the world's great despotisms. Indeed, to avoid a return to such conditions was one of the main reasons for Jefferson's interest in both public education and a separation of church and state. It is not impossible that under certain circumstances the people might again acquiesce in illiberal forms of government, might again prefer to be ruled without their free, recurring consent. But the people never have a right, by whatever means, or for whatever reasons, to destroy liberty for others, for their own posterity, or for themselves. A well-constructed liberal society will not permit the people to participate in movements or parties that directly threaten the preservation of liberal society itself. The people, in other words, should be far-sighted enough to want to withhold from themselves the possibility of choices directly antithetical to the continuation of liberal democracy. Through vast legislative majorities, Americans have shown an eagerness to do this, but Holmes, Brandeis, and their followers have made it impossible.

The history of the Weimar Republic in this regard is tragic and never to be forgotten. Established in 1919 at the behest of the Allies, it sought to be the most progressive democracy of its day, incorporating every principle and device of modern liberal political theory. At least two of these it derived from Mill: proportional representation and, even more important, the legitimation of all parties, including those devoted to the overthrow of the Republic. Thus were the Nazis and Communists tolerated in principle, from the beginning, although neither party was itself committed to the rule of law, and both openly despised the government. After his failure at a putsch and subsequent imprisonment, Hitler determined that he had to use primarily republican means (always accompanied by *some* violence) to destroy the republic—he had to win the votes necessary to take over the army that had squelched his coup. Only then could he establish his party's dictatorship. As Germany began to return to prosperity, neither of these totalitarian parties seemed to threaten very much harm: their vote was small and their seats in the Reichstag few. Then, quite unexpectedly, an ever-deepening and worldwide depression struck Germany after 1929, and a people inexperienced in democracy quickly began to lose patience with the Republic's divided and paralyzed government.

The fully legalized Nazi and Communist parties saw their representation in the Reichstag and influence in the presidential elections soar dramatically in a very short time. Soon it was only a question of which of the two parties would be most instrumental in overthrowing the Republic. Confused, divided into a multitude of proportionately represented parties, insufficiently attached to republican government, longing for decisive authority of some sort, and too readily attracted by irrational appeals to nationalism, enough of the Republic's citizens gave their votes to Adolf Hitler in 1933 to bring him to power. Thus, those who formed the constitution of this ill-fated but most progressive republic also laid the ground for its destruction by not protecting the German people from their own inexperience, impatience, gullibility, and passions. If Hitler lacked support in 1933, it was not too many years before he had the enthusiastic support of a substantial majority of Germans. By then, the Republic had been completely dismantled and its supporters eliminated. Practical resistance to the party which had overthrown the Republic through its own laws became impossible. Tyranny and a brutal war were the result.

Thus it is a question of some interest whether the American people have a right to bring democracy to an end for some or all by constitutional means. For it would follow, if they have such a right, that all parties advocating such changes in our constitutional order may not be proscribed, providing always that they abide by the law as it currently stands. There is no provision of the Constitution which explicitly prohibits such changes if extraordinary popular majorities are available to bring them about. But a purely procedural view misses the wood for the trees and misconstrues the spirit not only of the Constitution as a whole but of the amending process itself. Amendments to the Constitution were provided for as a means of improving, not destroying, democracy. The founders could not be sure they had not erred in some way, and new circumstances might require alterations in our supreme law. From the Preamble, with its marvelous evocation of the "blessings of liberty," to the provision for amendment, the Constitution is replete with signs of strenuous and unremitting republican devotion. The only specified exception to amendment is itself evidence of this devotion, for it presumes that the Senate, where the states are never to be made unequal, will persevere as part of a representative republic. Clearly, the people were not expected to reject the dedication to republican government which the founding generation shared and bequeathed to future generations. If, nevertheless, the Congress and the people should grow so corrupt as to approve anti-democratic amendments to the Constitution, it would be the duty of every American who remembers the Declaration of Independence and understands the original Constitution to oppose the popular will by persuasion, by refusal to obey, by resistance, and if necessary by force.

This conclusion Justices Holmes and Brandeis could no longer draw by 1925. They had ceased to believe in the inalienable rights of man and were therefore willing to follow "the dominant forces of the community" wherever they led, even into proletarian (and why not fascist?) dictatorship. Under such circumstances they would not call for applying their own vaunted "clear and present danger" rule to save the republic, or vow armed resistance if it should fail. Their power of resisting "dominant forces" had disappeared as soon as they ceased to believe in an objective standard for determining the justice or injustice of governments. No longer convinced of the intrinsic rightness and superiority of liberal democracy, they were perfectly willing—without any sign of reluctance—to insist on extending the freedom of speech and press to groups they knew were devoted to its extinction. Full of new ideas that to their minds had superceded the antiquated notions of the founders, these justices of the Supreme Court could look upon the possibility of the passing of their democracy with the detachment of a scientist considering the extinction of a species.

6

The Imprudence of the
"Clear and Present Danger" Rule

H OLMES'S AND BRANDEIS'S NEW APPROACH to the Constitution
is no better prudentially than it is philosophically or constitutionally. The "clear and present danger" rule asserts that the
First Amendment's freedom of speech and press protects the expression of (and organization for) all political ideas, however revolutionary,
to the point that the danger of the commission of crimes such as treason, espionage, assassination, and revolution becomes imminent. Quite
apart from questions of constitutional interpretation and political theory,
how useful is this rule for maintaining ordered liberty?

TEN DEFECTS

Its first defect is that it grants to obviously hostile movements the sort
of moral blessing that goes with open public legality. Such a blessing
weakens the repugnance good citizens spontaneously have and ought
to have for those who would undermine their freedom and confuses
them as to the nature and durability of their political order.

This dulling of political sensibilities reveals a second and more serious defect, for the new rule gives license to the most divisive and mortal

hatreds that might arise among citizens, allowing those who wish to make victims of others to organize and spread their propaganda freely. The ordinary political give-and-take of liberal society becomes a life-and-death struggle among warring factions. The "domestic tranquility" which numbered among the ends sought through the Constitution, as well as agreement on the essentials of unity, peace and security, comes to an end. Viewed from the vantage point of the philosophy of the Declaration of Independence, the "clear and present danger" rule grotesquely sanctions a return to the condition that preceded civil society—the state of nature—as an acceptable and necessary feature of civil society itself.[1]

A third prudential defect of the "clear and present danger" rule follows from the second. Legalizing revolutionary parties gives status, standing, and influence within the constitutional order of free society to groups whose prime interest is to bring about the weakening and collapse of that order. In other words, long before they are in a position actually to overthrow liberal society, they may grow large enough to exercise considerable influence on decisions affecting its political health and hence its susceptibility to overthrow. Indeed, it is as though a man has authorized a cancer to grow within his body. This is precisely how communist and fascist parties have functioned in democracies like the Weimar Republic before World War II, or those France, Italy, India, and Japan since.

To this obvious danger must be added a fourth, less obvious but equally well demonstrated by history: such totalitarian parties are hardly likely to confine their efforts to open and legal measures for weakening liberal society. Legalization makes the infiltration of key positions in trade unions, universities, and government immeasurably easier for such parties, facilitating strikes, indoctrination, sabotage, espionage, and many other pernicious activities surreptitiously undertaken to hasten the collapse of liberal society. In short, such organizations pose as ordinary parties but in fact are hostile political armies, under strict discipline, working both openly and secretly to bring about a revolution.

A fifth defect follows from the third and fourth, and involves the link between internal and external enemies. Communist parties always retained special ties to the USSR, and sometimes were candid enough to say that in a war between their own country and the Soviet Union they would take the latter's side. In the struggle between East and West this circumstance created a dangerous asymmetry, with all western powers harboring internal enemies to which they had given legal status, and all eastern powers allowing no such forum to pro-western or pro-democracy groups, but instead ruthlessly rooting them out. This difficulty which beset the West alone was always worrisome and in crises, where a united effort by the whole people would have been necessary, could have proved extremely serious.

The previous five defects arise out of the legal status Holmes and Brandeis grant revolutionary parties. An equal number of defects are connected with the other part of their rule, which stipulates under what circumstances government may restrict speech, press, and organization of groups advocating or preparing for revolutionary overthrow.

Sixth, to begin with, once the groups involved have become so dangerous—which could well mean large and powerful—will the government find it practicable at that time to declare them illegal, arrest their leaders, stop their presses, and prevent the act of overthrow itself? It turns out that precisely when the rule must be applied is the time it is least likely to work, if it can be applied at all. It would have been practically impossible for the Weimar Republic to have closed down either the Nazi or the Communist parties in 1932 or 1933. The rule was not applied even in the face of acts of criminality in this country during the 1960s and 1970s.

Seventh, moreover, will it not be most difficult to resist the claim that parties tolerated when small should be all the more tolerated when the people are flocking to them? The size of their membership, it will be forcefully argued, is sufficient to justify their continued legality. Holmes and Brandeis themselves succumb to the force of this claim in

Gitlow when they grant the dominant forces of the community their way. This argument will reinforce the already plausible claim that it is too late to suppress a popular political party, however pernicious.

An eighth defect comes from the word "present" in the rule, for its apparent precision vanishes on a moment's inspection. When is the danger of a revolutionary takeover "present"? Is it a split second before the orders for takeover are given? A month before? A year before? How many of the elements necessary to a revolution must be manifest? How will the government know how imminent the danger is if it has no *prima facie* probable cause to infiltrate a legal party—which the party in question, on Holmes's and Brandeis's definition, certainly remains until it constitutes a "present" danger? Moreover, does not a judgment about the "danger" require an assessment not only of when the revolutionary forces are about to strike, but of the government's ability to thwart its efforts, and to do so with the least harm to itself or to innocent citizens? Common sense answers in the affirmative, but Holmes and Brandeis make no such provision. So the definition of timing, or "presentness," will either be precise and too late, or so vague that, paradoxically, it will allow the government to act long before the danger is in fact "present."

The ninth of these defects follows on the eighth, for the Holmes-Brandeis rule leaves to the judiciary the certification of a danger as both clear and present. Judges or jurors will have to decide, on evidence supplied by the executive, whether the danger of revolution or allied crimes is imminent. But such judgments are manifestly not the kind judges or juries are best fitted, or chosen, to make. They are prudential or political rather than legal judgments, and least of all can be reliably made by courts in times of great internal stress, amid fearful pressures—that is, under the conditions likely to prevail in a society that is approaching revolution.

Finally, tenth, there is an overestimation both of man's general capacity for rationality and government's powers of prediction and control implicit in the "clear and present danger" rule. It cannot accommodate unforeseeable circumstances involving great catastrophes such as depression or war, when deep passions and prejudices rather than reason are likely to master the people. And the notion that government action may be curbed until the last moment, while we call for education and appeal to reason, shows an almost sophomoric ignorance of the political fanaticisms of the twentieth century. The Russian revolution of 1917 utterly transformed world politics, and the appearance of fascism and Nazism completed the change. Ours is not a world unified by a common commitment to reason and human rights, the rational world of only conservative and liberal parties vying with each other for electoral supremacy within liberal democracy. For some time now it has been a world where political fanatics abound—communists, Nazis, the Klan, the Black Panthers, the Weathermen, the Symbionese Liberation Army, the Aryan Nation, the followers of the Ayatollah, the "militias"—to mention only those of which we have some experience in this country. These fanatics are all determined to establish some unpleasant form of tyranny, stripping others of their rights, never hesitating to sacrifice the innocent. Holmes, Brandeis, and their intellectual heirs imagine themselves in the naïve and progressive world of the nineteenth century. Like Mill, they act as if nothing has occurred to change the rational optimism that dominated Europe and America prior to World War 1. As the world has grown wilder, and the enemies of freedom stronger and more diverse, they have persisted in presuming the world a calmer and better place and our enemies capable of being handled by friendly persuasion.

A SINGLE REVOLUTIONARY SPARK

The sole alternative to the legal fiction of "clear and present danger" is the principle that preceded it and has never completely yielded to it. By way of contrast, this principle involves what might be called the "clear danger" rule, omitting the requirement that a "present danger" be demonstrated. But it never had a name, and is probably best left unnamed, since the phrase "clear danger" does not unambiguously express it. Far from ambiguous, the older understanding holds simply that both Congress and the state legislatures have the constitutional power to make it a crime to advocate, promote, prepare, or incite to the commission of a crime. This holds especially for the crime of overthrowing or destroying American society or its government. Americans are not free to advocate crimes, though they may criticize all laws and seek even drastic changes in the criminal code by legal means. Once we grant the necessity of adopting this principle for the effective working of liberal democracy itself, its application turns out to be legally much simpler, much clearer, and much less arbitrary than that of the Holmes-Brandeis rule.

We must not forget that this "clear danger" principle used to be the accepted rule of the Supreme Court and all the courts of the nation. It reigned unchallenged from long before Justice Story wrote in 1833, to opinions both Judge Learned Hand and Justice Holmes himself wrote in 1919, persisting in the opinions of such men as Justices Sanford and Jackson at least as far as the year 1951. Judge Learned Hand was clearly correct when he maintained in 1917 that "one may not counsel or advise others to violate the law as it stands. Words are not only the keys to persuasion but the triggers of action, and those which have no purport but to counsel the violation of law cannot by any latitude of interpretation be a part of that public opinion which is the final source of government in a democratic state."[2] Or as a unanimous Court said in 1890, if certain actions are criminal, then "to teach, advise and counsel their practice is to aid in their commission, and such teaching and counseling are themselves criminal and proper subjects of punishment, as aiding and abetting crime are in all other cases."[3]

No one applied the principle to revolutionary groups better than Justice Sanford, who in recent decades has served as a whipping boy for the army of Holmes-Brandeis innovators. Sanford does not think the state obliged to expose itself to the machinations of its enemies. As he said in the majority opinion in *Gitlow*,

> A single revolutionary spark may kindle a fire that, smouldering for a time, may burst into a sweeping and destructive conflagration. It cannot be said that the State is acting arbitrarily or unreasonably when in the exercise of its judgment as to the measures necessary to protect the public peace and safety, it seeks to extinguish the spark without waiting until it has enkindled the flame or blazed into the conflagration. It cannot reasonably be required to defer the adoption of measures for its own peace and safety until the revolutionary utterances lead to actual disturbances of the public peace or imminent and immediate danger of its own destruction; but it may, in the exercise of its judgment, suppress the threatened danger in its incipiency.[4]

In the application of this principle of traditional American jurisprudence, the burden remains on government to demonstrate in court that a given individual or group is directly encouraging a particular crime. Admissible evidence will consist of whatever might ordinarily prove such an objective, including speeches, writings, attendance at reported meetings or actions. Nor is this essentially different from what would have to be proved in connection with the "clear" part of the "clear and present danger" rule. But law enforcement will not have to wait for education, rational persuasion, or a crisis to prevent the individual or group encouraging the crime in question from expanding their influence. Government may act long before temporary or extended crises, false accusations or promises, or deep discontents fanned into fierce hatred allow them to have a divisive and dangerous effect.

The most serious evidence of hostility to liberal democracy is the advocacy of violence for the sake of either overthrowing the government or inflicting political or other forms of harm on a certain group of citizens. Another grievous threat comes from groups which use democratic means for accomplishing the same ends. In practice such groups also tend toward the paramilitary, and often use or threaten violence in some way—for which they are already punishable. But even if they do not and are as peaceful as lambs, their purposes are intrinsically noxious to the principles of the Declaration and liberal democracy and need not be permitted to disturb its tranquility. Most of the groups that have proved worrisome in recent decades have been given to violence and often could have been prosecuted even under the prevailing "clear and present danger" rule. But the government should be able to act against them long before the crimes and harms they encourage come to pass. All that is required is clear evidence of their intent, which is often openly proclaimed. Such prosecutions would again make plain to the body of lawful citizens the principles holding them together as a liberal democracy and assure them that their government is strong enough to defend both itself and them against attack.

Instead, we have seen the beginnings of a headlong descent into anarchy, understood as the absence or inaction of government. Not merely revolutionary groups but groups and individuals spread throughout society have been calling with impunity for the commission of serious crimes. To date the harm they have done has fallen short of wrecking the country, but pernicious precedents of governmental permissiveness and weakness have been set that could, in a crisis like the Vietnam War, make it impossible for liberal democracy to survive. When Quakers were freely calling for non-registration for the draft, teachers' unions for strikes that violate state law and their own contractual obligations, church groups for giving sanctuary to illegal immigrants, the national habit of obedience to duly constituted law was seriously weakened, and the door opened to increased lawlessness by both the wicked and the well-intentioned. Similarly, when Supreme Court decisions placed severe limits on police discretion and extended the rights of defendants, they strengthened the dangerous impression that the legal system worked more for the lawbreaker than for the law-abiding citizen.

Once a group has been convicted of seeking either the overthrow of liberal democracy or serious harm to some of its members, further laws to minimize its influence are equally constitutional. It is well within the authority of government to insist that public officials, teachers, lawyers, the personnel of war industries, trade union leaders remain loyal to the Constitution and free of membership in such groups. As with many other matters of legislation, the problem of outlawing and controlling groups directly hostile to liberal society is not always easily solved. Legislatures and administrations may occasionally err—though we should remark how little prone to excess they have been in the past, being more often inclined to leniency than severity. Nevertheless, such errors as might occur are reviewable by the courts as well as by later legislatures and administrations, and it is better to run the limited risks they involve than to follow the "clear and present danger" rule, with its immediate costs in divisiveness and much greater long-range risks.

Despite all that has been said here, some people will still passionately insist that liberal society becomes no better, morally, than the worst totalitarian tyranny when it suppresses parties hostile to itself. This is like insisting that the policeman and the murderer are equally culpable for using guns, or that Hitler and his victims were equally culpable for waging war. Such people fail to realize that the central virtue of liberal democracy is its protection of the life, liberty, property, and pursuit of happiness of its citizens, and *not* its allowing them a right to encourage violation of its laws, saying and doing as they please. This is no part of the freedom they retain, and if they retained it, freedom itself for all in society would come to an end. Liberal society does require a degree of intolerance: it must be prepared to put down its internal enemies. But even so its members are infinitely freer, infinitely more secure than the members of totalitarian societies. By not tolerating the parties of liberal democracy, communist and other dictatorships make sure the rights of their citizens *cannot* be protected from government. And by tolerating only the communist (or dominant) party, they make sure they have an instrument for fastening the most severe dictatorship on their citizens. On the other hand, when sound liberal democracies refuse to tolerate parties opposed to liberal democracy, they protect themselves from being divided or overthrown from within, and thus give a more formidable guarantee to the preservation of liberty and equality for their citizens. Beyond this minimal but fundamental prohibition, they do in fact allow many parties and opinions to flourish—quite contrary to all one-party systems. In short, political intolerance in liberal societies is narrow and protects liberty; political intolerance in totalitarian societies is broad and guarantees servitude.

The flawed constitutionalism of Holmes and Brandeis, manifest in their "clear and present danger" rule, has dominated our jurisprudence for decades. Republican self-government has already suffered badly because of it, and in the tempestuous future is likely to suffer even more. The intellectual supporters of the rule have been living in a dream world, and by misusing and abusing the awesome power of judicial review, have foisted this dream on an unwilling nation. The "clear and present danger" rule has utterly no foundation in the original Constitution or Bill of Rights. Its philosophical ground is shaky, filled with contradictions, and in no way merits replacing the moral and political principles, still cherished by the American people, which Jefferson wrote into the Declaration of Independence. Its practical effect has been to do great harm to the body politic long before the crimes it is meant to prevent have become imminent—at which time it stands very little chance of preventing them. Constitutionally, philosophically, and prudentially the "clear and present danger" rule has nothing to recommend it.

Liberal societies must have the right to defend themselves against internal enemies long before they can actually bring about the evils they threaten. For internal enemies there will be, with or without vast tyrannies abroad to encourage them, and their crimes must be prevented or punished. To this task liberal societies will bring their own special virtues: a reluctance to restrict the liberty of their citizens unduly, a disposition to draft laws with care, and an almost fastidious judicial system—all within the context of representative democracy. But they must again come to realize, as the people still sense better than many of their leaders, and as the old leaders sensed far better than the new, that liberalism requires rigor against enemies, and that our own government is not the main enemy. In this the United States can still serve as a model not only to older liberal societies that have been faltering or weak in their policy, but also to newer ones and to those countries that still aspire to become liberal democracies. To its friends abroad it can demonstrate that the regime of liberty need not lead to internal divisions, weakness, and eventual collapse. The lesson will not be lost on its enemies.

PART II

DOES THE FIRST AMENDMENT

PROTECT OBSCENITY?

7

Liberty without Morality?

ALEXIS DE TOCQUEVILLE, our most profound foreign visitor and commentator, could claim in 1832 that travelers to America "all agree in remarking that morals are far more strict there than elsewhere." So great was this strictness that "In America all books, novels not excepted, suppose women to be chaste, and no one thinks of relating affairs of gallantry."[1] One hundred years later, America was still morally strict, but not to the same degree. By the 1940s and 1950s, books and magazines appealing to lust and movies portraying physical passion without moral restraint had begun to appear, but they were still considered in bad taste and of doubtful legality.

During the 1960s and 1970s this situation changed radically. For several decades already, intellectuals had been crusading to free the sexual appetite from conventional restraints they mocked under the names of Puritanism and Victorianism. This effort led to the debasing of public morality in novels, poetry, essays, cheap paperbacks, magazines, movies, songs, and higher education. By 1957, the Supreme Court had taken a modest though decisive step toward joining this movement; by 1966, it had practically foreclosed the possibility of prosecutions for obscenity; in 1973, while in principle drawing back from this extreme, it also retreated further in practice by allowing only pornography to be legally punishable as obscenity. Suddenly every appeal to lust short of pornography was free to appear in the media, and so of course it did. The last medium to fall was television, and even that previously sacred zone known as "family viewing time" was by the mid-1970s subject to a vulgar hedonism. So far has the situation degenerated that today, while many claim constitutionality for pornography itself, few older liberals seem willing to defend the constitutional tradition against them.

MORAL REVOLUTION

What understanding of human life is propagated through the media? The incessant artificial stimulation that fills our world is a mixture of the childish, the sleazy, the frivolous, and the brutal, with a pervasive concentration on sex that makes its immoral and illegal use attractive, or at least no longer shameful, and its moral and legal use unattractive. The result is a steady erosion of old values and laws. In this obsessive portrayal of sex, we find only a shallow animal sensuality that strips sex of its connection with admirable traits of intellect, character, even passion, and hence from lasting love and marriage. Our outlook has become that of the adolescent who never grows up and never thinks of sex as a husband, parent, citizen, or statesman does, thus freeing it from any sense of responsibility. The old theme of seduction has practically disappeared, since the woman—in this new model—is more likely to surrender her virtue voluntarily and quickly than have it beguiled from her. Rape as a theme is explicitly taken up much more frequently in the media than it has ever been, and perhaps remains the only evil. As a general matter, sexual restraint is treated as antiquated repression inconsistent with our nature and sexual intercourse of almost the most casual kind as never to be forborne. Nothing more in this regard is expected of women than of men, of adults than of adolescents, of community leaders than of criminals and ne'er-do-wells: all have license to indulge unrestrained appetites. Movies and books, of course, have gone far beyond television in portraying explicit sexual activity of every kind, but it is not moral scruple or a sense of public responsibility that prevents any of the media from going even further. They are restrained only by the fear of citizen outrage and public regulation—threats which have grown weaker over the years, but which now may be reviving as the menace of unfettered pornography makes itself felt.

The new dispensation has been in force for only thirty years or so, but such is the unprecedented power of the mass media that a perceptible alteration in the American character—its ideals, modes of speech, thought, feeling, and behavior—has already taken place. It may not be accurate to say that we have left civilization and returned to the jungle, for animals follow simple, natural impulses. What we are now engaged in is not only a starving or warping of our uniquely human faculties, but in many ways a corruption of the nature we share with beasts.

Americans have not reacted uniformly to this revolutionary attack on their morality. At one extreme we have those who deny that the mass media have any lasting effect at all, tending to regard them instead as rather superficial instruments of entertainment rather than formative instruments of education. Others would claim that the picture painted above is entirely one-sided, omitting all those great recent dramatic and literary accomplishments which add luster to, and alone justify, what is admittedly a tawdry scene at best. Some argue that the prospects for improvement have yet to appear in this temporary stage, with its excesses of defiant assertiveness spawned by the excesses of past moral and legal repression. They look forward to the serenity without obscenity that will characterize the next and final stage of culture, when art will finally be in accord with nature. Some believe that individual artists deserve First Amendment protection, yet acknowledge that the presentation of sex (others will assert this of violence but not of sex) by the mass media is distinctly unwholesome. Finally, many, filled with disgust, are more apt to liken these influences morally to a sewer and find it hard to believe that the First Amendment was intended to protect them. The revulsion felt by ordinary people at what to them are clear abuses of liberty has figured prominently in presidential politics and influenced the composition of the federal judiciary.

What the Constitution compels or permits, and its relation to what is philosophically sound and prudent in practice, are issues of great complexity. There is no doubt that we have moved from a moderate to an extreme liberty under the impress of a judicial revolution that postdated, but grew out of, Holmes's and Brandeis's libertarianism. After having extended First Amendment protection to obviously hostile and alien revolutionary movements, the judiciary now conceives the Amendment as sheltering works inspired by the supposedly friendly forces of Art and Science and dedicated to sexual emancipation. Attacks on sexual restraint, in the form of increasingly open appeals to lust, have been given First Amendment protection with growing frequency. After all, if sex is natural and good, are not all constraints on it purely conventional, and perhaps even harmful? This puerile appeal American intellectuals could not easily resist. Associating sexual constraint with revealed religions of which they have long been contemptuous, not understanding liberty's need for such constraints, they bridle at prohibitions of obscenity that limit their freedom to write and read what they wish. Often believing, as Americans are prone to do, that men are spontaneously good without education or training, they have not grasped the full moral consequences of emancipating the sexual urge. They have not realized how much harm comes from this emancipation, or that it entails emancipating all urges, including the urge to violence. They did not anticipate how quickly the acid of the mass media, once liberated from moral restraint, would start to dissolve moral fiber built up over many centuries. Above all, they have managed to overlook a basic fact: for men to live together as a civilized nation devoted to their common freedom rather than as a loose collection of individuals devoted to their own pleasures, moral virtues are necessary. A nation of profligates, cheats, and cowards, of people incapable of controlling their own lust, greed, rage, and fear, cannot, by the nature of things, use its freedom properly or long endure.

The moral interest of liberal democracy, while in some ways coinciding with elements of religion, is nonetheless wholly independent of it and founded on completely natural and rational grounds. The views of both Jefferson and Washington have some relevance here. Between these two there were many differences, but not on the matter of the Republic's general need for virtue and morality. In Europe Jefferson was equally repelled by city mobs and dissolute aristocrats. Whoever goes to Europe for an education, he warned,

> acquires a fondness for European luxury and dissipation, and a contempt for the simplicity of his own country; he is fascinated with the privileges of the European aristocrats, and sees, with abhorrence, the lovely equality which the poor enjoy with the rich, in his own country. . . . [H]e is led, by the strongest of all the human passions, into a spirit for female intrigue, destructive of his own and others' happiness, or a passion for whores, destructive of his health, and, in both cases, learns to consider fidelity to the marriage bed as an ungentlemanly practice, and inconsistent with happiness; he recollects the voluptuary dress and arts of the European women, and pities and despises the chaste affections and simplicity of those of his own country.[2]

Note that Jefferson emphasizes sexual morality as part of morality in general, the corruption of which he connects with aristocracy rather than democracy.

Jefferson cites improving the morals of the citizens as one of the purposes of primary education, and this improvement was to reach a high level at the university, where an effort would be made to "enlarge their minds, cultivate their morals, and instill into them the precepts of virtue and order." They were to be "examples of virtue to others, and of happiness within themselves."[3] Imagine a superintendent of education saying something like this today.

While Washington attributed much more importance than Jefferson to the role of religion in supporting morality, they did not differ about democracy's need for morality. This passage from Washington's Farewell Address is well known: "Of all the dispositions and habits, which lead to political prosperity, Religion, and Morality are indispensable supports. In vain would that man claim the tribute of patriotism, who should labor to subvert these great pillars of human happiness, these firmest props of the duties of Men and Citizens."[4] And in words undoubtedly added to modify Montesquieu's famous dictum about the need for virtue in small democratic republics,[5] Washington observes that "'Tis substantially true, that virtue or morality is a necessary spring of popular government. The rule indeed extends with more or less force to every species of Free Government. Who that is a sincere friend to it can look with indifference upon attempts to shake the foundations of the fabric?"[6]

What the founding generation meant by virtue, in its higher reaches, can be gathered from the life of Washington himself, who had no superior, and few peers, in exemplifying the virtue he extolled. On one of the few occasions that a great and virtuous man has written the biography of another, John Marshall wrote his extensive *Life of George Washington*. In his concluding account of Washington's character, Marshall states that

> No man has ever appeared on the theater of public action whose integrity was more incorruptible, or whose principles were more free from the contamination of those selfish and unworthy passions which find their nourishment in the conflicts of party. . . . Endowed by nature with a sound judgment, and an accurate discriminating mind, he feared not that laborious attention which

made him perfectly master of those subjects, in all their relations, on which he was to decide; and this essential quality was guided by an unvarying sense of moral right, which would tolerate the employment only of those means that would bear the most rigid examination; by a fairness of intention that neither sought nor required disguise: and by a purity of virtue which was not only untainted, but unsuspected.[7]

We can see from Marshall's description that Washington's moral virtue, while politically of great use to the republic, was valued not simply for that reason: it was admirable in itself. This elevated view of virtue is different from and superior to anything derived from the pages of Locke's political philosophy. It shows that the founders managed to make an amalgam of Locke and older views, just as the American people have in practice managed to combine Locke's rationalism with elements of Christianity. Were Jefferson and Washington correct? Does Lockean liberty require the restraint of moral virtue—or can liberty subsist on self-interest alone?

THE LEGAL TRADITION

In 1966 Justice William O. Douglas voted with the Court to clear an eighteenth-century classic of pornography, *Fanny Hill*, of the charge of obscenity under a Massachusetts law. He claimed that "the First Amendment, written in terms that are absolute, deprives the States of any power to pass on the value, the propriety, or the morality of a particular expression."[8]

Justice Douglas seemed to forget that the First Amendment is directed against Congress, not the states. Nor did he mention the Court's long, unbroken tradition of upholding obscenity laws. Yet seven years earlier he had cited as "our constitutional ideal" the decision in *Near v. Minnesota* (1931) in which Chief Justice Hughes had gone beyond

Blackstone himself in citing restrictions on the press.[9] Not only are there abuses of the press deserving of subsequent punishment, as Blackstone had argued, but four in particular merit *prior* restraint, including one by which "the primary requirements of decency may be enforced against obscene publications." In short, in 1931 "our constitutional ideal" maintained that society has an interest in decency and morality, and may even go so far as to keep publications from seeing the light of day to protect that interest. What could have made the Court reverse itself so radically between 1931 and 1966? To answer that question, we must follow the main line of constitutional development through 1957, when the Supreme Court first stumbled in the thicket of obscenity law, only to end less than a decade later in what amounted to the abolition of obscenity laws.

The single most important fact to bear in mind, when approaching this constitutional question, is that the Supreme Court, as a body, has always excluded obscenity from the realm of protected speech and press. True, the Court has seldom tried to explain or defend this remnant of Blackstonianism. Moreover, under the influence of recent intellectual currents, its appreciation of the moral foundations of society has been so weak and its awe of art, science, and individual liberty so great as to permit the sacrifice of the former to the latter. Nevertheless, while drastically reducing limits on obscenity, the Court has never reached the point of removing them entirely. Government may still ban obscenity, consistent with the First Amendment.

In England, common law prosecutions for obscenity go back as far as 1727. Blackstone, writing in the 1760s, did not use the term "obscene libel," but he plainly had such things in mind when defining libels in the most general sense as "any writings, pictures or the like of an immoral or illegal tendency." And he cites "immoral libels"[10] as one of the six excluded from the liberty of the press and punishable at law. Even today, hardly anyone claims that the framers of the First Amendment *meant* to emancipate obscenity from its common law restraints, yet there is practically no direct evidence from the debates one way or the other. In all likelihood no one at the time saw it as a national problem or believed it *should* be emancipated—a view supported by the fact that the first common law prosecutions for obscenity (one involving obscene pictures, in the Philadelphia of 1815, the other for the book *Fanny Hill* in the Massachusetts of 1821) occurred despite, or rather consistent with, guarantees of the freedom of speech and press in the state constitutions of both Pennsylvania and Massachusetts. Of similar import is that, beginning in the 1820s, state after state passed anti-obscenity statutes, again without constitutional hesitation.[11]

Such statutes were universally understood to be legitimate exercises of state police power, a power inherent in state authority and hence among those the Tenth Amendment reserves to the states. The term "police power" has a curious history. In Blackstone, offenses against the "public police and economy" are a miscellany—some quite serious—involving violations of public propriety, decency, and orderliness.[12] In this country, the "police power" of the states was first mentioned on the Court by John Marshall in 1827,[13] but it did not come into regular prominence until the last quarter of the century, when the states saw fit, under their police power, to regulate various aspects of modern industrial society. While all members of the Court acknowledged the existence of the "police power," there were serious differences about its extent, and in particular about its relation to economic liberty. There were no comparable differences about its relation to morals.

We may gain some idea of the unanimity and consistency of the Court's views by considering a few passages from notable decisions:

> The people, in their sovereign capacity, have established their agencies for the preservation of the public health and the public morals. . . . (1880).[14]

> We hold that the police power of a State embraces regulations designed to promote the public convenience or the general pros-

perity, as well as regulations designed to promote the public health, the public morals or the public safety (1906).[15]

The liberty safeguarded [by the Constitution] is liberty in a social organization which requires the protection of law against the evils which menace the health, safety, morals and welfare of the people (1937).[16]

Public safety, public health, *morality*, peace and quiet, law and or-der—these are some of the more conspicuous examples of the tra-ditional application of the police power to municipal affairs (1954).[17]

The final passage was written by Justice Douglas. Further, Justice Holmes, half a century earlier, had favored granting the states great lati-tude in exercising their police powers in economic affairs. As Holmes said in his *Lochner* dissent, "I think that the word liberty in the Four-teenth Amendment is perverted when it is held to prevent the natural outcome of a dominant opinion, unless it can be said that a rational and fair man necessarily would admit that the statute proposed would infringe fundamental principles as they have been understood by the traditions of our people and our law" (1905).[18]

Examples of the exercise of the police power in the area of moral-ity are state laws regulating not only obscenity, but marriage, educa-tion, the content of movies, gambling, alcoholic beverages, and red-light districts. Although the Constitution delegates no such powers to the national government, something like it developed on that level as well through an oblique application of power Congress does possess. Con-gress has forbidden the importation of obscene materials (starting with the Tariff Act of 1842), the mailing of them (starting in 1865, and then enlarged in the famous Comstock Act of 1873), and even their trans-portation by common carrier (1897). Citing its earliest opinion on the postal authority (1878), the Court later ruled that "Congress may 'also classify the recipients of such matter, and forbid the delivery of letters to such persons or corporations as, in its judgment, are making use of the mails for the purpose of fraud or deception or the dissemination among its citizens of information of a character calculated to debauch the public morality'"(1904).[19] In fact, the first clear obscenity case to reach the Supreme Court involved the mails (1896), and the first case charging a book of great stature (James Joyce's *Ulysses*) with obscenity, though it never reached the Court, involved its importation (1933).

WHAT IS OBSCENITY?

We have established, through an examination of constitutional history, that the First Amendment has never protected obscenity, that the states have always been thought to have direct authority to suppress it, and that the federal government as well has used certain of its powers in an effort to "promote the general welfare" by helping suppress it. This explains the entirely negative constitutional view the Court has always taken of obscenity. But what is this "obscenity," which various levels of government, each in its own way, may suppress?

In the first recorded obscenity case in this country, the Supreme Court of Pennsylvania reviewed a trial involving a painting of a man and woman in an "obscene, impudent and indecent posture." Its exhibit was charged with intending to "debauch and corrupt" the morals of youth and other citizens of the commonwealth, and "to raise and create in their minds inordinate and lustful desires."[20] Seventy years later, in the first obscenity case to reach the Supreme Court, the trial judge followed the practice of the day in adopting from English law the rule Lord Chief Justice Cockburn, in *Regina v. Hicklin*, had first formulated in 1868: "I think the test of obscenity is this, whether the tendency of the matter charged as obscenity is to deprave and corrupt those whose minds are open to such immoral influences and into whose hands a publication of this sort may fall."[21]

In the 1930s this test was subjected to important qualifications by lower American courts, but it was not formally altered by the Supreme Court until 1957 in *Roth v. United States*, in which the Court opened its opinion with a more exact definition of obscenity: "Obscene material is material which deals with sex in a manner appealing to prurient interest." A footnote defines "prurient interest" as "having a tendency to excite lustful thoughts," and enlarges on the key term, "prurient," with the words "itching, longing; uneasy with desire or longing, of persons, having itching, morbid, or lascivious longings; of desire, curiosity, or propensity, lewd." And "pruriency" is "the quality of being prurient; lascivious desire or thought." [22]

The stress on exciting prurient or lustful thoughts and desires is present in both the 1957 and the 1815 versions, though not in Lord Cockburn's test. On the other hand, the new term "prurient" introduces a recondite, scientific tone into a definition originally intended to be plain to every decent person. This impression is corroborated by the fact that only the 1957 definition lacks a reference to moral corruption. And it may be of more than passing interest to note that the Court's later attempt (in 1973) to revive some understanding of the harm done by obscenity led Chief Justice Burger to speak once again of its "corrupting and debasing impact." Nevertheless, educated men of an earlier time did not have to explain why it was that obscene materials had an immoral and corrupting influence. To the public, educated and uneducated, this would have been so obvious as to require no explanation. But times have changed, and the intellectual currents of the twentieth century, challenging old ideas and restraints, have made such explanations necessary. Today we must explain what the Philadelphia indictment of 1815 called the "manifest corruption and subversion" of the youth and others by obscenity, and why it in fact offended "the peace and dignity of the commonwealth of Pennsylvania," as claimed. [23]

Other important elements of obscenity law were also changed in *Roth*. The Court rejected the *Hicklin* rule's test of obscenity, claiming that it made the obscene effect of a publication depend particularly on how it affected the most vulnerable parts of the population—that is, women and children. Instead, the Court recommended a test that had developed in lower American courts: "whether to the average person, applying contemporary community standards, the dominant theme of the material taken as a whole appeals to prurient interest." This peculiarly inept pronouncement was a marked regression from the *Hicklin* rule and became a veritable breeding ground for difficulties the Court soon had to face. The removal of the special consideration the *Hicklin* rule gave to women and children exposes them to obscenity in a new way. Now, only what the "average person" would find obscene can be prohibited, without reference to particularly vulnerable audiences like children. In addition, the "average person" may judge only by the "dominant theme" of the work as a whole, not by particularly effective passages. On both counts *Roth* is much more permissive. And if it has been argued against the *Hicklin* rule that no difference should exist between men and women in this area, to date no one has dared argue against the special vulnerability of children.

The Court made an even greater error when it referred in its new test to "contemporary community standards," for the term suggests the variable nature of these standards, and thereby prepares the way for their alteration. A question is also raised by the reference to the average person applying contemporary community standards: what other standards could the average person apply, if we are talking about his own? The Court included all these new elements in the confidence that they marked real progress over the prudish and restrictive *Hicklin* rule. Once standards were loosened, the demand to loosen them further could hardly be resisted. The floodgates were opened, and the restoration of any sanity to standards of decency has become very difficult. The good sense of previous generations is forgotten, and the justification of obscenity laws must be sought anew.

OBSCENITY LAWS AND CIVILIZATION

Why and to what extent do free societies have an interest in the morality of their citizens—that is, in their possessing certain virtues and lacking certain vices? How are these moral results to be achieved? How much depends on sound education? What can be done by criminal law? Let us start with obscenity, understood quite traditionally as lewd and indecent material appealing to lust and sensuality and shocking to the sensibilities of the decent citizen. The decent citizen is one who generally abides by the laws, and respects the rules, manners, and institutions necessary to a free civilized society. Such a society must be characterized by the rule of reason and proper habits rather than raw passion, by stable families and communities that provide the kind of upbringing and support necessary to produce good citizens. Such citizens must be capable of ruling themselves and treating their fellow citizens and their common public institutions with care and respect. In short, free civilized society cannot be largely composed of individuals driven by their appetites, disorderly and impulsive, who have no respect for others or for the law, and increasingly none for themselves, as they sense their uniquely human worth degenerating.

If the foregoing is correct, all forces calling us back to a primordial condition, appealing to appetites and passions, and ignoring moral and legal constraints that must be placed on them, are dangerous to free civilized society. Even liberals worry about the effects of violence in the mass media, and all but the most extreme libertarians on the Court have been willing to concede a state interest in keeping obscene materials at least from the young. Such views are obviously predicated on the assumption that our dispositions, desires, and ideas *can* be harmfully influenced by what we see, read, and hear—by books, pictures, pamphlets, movies, music. Obscenity, whether in the form of dirty pictures, novels like *Fanny Hill*, or x-rated movies, portrays human beings in such a way as to make sexual pleasure an end in itself, however obtained. Its appeal is solely to lust—not to love, not to concern for others, not to the traits of mind and character deserving consideration in choosing a mate, not to the enduring tie of marriage, not to progeny, but to lust alone. While sexual appetite is no doubt natural, obscenity separates it from all other socially and politically relevant aspects of our nature. Indeed, obscenity separates sex from the reproductive function, for which it exists in the animal kingdom, from the raising of children and the stability of the family, from the rule of reason essential to the dignity of the individual and civilized society.

In order fully to appreciate the harm done by obscenity, we must become aware of how much of our ordinary, decent behavior is *not* spontaneously natural to us but the socially inherited product of reason and experience working over centuries to bring our raw natural appetites under control. Take a simple moral quality like consideration or politeness in its sexual application. To behave well reliably in this area, we must be strongly influenced by our parents, elders, and community during our formative years. Left alone, we remain rough creatures, more likely to grab at what we crave than to consider the desires and dignity of others.

It is the civilizing process alone, repeated in the upbringing of every child, that leads men to treat women with respect rather than to dominate them by brute force, that tests affection through courtship, that forms the very emotion of love itself, considered not as a transient physical impulse but as a deep and enduring devotion, and that cultivates in parents a reliable willingness to care and sacrifice for their children over a long period of time. It is the civilizing process that teaches us to distinguish proper from improper objects of sexual attention— for instance, to abstain from incest, to avoid taking advantage of the young, and to respect the ties and affections of others. It is the civilizing process that teaches us to distinguish proper from improper sexual attention—for example, to avoid harassment and vulgarity, not to mention rape, seduction, and other forms of compulsion or enticement.

The civilizing process, the process by which we are changed from hairless near-apes into the rational and moral animals we are *in potentia*, cannot be successfully carried out without the support—the unswerving, general and dominant support—of the community of opinion and law. Community opinion acts through praise and blame and in support of the parents' praise and blame. Community laws and punishments act in support of parental punishment. The process by which we are made into civilized, responsible, and therefore free, individuals is one in which all the forces of family and community, education and coercion, work together to place under both internal and external controls those impulses in us that resist civilization, whether they derive from our untutored human nature or from defects in society itself.

Unless we understand the difficulties which had to be overcome in achieving civilization and producing the rational self-controlled individual, unless we see that these difficulties never disappear but constantly threaten to bring back a savage state approaching anarchy, unless we realize that this anarchy will itself be a prelude to despotism, we cannot appreciate the task confronting civilized societies and *above all* societies which place the highest possible premium on individual liberty. For free societies must realize that they are not the spontaneous product of primordially free individuals: they derive from, and are constantly dependent on, the controls needed for civilization. And they require these restraints much more than regimes that do not depend on individuals' enjoying a broad personal liberty to judge and act as they please. Only in free societies does what actually pleases most individuals— whether it is consistent with sustaining the regime or inconsistent with it—make a crucial difference. Only free societies require of all their members the moral dispositions and capacities that make cooperation in self-government possible. In other societies, what pleases the rulers, who have the power to compel the people, is all that matters.

We need not undertake here an analysis of all elements of the human soul that the media can influence to the detriment of republican self-government. Nevertheless, four that must be prominent on anyone's list are lust, the inclination to violence, the love of domination, and fear. Each of these, when tamed and controlled in such a way as to serve rational and moral ends, is useful both to the individual and society. Lust can be subordinated to love and marriage. The inclination to violence can be directed against internal and external enemies or molded into the disciplined desire for just punishment. The love of domination can be transformed into responsible ambition, directed toward political, economic, athletic, and other worthy endeavors and turned inward as the mastery of oneself. Fear—the watchman of our preservation—can be made manageable or overcome, even to the point of allowing great sacrifices and the bearing of great pain.

In each of these cases it is exceedingly difficult to achieve the civilized end sought. All the powers of parental upbringing and community affirmation are required, and contrary influences from the mass media, obstructing, weakening, or subverting these powers, are dangerous to the community and the individual. Opinions or portrayals that arouse sheer uninhibited and uncontrolled lust are dangerous, and so too are stimuli to violence, domination, and tyranny, as well as to flinching at necessary tasks or trembling in the grip of uncontrollable terror. State legislatures, and to some extent Congress, have a right and a duty to prohibit the propagation of such influences through the mass media. And they do so on the authority of their power to promote public morality, public safety, public tranquility, and the general welfare, thereby preserving the conditions necessary to a free civilized society.

The First Amendment was never intended to protect speech and press posing such threats to society. This is not a question of taste, of what one person dislikes and another likes, but of the objective needs of a free society. It is a question of fact, of cause and effect, not essentially different in this respect from the science of medicine. The founding fathers sought to establish a society with unprecedented freedom of thought and expression, but they had no intention of allowing a freedom so broad that it would destroy free society itself. From speech and press they sought the expression of grievances and public discussion more than anything else—that is, rational debate about public affairs. No doubt they wanted to free philosophy, science, and literature as well. But there had to be limits, and whenever the individual's expression of thoughts or emotions violated these limits, carefully wrought for the preservation of civilized society and ordered freedom, the individual guilty of the abuse had to give way, not society.

It is also clear that free society's claim, in the interest of its own preservation, is superior to the claim of art or expression to absolute freedom. If society, by setting moral and legal limits, can prolong its own existence, it will furnish ordered freedom to generations of individuals, all enjoying its blessings, including art. If it fails to set these limits, its existence as a stable free society is jeopardized, and hence its ability to pass on its freedoms and culture to future generations. Setting the proper moral tone is not only necessary for the higher good of society but for enduring intellectual and artistic endeavor as well, which even with the necessary restrictions is afforded much more protection in free society than elsewhere. When science and art ask more, in the name of freedom of thought and expression, they act as though they were self-subsistent, capable of supporting and protecting themselves, whereas they are in fact completely dependent for sustenance and protection on the societies of which they form a part. They share the destinies of these societies, and must therefore, to some extent, fly on pinioned rather than unpinioned wing.

Libertarians speak unceasingly as if the glories of science and art depend completely on the extreme freedom they have demanded in the last thirty years. This argument implies that the moderate regulation of the press in this and other free countries during the nineteenth century and first half of the twentieth had a debilitating effect on science and art—an effect that can be expected to diminish as the regulation diminishes. Both parts of this claim are patently false. Our greatest novelists, Hawthorne, Melville, and Twain, flourished during the Victorian period, and it is certainly unclear that their works would have benefited from the permissiveness of 1966. On the other hand, the contributions of D.H. Lawrence, Henry Miller, and the like to serious literature and to society are much more questionable. In any case, their achievements were bought at the heavy price of flooding the field with *Fanny Hill* and the obscene products of countless reprobates whose main concern is profit, not literature. With respect to motion pictures, it is hard to maintain that those filled with provocative sex, excessive violence, or both, are better because of it, or that movies in general since 1966 have been superior to those produced under the old dispensation. Again, for the one or two possible exceptions to this rule the country has had to pay a thousandfold in salacious and tawdry vulgarity and brutalizing violence displayed before general audiences, the effect of which has been steadily to lower both the moral standards and aesthetic taste of the people. And the whole libertarian argument collapses like a house of cards if one recalls the standard libertarian view (best expressed by Justice Douglas) that literary quality is purely relative or subjective, a matter of idiosyncratic taste. Grant this and it becomes impossible to claim that art is *improved* by the removal of restrictions, or that art itself is in any way deserving of special constitutional protection. Relativism destroys, rather than bolsters, libertarianism.

THE MASS MEDIA

The object of the regulation of the press is to prevent or punish definable harms to the society as a whole or its individual members. Society is harmed, its civilizing capacity damaged, and its capacity to endure placed in question when its essential institutions (like its laws) are directly threatened with violation; it is also harmed when appeals are made to powerful appetites which, as evoked, would destroy these essential institutions. No doubt it is one thing to say, explicitly, "Commit adul-

tery," or "Adultery is acceptable behavior," and another to appeal so vividly to lust as to generate an increase in adultery and other such offenses.
But both are directed toward clear social harm, and society has a right
and duty to prevent both. The regulation of the press must not depend on whether ideas are involved, since "ideas" are always involved.
Implicitly, dirty pictures—the bread and butter of simple pornography—convey their message quite vividly, with or without captions: lust
is good; do whatever you wish to satisfy it. Pornography is certainly to
be distinguished from a lecture explicitly glorifying the life of unrestrained sex that even without a slide presentation may use evocative
imagery to heighten its message. Yet despite differences in cerebral appeal, both can have the same harmful effect, and it is the effect, not the
means, that should interest society and justifies prohibitive legislation
in the most dangerous cases. The same principle that entitles society to
ban obscenity allows it to criminalize the publication of material which
encourages adultery, premarital sex, incest, and the like.

  While our discussion has focused on issues of sexuality, the same
reasoning applies with equal force to other serious threats to the essential institutions and rules of a civilized republic. Incitement to violence
without justification is obviously a serious threat, though not all portrayals of violence are incitements to it—some actually arouse repugnance. It would be mistaken, moreover, to treat all violence as equally
unjustified—mistaken when judged by the standard of the Constitution and the philosophy underlying it. Nevertheless, the violence, brutality, and sadism pervading the mass media weigh heavily on society.
Almost subconsciously all citizens, young or old, have begun to feel
that society is dominated by repulsive and fearful elements and life itself
filled with dread and insecurity— that brutishness is our natural state.
Nor are these feelings entirely unfounded. These effects, particularly as
they occur in the movies, on television, and in popular music, and as
they show themselves in the young, are of great interest to society even
when they do not amount to the stimulation of violence. For this com-

bination of lawlessness, brutality, and fear begins to spawn human types and moods that are much more conducive to violent ideologies and regimes than to moderate democracy.

We must admit a fact that should be obvious: the mass media constitute a new way of educating the nation, forming in the minds of citizens an understanding of the good life approved by those in the media. This new mode of education is able to replace old ideas with new ones in the minds of both young and old more rapidly than anyone thought possible and could not be ignored even if it did not cause clearly identifiable harm. The view of good and evil—personal, moral, political—that the media disseminate is of prime interest to society. In recent decades it has given continuous powerful support to a dangerous counterculture. It is nearly futile to teach in the home, the schools, and the churches a moral outlook fundamentally contradicted by the mass media. Society must therefore find a way of assuring that its view of the good citizen be conveyed not only in the schools but in those media, like television, the movies, and popular music, that have an especially profound impact on the public.

We have allowed the mass media, under the influence of contemporary libertarianism, to inject into our body politic the very kinds of corruption Jefferson witnessed in Europe among aristocracy and mob alike. Profligacy, dissipation, brutality, lawlessness, and lack of rational control over the passions have all been brought into the living room, the neighborhood theater, the local drugstore, and record shop—and this not only without a struggle from educational and political authorities but with the blessing of the highest court in the land. Jefferson—and probably all of the founders, without exception—would have been appalled at this loss of understanding of democracy's moral prerequisites. And he would no doubt have wondered—with some sense of urgency, if not desperation—what could possibly be done to restore this understanding and then to regulate the media in such a manner as to restrain the worst and encourage the best.

8

The Sexual Revolution

Pressure against old obscenity laws has come from publishers, authors, psychologists, and a host of intellectuals. Lawyers, far from serving as the conservative ballast both Hamilton and Tocqueville hoped they would be, have not been bashful about furnishing their clients with the requisite arguments to justify the liberalization of obscenity law. Such arguments have rarely revealed any appreciation for the moral needs of free society, since it is generally supposed that individual freedom is the only consideration and that more of a good thing must itself be a good thing. Some oppose suppressing obscenity because of a mistaken, but sincere, belief that the First Amendment protects all speech and press and that any regulation will eventually mean total regulation. Most who oppose obscenity laws, however, are simply active opponents of the old morality of restraint, which they identify as Christian, and zealous proponents of a new morality. Their eager anticipation of the fruits of sexual revolution has the effect of making their historical investigations of the First Amendment less than impartial.

The writers we have chosen to examine in this chapter have had important roles in the cultural, political, and legal challenges to the restriction of obscenity. D. H. Lawrence, with whom we shall begin, is an important literary figure of the twentieth century. His novel *Lady Chatterley's Lover* was also made into a movie and in both forms became the center of legal controversy both here and in his native England. By Lawrence's own admission, his book presents a new sexual morality, but he vehemently denies it to be pornography, which he believes should be censored rigorously. The Kronhausens, psychologists who in a popular mid-century book entitled *Pornography and the Law* distinguished between erotic realism and pornography, place great value on the former but find positive value in the latter as well. Naturally, their conclusion is that obscenity laws should be abolished. We shall also look further into the views of John Stuart Mill, whose name and reputation are sometimes used to justify a further extension of liberty in this area. His ideas, by virtue of their widespread dissemination and popularization, have led many to read his "liberty of thought and discussion" into the First Amendment. Holmes and Brandeis used his ideas without citing him; others use his ideas without knowing whence they came. In the next chapter, we shall discuss the fruit of these cultural and political challenges to obscenity law in the constitutional attacks by Charles Rembar and Justice William O. Douglas.

D. H. LAWRENCE

Lawrence would censor pornography because it is degrading and harmful. It is "the attempt to insult sex, to do dirt on it."[1] There would be little difficulty, he thinks, in distinguishing it from literature and art, especially from writings that convey the naturalness and beauty of sex, like his own *Lady Chatterley's Lover*. In this work Lawrence does all a modern *littérateur* can do to popularize the life of natural eroticism. In his view, the only proper restraints on passion must grow out of passion itself: physical passion spreads into tender love, from which self-denial comes naturally. To teach this and similar lessons about the

natural primacy of sexuality in man, Lawrence describes a romance between the wife of a British aristocrat (rendered paralyzed and impotent in the First World War) and the estate gamekeeper. Lord Chatterley
symbolizes an artificial and increasingly decadent society and his gamekeeper the preservation of the natural life. The novel reaches its climax
in an abundance of sexual detail such as had never before been set down
by gifted pen. This detail is meant to act on the souls of male and female readers alike, and indeed with greater force on the female to coun-
teract her greater modesty, for Lawrence devotes a disproportionate
number of pages to Lady Chatterley's perceptions and feelings. Both
men and women are to be emancipated from harmful moral restraint
and made eager for the experience shared by the protagonists.

It does not suffice to say that the work "advocates" adultery in certain circumstances: it "incites" to it, to adultery as such, and to much
more than adultery. Since the great variety of human circumstances
which might oblige people to refrain from entering a life of sexual love
go unmentioned, one may fairly conclude that Lawrence believes that
conventional restraints placed by society on sexual love—whether before or after marriage—must bow to the imperious demands of primordial nature. Feelings of obligation are co-existent with love, and
cease when love ceases. The life of natural inclination alone is the good,
the pure, and—in this sense only—the sacred life.

Yet Lawrence does not present his case fairly to the reader. Instead
of beginning with natural or primordial man and woman, he chooses
two unusual people who, whether by endowment or upbringing, have
many virtues. Their physical passion expands rapidly into something
more than the desire for an embrace. He takes leave of them separated
from each other temporarily but with their juvenile ardor still burning
as they anticipate future physical reunion. But is this what can be expected of the relation of the sexes by nature? Has not Lawrence, without acknowledging it, retained vital elements of the civilizing process
provided by society? For one thing, the gamekeeper does not overpower

or beat the lady, as primordial man might well have. Indeed, apart from his initial willingness to take advantage of her and betray her husband, he is more chivalrous than most. Their zest for each other is depicted, quite without reason, as being constant and exclusive rather than transient and variable. Nor should we overlook the fact that these lovers could rest secure in the confidence that the English police force and soldiery would, like Lord Chatterley in the Great War, run any risk to protect the two of them from rapine or other external violence that might threaten their affair. In the background civilization and the state are there, unrecognized and unappreciated.

How much of this portrait of the lovers is natural to mankind? Lawrence is too sanguine about the original relation between the sexes. Only the development of political society and civilization could give rise to or protect the kind of love depicted in the novel. In other words, something other than mere unfettered sexual instinct makes the romance possible. Societies require sexual restraint as well as sexual impulse, and they have not found such restraint forthcoming from impulse left to itself. Societies are everywhere sustained by families, and wherever there are families there are prohibitions and demanding duties, not simply liberties. Moral and legal regulation of sexual behavior makes it more orderly, dependable, and responsible than it would otherwise be. Restrictions on intercourse, marriage, and divorce, and a network of obligations and rights within each family are necessary because the free will of the individual cannot always be relied upon. This is not to say that a given set of regulations of a given country is the best it could possibly have. But an immense burden of proof lies on the reformer, who must consider not only the changes he proposes but those unintended consequences that could accompany them. Further, reform differs utterly from extirpation. To extirpate moral and legal restraints on sex is to extirpate society itself. And as Tocqueville saw with unequaled clarity, there is a vital connection between the virtuous family and the well being of American democracy. [2]

THE KRONHAUSENS

An even more extreme position than Lawrence's has been taken by the authors of *Pornography and the Law* (1959). Drs. Eberhard and Phyllis Kronhausen, in a novel declaration of independence, proclaim the right of every human being to use his body sexually as he sees fit, short of harming or deceiving others. Since this cannot be a mere civil right, it must be a natural right. Armed with this bold (and baldly stated) premise, we have no reason to believe that such phenomena as prostitution, fornication, adultery, bigamy, polygamy, polyandry, sodomy, exhibitionism, the making of improper advances, and a multitude of more perverse expressions of the sexual self should not be the moral and legal right of every individual. This new laissez-faire of the organs does not permit rape or seduction, but it forbids only the most palpable harm to others, precludes considering harm done to oneself, and leads us to no lofty conception of sexual conduct. To this barely human right of man, ideas of love, duty, respect, and restraint are needless accretions, since it exists in autarchic perfection whether or not they are present. Whatever the deficiencies in Freud's conception of man, he at least perceived the need for society to inhibit the libido more extensively. Not so the neo-Freudian Kronhausens, who judge a society by the sexual freedom it bestows and thus supply democracy with what they think is its ultimate justification. Sexual freedom can be the privilege only of a free society, they say, and the more democratic a society, the greater the sexual freedom of its members. They cite Communist Russia in the 1920s as promulgating the most liberal sex legislation of modern times.[3] They look forward to the Eden of free and natural love, when both the coercive state and sexual perversion shall have withered away.

Pornography and the Law is a study intended for the instruction of the jurist as well as the layman. The Kronhausens wish to provide a guide for the Supreme Court to distinguish the obscene from other literature. They begin by distinguishing between pornography and erotic realism. Obscene books (pornography is called hard-core obscenity) stimulate lustful desires and keep doing so throughout, making strong appeal to unrealistic sexual fantasy. Erotic realism—epitomized by Lawrence's *Lady Chatterley's Lover* and Edmund Wilson's *Memoirs of Hecate County*—is, they say, another matter. The authors of erotic realism depict the "appropriate emotional states which accompany sexuality under a variety of conditions."[4] So essential is erotic realism to the education of the young, that its *chef d'oeuvres* should be part of a compulsory public school program for sexual instruction. As for obscene literature (including pornography), the Kronhausens disagree with the Supreme Court's willingness to see its publication prohibited. Contrary to the opinions of Justice Harlan and others, obscene writings do have redeeming social value. Although they sometimes stimulate erotic fantasies which may lead to prohibited sexual behavior, more often than not they serve as a safety valve for the sexually deviant and potential sex offender.[5] We are never told how much more often they inhibit rather than stimulate sexual crime. Nor do we learn of any restrictions the Kronhausens would place on the production or sale of pornography. Evidently it is worth risking the health of the many to alleviate illness in the few.

The authors also brandish an ad hominem argument against those who advocate the censorship of erotic materials: censorial urges are the product of an overt or tacit subscription to the "Pauline doctrine of carnal sin" and to the view that "sex is inherently evil, dirty, and dangerous, or at least potentially so, if not carefully checked and circumscribed by a number of social prohibitions."[6] They do not consider the rational wisdom in the story of Adam and Eve, and they fail to state, let alone refute, the reasoning of those who would no more abolish sexual prohibitions than laws against murder. The Kronhausens correctly perceive that the most urgent sexual problem of the child is handling the lustful emotions, but they recommend dispelling the shame attached to these emotions by our moral tradition.[7] They fail to realize that shame is society's means of assisting weak reason. Unrestrained intercourse and complete shamelessness make reasonable society, a reasonable life, and social existence impossible. Puberty arrives before mental maturity, and full thoughtfulness is difficult to attain. The sexual freedom of adolescents conduces to impulsive behavior based on physical passion alone, making for frequent and unwise liaisons and the production of unwanted children by unfit as well as unmarried parents. The sexes come to regard each other as objects of selfish exploitation rather than of considerate and enduring, if possessive, devotion. Once dalliance becomes habitual and self-control declines, the loss of self-respect as well as the respect of others follows, and it becomes probable that fly-by-night lovers will become fly-by-night mates—unless, through sheer revulsion, they plunge into a bitter and withdrawn asceticism.

Shame, modesty, politeness, and fidelity strengthen the intellect, deepen the heart, and restrain the appetites of the human species. The rational and social nature of man learns through society to perfect itself; after countless centuries the original male and female human animal has been transformed into the gentlemen and the lady, and their children, after an upbringing of little more than a decade, into young gentlemen and young ladies. This heritage is threatened by those who inveigh against shame as such rather than against a morbid and excessive shame. To be understood, their new abstract geometry of the sexes must be grasped in its purity, not in any admixture, such as we find in *Lady Chatterley's Lover*, with the moral heritage we still possess. Today society still teaches restraint, though it increasingly permits or encourages shamelessness and promiscuity. For a view of what a society based on the extirpation of shame might be like, we should remember Aldous Huxley's description of the relation between the sexes in *Brave New World* and his disgust at its canine casualness, as well as his fear at its autocratic political implications.[8]

The claim that there is a healthy and unhealthy condition and control of sexual desire, that people must be guided toward wise choices and held to their responsibilities, and that natural sexual inclination alone is a weak reed for individuals and societies to lean on, is not traceable to any notion of sex as sinful or dirty. It was most plainly stated in the ancient world by Aristotle. It has been held by believers in a divine principle and atheists alike. But the Kronhausens are scornful of those who want to retain old beliefs. They refer to the ancient "taboos" on incest, homosexuality, and sodomy with the cold disrespect of the scientific enthusiast. They display Kinsey's statistics on what actually occurs in the United States (in contravention of what people say should be done) and take the increasing incidence of premarital relations as a sign of progress, of healthy nature coming into its own. In their zeal for sexual emancipation, they are eager to have young and old shaken loose from the anachronisms of conscience, so that future generations will be free. They are revolutionaries disguised as scientists.

The Drs. Kronhausen classify *Lady Chatterley's Lover* as erotic realism, created by a "prudish but intellectually honest writer." [9] Their definition of pornographic or obscene writings emphasizes two points: such writings attempt to evoke lust in the reader throughout the work, paying little attention to anything else, and they also accentuate those varieties of sexual relations which are the most forbidden or unusual. Early in their book the Kronhausens tell us that erotic realism, by contrast, does not aim at exciting sexual passions, adding toward the end that it "satisfies the natural and desirable interest in sex without turning it into morbid channels, confusing and linking it with violence, or keeping it antiseptically detached from the sensations which should accompany it, and by connecting the sexual impulse with those love-feelings which are its highest perfection." [10] Yet they admit soon afterward that erotically realistic literature or art may cause an "erotically stimulating effect," a "momentary psychological and physiological sex response," and also that "Erotic realism in literature frequently deals with rather 'shocking' aspects of sexuality: perversions and deviations of the natural sex drive, cruelty, and a variety of pathological emotions. But this does not detract from the literary or clinical value of such books." [11]

Yet these are traits it shares with pornography, so that the two are not sharply distinguishable after all, even if erotic realism does not concentrate wholly on evoking lust scene after scene as pornography does. If erotic literature and art tend to lead to sexual acts, this is natural and good, say the Kronhausens. Granting that *Lady Chatterley's Lover* is not pornography, it would be inane to speak of its sexual scenes as if their sole effect, or intention, is a "momentary psychological and physiological response." This the Kronhausens know, since they esteem its therapeutic qualities above all else. Nor need we question, as well we might, the realistic accuracy of Lawrence's most important sexual descriptions. It suffices to say that these descriptions constitute the dramatic and psychological climax of the book, making intelligible all that precedes and succeeds them. Lawrence's aim was to incite lust—a natural and healthy lust, by both his and the Kronhausens' standards. [12] This incitement, in its immediate context, is meant to justify the double adultery of Lady Chatterley and her gamekeeper. Nevertheless, by wrenching lust from the context of responsibility and restraint which ought to surround the sexual relations of men and women, the book has justified immoral and illegal behavior going far beyond adultery, violating obscenity statutes along the way.

JOHN STUART MILL

We return now to the philosopher who went farther than any before him in defending both individuality and freedom of thought and discussion. Yet Mill can hardly serve as a pillar of The Morality of the Future, sexual or otherwise. His stress on individuality did not take him

in the direction of libertinism. He sought rather to overcome the con-
formist mediocrity of an increasingly democratic age, stirring individuals
to make of themselves the best, the happiest, and the most useful human beings they could. Distinguishing the higher pleasures of the soul—
intellectual, moral, and aesthetic—from the lower pleasures of the body,
Mill maintained that we share a common human nature that provides
the standard for human happiness.[13] Liberty in the choice of ways of
life and thought is the opportunity society must allow us that we may
find the greatest possible good for ourselves, not simply that we may
live as we please. In our nonage, society has the duty to cultivate our
rationality and train our passions to obey reason. Lacking self-restraint,
adults cannot be trusted to care for themselves without harm to others.
Possessing it, they can emancipate themselves from conformity and cus-
tom and ask themselves, "what do I prefer? or, what would suit my character and disposition? or, what would enable the best and highest in
me to have fair play, and enable it to grow and thrive?"[14]

This is not to deny that Mill calls for "different opinions," "different
experiments of living," "varieties of character," "different modes of life."[15]
But these differences are not valued for their own sake or for any vulgar
end. On the contrary, human beings are to become "a noble and beautiful object of contemplation" by having "high thoughts and elevating
feelings." The differences among them must indeed be taken into account in choosing their modes of life, otherwise "they neither obtain
their fair share of happiness, nor grow up to the mental, moral and aesthetic stature of which their nature is capable." What is wanted are "great
energies guided by vigorous reason, and strong feelings controlled by a
conscientious will." While people cannot justly compel an adult to
benefit himself in ways they think fit, "They should be for ever stimulating each other to increased exercise of their higher faculties, and increased direction of their feelings and aims towards wise instead of
foolish, elevating instead of degrading, objects and contemplations."[16]
A person who does harm only to himself—one "who pursues animal

pleasures at the expense of those of feeling and intellect," for instance—
must expect that others will have a lower opinion of him, though they
may not punish him for it.[17]

Clearly Mill did not understand his principle of liberty in the same
way as those who are confident that it justifies eradicating obscenity laws
and freeing sexuality from social constraint. Oddly enough, Mill omits
any direct consideration of obscenity law from *On Liberty*, even though
Parliament had passed the new Obscene Publications Act only two years
before. He does maintain, in a footnote, that "there ought to exist the
fullest liberty of professing and discussing, as a matter of ethical conviction, any doctrine, however immoral it may be considered,"[18] but it
is hardly apparent that obscene novels or pornographic pictures involve
the "professing" or "discussing" of a "doctrine." Nevertheless, to look at
the matter from the other direction, Mill never positively excludes obscenity from the liberty he proposes. Moreover, the principle he lays
down for determining exceptions—what amounts to the "clear and
present danger" rule— is not readily applied to obscenity. Yet here he
again speaks of all "opinions" being free unless they serve as a "positive
instigation to some mischievous act,"[19] and an obscene novel is not what
we normally think of as an "opinion."

Mill advances a corollary standard for determining generally when
an individual's action only concerns himself and when it concerns others: "Whenever, in short, there is a definite damage, or a definite risk of
damage, either to an individual or to the public, the case is taken out of
the province of liberty, and placed in that of morality or law."[20] Mill
could have easily likened the worst forms of obscenity (as "pollutions
of the soul") to the adulteration of food, which he does authorize government to prevent, and could have made special provision for children as well. While he mentions acts which, "if done publicly, are a
violation of good manners," and includes within this category "offenses
against decency," he does so without any further explanation. And while
he charges with "moral crime" parents who bring a child into the world

without a fair prospect of providing not only "food for its body, but instruction and training for its mind,"[21] he never makes a similar charge against people who sell or distribute obscene materials to the young. So Mill never applies his principle, which conditions public intervention on "definite damage, or a definite risk of damage," to obscenity, considered as damaging to the higher elements in human nature.

One of the best recent writers on Mill discusses the difficulties raised in his teaching more extensively than our examination permits. "When he spoke of 'experiments in living,'" Gertrude Himmelfarb says, "there is nothing in *On Liberty* to suggest that sexual experiments were what he had in mind; certainly there is nothing in it remotely suggestive of what was even then being spoken of as 'free love.' A quotation she selects from an 1870 letter of Mill's could not be more clear: "I think it most probable that this particular passion will become with men, as it is already with a large number of women, completely under the control of reason. It has become so with women because its becoming so has been the condition upon which women hoped to obtain the strongest love and admiration of men. The gratification of this passion in its highest form, therefore, has been, with women, conditional upon their restraining it in its lowest."[22] In sum, "Mill himself was not a moral relativist; he firmly believed that sobriety was inherently and absolutely superior to drunkenness, chastity to promiscuity, even altruism to self-interest."[23]

Yet many elements of the argument in *On Liberty* understandably draw superficial readers toward moral relativism, tempt them to think only of liberty, and not of morality, as a fixed point in society, and might even lead them to extend liberty so far as to threaten its very survival. This threat could come either from a revolution by opponents of liberty, or more slowly from social and political disintegration brought about by the encouragement given to the most deep-seated differences in thought, expression, and modes of living.

9

Extremism on the Court

I N 1966 THE SUPREME COURT decided three cases dealing with obscenity. By far the most important was *A Book Named "John Cleland's Memoirs of a Woman of Pleasure"* (better known as *Fanny Hill*) *v. Attorney General of the Commonwealth of Massachusetts*. Another, *Ginzburg v. United States*, involved the use of the mail for transmitting obscene publications. The third, *Mishkin v. New York*, dealt with the preparing and publishing of obscene books. The Court affirmed the guilt of both Ginzburg and Mishkin while seriously weakening the principles laid down in *Roth* nine years before and thus freeing *Fanny Hill*, a classic of pornography, from the charge of obscenity.

CHARLES REMBAR FOR THE DEFENSE

Charles Rembar was the attorney who fought successfully to free *Lady Chatterley's Lover* (1959), Miller's *Tropic of Cancer* (1964), and *Fanny Hill* (1966) from charges of obscenity. In the *Fanny Hill* case, he managed to persuade the Supreme Court that if a work has even the slightest social or artistic value, the First Amendment protects it from prosecution as obscenity, regardless of how obscene it might otherwise be. Judging from his book, *The End of Obscenity*, published two years later, this view is based on a combination of bad history and willful disregard for constitutional tradition. According to Rembar, the founding fathers were "eighteenth century students of John Locke, divided on many points but united in a rational libertarian philosophy."[1] By the First Amendment they intended, on his account, to ban prosecutions on the grounds of heresy, sedition, and obscenity and to protect all thought and expression against legislative majorities. Having thus erroneously credited the students of Locke with the philosophy of John Stuart Mill, Rembar dismisses the long legislative and judicial history—completely benighted, he believes—in which the states, the national government, and the Supreme Court all gave voice to a contrary interpretation of the First Amendment and a coordinate belief in governmental police powers. To him, the Supreme Court's often-repeated (and never relinquished) insistence that "obscenity is not protected," not to mention legal history itself, prove nothing.[2]

Rembar claims that the attempt on the part of legislatures to promote public morality amounts to nothing more than an effort by popular majorities to advance the sexual morality they prefer and suppress sexual alternatives they dislike. He distinguishes sharply, in other words, between the fixity of free speech and press and the changeability of sexual morality, without ever reflecting on the purpose of sexual morality— that is, on its social, intellectual, moral, and political functions. From what he says, one might conclude that there is no need for sexual morality at all, and that its continued existence is simply a vestige of outdated religious superstition. Let men and women return to nature, he seems to say, and not only will they be happier, less repressed, and freer, but the very need for obscenity—for an appeal to unlawful lust symptomatic of our ill health—will simply disappear. Hence the double meaning of the title to Rembar's book, *The End of Obscenity*: the end to legal prosecutions, and the end, in the not-too-distant future, to the phenomenon of obscenity itself.[3]

Rembar is upset by what he calls "the outrageously immoral fact" that only sexual taboos have been potent enough to bring forth censorial urges, and that "[n]othing has ever been censored on the ground that it had a tendency to promote dishonesty or cruelty or cowardice."[4] Rembar seems to have forgotten that the police power over public morality as a whole has in fact directed its attention to many things apart from sex—drinking, drugs, gambling, and the like. And some state statutes have concerned themselves with verbal incitement to group hatred and violence. The code movie producers once employed to police themselves contained prohibitions that went far beyond sex. Moreover, a well-known Supreme Court case involved a New York statute that banned "stories of deeds of bloodshed, lust or crime."[5]

Nevertheless, granting that states should indeed pay more attention than they do to materials promoting cruelty, unjustified violence, and excessive fear, it is still true that the appeal to lust, by the nature of things, is bound to be much more widespread, and hence more in need of control. It alone portrays something intrinsically pleasurable that entices without immediately awakening in the audience a sense of physical danger, easily obscuring the other, less apparent, dangers it entails. Its immediate effect on the integrity of the family and on the young make it an object of real, and not simply imaginary, concern.

Paradoxically, after denouncing legislatures (he calls them "censors") for taking interest only in sexual immorality, Rembar maintains that the urge to censor is total, reaching out toward religious and political matters, and generally striving "to preserve the common man from the ravages of intellect."[6] What he wants us to imagine by the word "censor" is a leering fanatic of the extreme right. What we must in truth imagine are ordinary people and their representatives trying to protect themselves and the body politic from the puerile sexual and political visions of people like Rembar who prefer to outflank democracy by appealing to the courts. The First Amendment was meant to protect, not destroy, republican government, and this the people and the legislators seem to understand a good deal better than many intellectuals, who would like to use the Amendment to impose their own view of society on an unwilling public, frustrating large democratic majorities with the assistance of a tiny judicial elite.

It might seem that Rembar would share the literal or "absolute" reading of the First Amendment of Justices Black and Douglas. Instead he creates his own qualifications of the Amendment, without of course trying to trace them or the principles underlying them to the founders. Children, he grants, might require protection against obscenity that the First Amendment cannot allow adults, but he refrains from saying why. Is it because of some harm to which children are peculiarly liable—a rather dangerous admission, since it would admit to possible bad effects of obscenity? He is also willing to grant that the First Amendment primarily protects speech and printed matter and may therefore allow for a different treatment of movies and television. He further concedes that the requirements of public decency might necessitate limits to obscene expression—limits perhaps rooted in some consideration for the sensibilities of the general and, in his view, narrow-minded and censorious public. Such limits might also be rooted in the fear that an affronted and enraged public could rapidly become disillusioned with the First Amendment interpreted in this manner.[7]

To his credit, Rembar does distinguish sharply between art and trash, and his object is to protect the serious writer, not the hack. But his definition of art or serious literature is such that anything written well is by that fact alone elevated to the category of the serious regardless of its content. Anything of literary, historical, or sociological value, as attested by expert witnesses, should not be found obscene. He candidly acknowledges that there is a dominant appeal to lust (a healthful lust, to be sure) in *Lady Chatterley's Lover*, that *Tropic of Cancer* appeals to a morbid kind of prurience, and that *Fanny Hill* is indeed a "classic of pornography." Without expert testimony as to their value, he concedes, it would have been impossible to save them.[8] But once Rembar

implies that some of this material is *harmful* simply because it propounds an unhealthy or morbid view of sex as he himself judges it,
can he sustain his stated willingness to sacrifice what he calls "worthless trash" to obscenity laws? After all, what is harmful ought to be less
protected than what is merely worthless—that is, lacking in positive
value. Either he would have to admit, with Lawrence, that perverted
views of sex should be prohibited, or more likely, he would have to accord First Amendment protection to all materials, regardless of their
healthfulness or worth. What he actually does (unlike Lawrence) is to
skirt the issue by stating that some intelligent people would "argue the
benefits of the pornographic experience," and that there would be disagreement about the value of even the "trashiest" works. His conclusion—that the law should not intrude upon such questions—indicates
that his argument before the Court carried him only half-way to his
destination, an eradication of obscenity laws as such. For Rembar, then,
if only in printed materials and for adults, anything goes.[9]

A JUDICIAL NADIR

In his 1966 concurrence, Justice Douglas helped free *Fanny Hill* from
a Massachusetts court's verdict of obscenity. In the process he did something quite unusual. To vitiate Justice Clark's strong and incredulous
condemnation of the book and buttress his own argument that courts
should not be making such judgments at all, Douglas appends to his
opinion an address by a Universalist minister, the Reverend John R. Graham. In this address, entitled "Dr. Peale and Fanny Hill," Graham pur-
ports to save the book from ill-deserved infamy and demonstrate its
immense superiority to Norman Vincent Peale's *Sin, Sex and Self-Control*. With an appendix almost as long as his opinion itself, Douglas
reduces constitutional interpretation to the level of the *Congressional
Record*, and—strange for a proponent of absolute separation between
church and state—lends official support to one side of a controversy with

strongly religious overtones and through a document that comes close to affronting a particular individual.

Douglas does not claim Graham's view as his own. He simply says he would "pair" it with Justice Clark's—that is, give it equal and opposite weight—if the Court had to render official judgments on the worth of books. But it seems unlikely that he would make so long an address so prominent a part of his opinion if he did not share its point of view. Be that as it may, those who read the case will either attribute Graham's opinions to Douglas or, at the minimum, will credit Graham's thoughts on the subject by virtue of their inclusion.

As Graham sees it, Peale represents the old Christian morality of self-control—a morality that does harm to human life by preventing self-expression and enforcing "conformity, rigid behavior and a lack of understanding." *Fanny Hill*, on the other hand, is in reality a subtle allegory which depicts Fanny growing in appreciation of self-expression ("self-expression is more human than self-control") and developing a "genuine love and respect for life and for people." So impressed is Graham by Cleland's literary performance that he extols it in superlatives: "I know of no book which more beautifully describes meaningful relationships between a man and a woman than does '*Fanny Hill*.'"[10] Graham, of course, admits that the allegory "may be missed by the average person who reads the work," but this is simply due to prejudice. We are left to infer that, elucidated by someone who has overcome prejudice, like Graham himself, *Fanny Hill* can only prove a blessing, perhaps to the young as well as the old. For, as he acknowledges at the outset, "Most parents would be pleased to find their children reading a book by Dr. Peale, but I am afraid that the same parents would be sorely distressed to discover a copy of '*Fanny Hill*' among the schoolbooks of their offspring." If Graham is "afraid" of this parental reaction, he must regard it as undesirable, one which his address is meant to overcome. It would not be too much of a stretch to conclude that he favors the use of *Fanny Hill* as an educational document which enlightened parents will positively insist upon their children reading. And why should the work not be employed in the education of the young, since it more beautifully than any other work "describes meaningful relationships between a man and a woman"?

If one compares this abstract paradisiacal description of *Fanny Hill* with the repellent details reluctantly supplied by Justice Clark in part three of his dissent, one wonders whether Graham might not have read an expurgated version of this acknowledged classic of pornography. Evidently Graham felt nothing in the long series of sexual encounters summarized by Justice Clark to be in the least offensive. No harsh note appears in his encomium, not even a single mixed reaction—and of course no details, no simple and candid account of what the parent or child might expect to find in a superficial reading of these pages before plumbing their allegorical depths. Taking Graham at his word, we must believe that he would commend the way of life undertaken by Fanny Hill at age fifteen as she works her way as a prostitute through every kind of sexual experimentation, for this is the best means of becoming a genuine human being. Only in such a manner as this, freely choosing our own course, can we express ourselves, act creatively, develop self-understanding, learn to love others. After all, "self-control and self-expression are at opposite ends of the continuum. As much as some persons would like to have both, it is necessary to make a choice, since restraint and openness are contradictory qualities. To internalize external values denies the possibility of self-expression."[11]

But at what age is the untrammeled choice of the individual to begin? The nostrum of self-expression assumes there is already a self to express. In the young, as yet untutored, human animal, however, there can be no self in the human sense, but only instinctual urges, unguided by conscience, reason, or ideals of any kind. And education, whether informal or formal, necessarily involves the conveyance of "external" values to the young. Is education as such therefore to be abolished—if that were possible? Or if it is education through such instruments as

Fanny Hill, tuned to true pitch by such teachers as Graham, will it be less a conveyance of "external" values to the young? Does self-expression have a natural basis, and self-control none? And more to the point, can human society endure if all its members seek to express themselves in the style of Fanny Hill? With a deeper understanding of the problem, John Stuart Mill required, like John Milton before him, a most thorough moral education of the young, without which they could make of themselves not genuine human beings rationally choosing but only beings unrecognizable as human. On the relation between self-expression and self-control, Mill said, "It may be better to be a John Knox than an Alcibiades, but it is better to be a Pericles than either; nor would a Pericles, if we had one in these days, be without anything good which belonged to John Knox." [12] The degeneration of present-day liberalism in such men as Graham is succinctly and aptly depicted by the change from the ideal of Pericles to the ideal of one infinitely lower than Alcibiades: Fanny Hill. And perhaps we may be pardoned if we are astonished at the irony of a Supreme Court justice, whose very title derives from the highest virtue of self-control, lending the prestige of his office to this new morality of libertinism.

Let us now turn to the body of Justice Douglas's opinion, where he speaks in his own name, to see whether body and appendix have any connection. Douglas begins with a bland, one-sentence summary of *Fanny Hill*, "The book relates the adventures of a young girl who becomes a prostitute in London," quoting Fanny's concluding reflections on the superiority of virtue to vice—surely the most unrepresentative passage in the work and, like Douglas's one-sentence summary, no clue at all to its dominant theme. His arguments against the *Roth* rule and for an absolute interpretation of freedom of the press follow. Justices are not competent to judge the redeeming social value or merit of any book. Moreover, the Constitution forbids the abridgment of the freedom of the press and makes no exception for obscenity: expression is placed beyond the control of both judges and popular majorities. It is unclear to what extent obscenity was a common law crime in the American colonies, Douglas claims, but even if it had clearly been an offense, the Bill of Rights was meant as a new dispensation. In proof of this last point, he quotes Madison on the unique importance to Americans of a written constitution protecting, among other things, the "freedom of the press."

In our evaluation of Justice Douglas's thoughts on the First Amendment, we can do no better than follow the lead of Douglas himself when he later warns his colleagues against permitting "fictionalized assertions of constitutional history" to obscure the true character of the Amendment. To begin with, the quotations from Madison only repeat the phrase "freedom of the press" and contribute nothing to our understanding of what he meant by it. Douglas admits that in 1790 a handful of states had obscenity statutes, but only because "the First Amendment was, until the adoption of the Fourteenth, a restraint only upon federal power." As we have seen, however, the First Amendment itself was never intended to protect abuses of the press, and both Madison and Jefferson agreed that the states had the authority to punish them. It was the Court (through its interpretation of the Fourteenth Amendment) rather than the amending process that placed this restriction on the states, and only in the twentieth century, long after that amendment was adopted.

Douglas goes on to claim that "Neither reason nor history warrants exclusion of any particular class of expression from the protection of the First Amendment on nothing more than a judgment that it is utterly without merit." And as if to show how seriously he means this, he cites the Court's recent ruling on libel in *New York Times v. Sullivan*. At this point the unwary reader might conclude that the Court has in fact freed libel as such—all libel—from restriction as a "class of expression" protected by the First Amendment. He does not tell us, as Justice Brennan does in the first sentence of his *Times* opinion, that the issue in that case pertains solely to "a libel action brought by a public official against critics of his official conduct." Libel, then, is still not generally tolerated by law. Nor does Justice Douglas give even the slightest indication of the long historical tradition of the judiciary, still adhered to by most of his own colleagues, according to which obscenity itself is excluded from First Amendment protection.

If Justice Douglas's arguments from history suffer from inaccuracy and incompleteness, perhaps his arguments from reason are better. The last part of the body of his opinion counters the argument that "erotica produces anti-social conduct." This, he maintains, has yet to be proved. Indeed, with the Kronhausens he finds it more likely that "literature of the most pornographic sort would, in many cases, provide a substitute—not a stimulus—for anti-social conduct." In a footnote he even refers those who are concerned about children and erotic literature to a lengthy statement by Judge Curtis Bok. According to Bok, such books (including the "literature of the most pornographic sort" mentioned previously?) need not be feared by parents who have faced the "biologic" facts of life with their children, and who have been "discerning with their children." In fact, reading such books will teach such children "what is in the world and in its people." Again, this comes close to a positive recommendation for at least some parents to keep the family bookshelves well stocked with erotic literature. But Judge Bok may not have been speaking about the full range of obscene writings currently available on the market to all who can pay the price.

Bok's reference to his daughters' finding certain books in *his* library certainly suggests a situation where they would not have an opportunity to obtain such books themselves. Moreover, his remarks are of no assistance whatsoever to parents who have not educated their children as well as he and for whom the general availability of almost every kind of obscene writing constitutes a considerable impediment to their children's moral education. Justice Douglas would have done better to consider sympathetically, rather than to scorn, those countless letters and postcards—many of them, no doubt, from worried parents—with which his office was flooded whenever an obscenity case presented it-self, even if, as he conjectures, they were copied from some "school or church blackboard." [13]

Douglas is not satisfied with asserting the absoluteness of First Amendment liberties and indicating the inherent difficulties in *Roth*—a path followed by his closest colleague, Justice Black, in his *Ginzburg* dissent. Black candidly tells us he has read none of the writings in these cases: his principle is independent of whatever merit or harm he might personally see in any of them. But Douglas has a unique and unprec-edented preachment to impart, for he attributes positive social value to so-called obscene writings. In fact, since he never in the slightest way attributes harm to them, we can only conclude that he thinks of them as an unmixed good. In the body of his *Fanny Hill* opinion we have discovered two reasons why this might be so: first, literature of even the most pornographic sort provides a substitute—not a stimulus—for anti-social conduct; second, erotic literature teaches what the world is like. Further, as we learn from the appendix, at least some erotic litera-ture (such as *Fanny Hill* itself) shows how sexual self-expression can help us become genuinely human. His evaluation of erotic literature becomes more positive in the course of his opinion, as it moves from fostering crime prevention, to realistic awareness, to what can only be described as a new gospel.

In his *Ginzburg* dissent Justice Douglas adds further to his esti-mation of these benefits. After discussing the testimony that various expert witnesses had given to the value of Ginzburg's various publica-tions, he presents some general observations on tracts for which pub-lishers have been sent to jail. Some of these "concern normal sex, some homosexuality, some the masochistic yearning that is probably present in everyone and dominant in some." Each of the three caters to its own kind of group, and a fourth, but unnamed, group, as we soon learn, "translates mundane articles into sexual objects." A similar classification had been set forth by Justice Brennan at the beginning of the Court's opinion in *Mishkin*, but with two differences: Brennan actually uses the technical term "fetishism" for what we have called Justice Douglas's fourth group, and more important, he speaks of "sadomasochism," not just of masochism.

Because of the degree to which Douglas dwells upon masochism in *Ginzburg*, his omission of the link with sadism is instructive. The problem arose in *Mishkin* because Mishkin's publications, according to Brennan, gave considerable prominence to the sexual beatings of one person by another (with the former's consent): one wants to beat, the other to be beaten —hence the term "sadomasochism." Justice Douglas's strange emphasis on masochism begins immediately after the sentence quoted above, in his discussion of the variety of sexual tracts for which people have been sent to jail: "Masochism is a desire to be punished or subdued. In the broad frame of reference the desire may be expressed in the longing to be whipped and lashed, bound and gagged, and cruelly treated. Why is it unlawful to cater to the needs of this group?"[14] Douglas may not mean what he seems to say, that the whipping, lashing, and the like, of masochists should not itself be treated as illegal, since it satisfies their needs. Certainly, interesting questions of consent are raised by this problem. What Justice Douglas in fact appears to have in mind is the meeting of the needs of masochists through literary tracts. What he calls the masochist "group" or "community" should be able to communicate with itself through publications, and such publications would ipso facto have social value. Additional value of a "therapeutical" sort—more effective in this respect than any "sermon"—might derive from this intramural communication.

THE CONGERIES OF MANKIND

Justice Douglas can only come to this conclusion about masochists and other "deviant" groups by positing a particular relationship between "normality" and "deviation," which he states in a single sentence: "Man was not made in a fixed mould." [15] Mankind is divided into different types, some "normal," some deviant. But "normal" is always in quotation marks, deviant never. "Normal" now signifies a mere statistical majority rather than a reference to a general norm or standard for judging what is natural, healthy, or good for mankind as such. Deviants are simply minorities of one sort or another, with their own "ideas and tastes." Masochists (and fetishists, sadists, etc.) are only "offbeat, nonconformist, and odd," not defective. The parallel is drawn with tastes in music: "Some like Chopin, others like 'rock and roll.'" [16]

We shall not dwell on the inconsistency between the fracturing of a common human nature in these passages and the concern in his *Fanny Hill* appendix for finding a truly human existence characterized by ideals deemed universally and objectively good. But we are struck by Justice Douglas's inconsistency regarding sadism. Why not forthrightly insist upon the right of sadists as well as masochists to find satisfaction, at least through the printed word? Are not sadists a deviant group—indeed, a much larger group, common observation would seem to indicate, than masochists? Would not the practice of sadism in print serve as a substitute for actual sadism? Might it not be therapeutic? But Justice Douglas's notable omission of sadism from his list must stem from a suspicion that it is too clearly linked with the possibility of "anti-social conduct," and that writings might very well stimulate and amplify this tendency. Perhaps—and quite reasonably—he had no desire to rely on the relevant parallel to his own pronouncement in *Fanny Hill* asserting that a link between erotica and anti-social conduct "has yet to be proven." Even so, he should still not have been deterred from including the right of sadists to publish sadistic writings, for on his principle of constitutional interpretation, only expression very closely "brigaded with illegal action" [17] lacks the protection of the First Amendment. In his view, writing as such, however stimulating to illegal action, remains protected.

Justice Douglas is more than inconsistent: his principles are both false and dangerous. To begin with, though his vocabulary is borrowed from psychiatry, he goes far beyond the views of many psychiatrists in likening psychological deviancy to differences in taste, and in apparently tracing them all to biological rather than social causes ("Man was not made in a fixed mould."). The masochist, who, according to Douglas, longs to be "whipped and lashed, bound and gagged, and cruelly treated," is still generally regarded by psychiatrists as a deviant and unhappy human being, not as just one of many natural human types. Justice Douglas does the masochist a disservice by removing his reason for seeking the therapy he needs. On the other hand, by using the term "deviancy" as a catch-all for all minority groups, he also does a disservice to the homosexual, who may in fact differ remarkably (and not merely as a matter of "taste") from the norm nature has set for purposes of reproduction. Douglas's greatest disservice, however, is to the country and mankind, for his cheaply bought relativism—already widespread among the educated—leaves our common ends and standards without any support but our choice of them, or rather leaves them without any support at all.

To be human is to share a common nature, whatever variations of lesser gravity for which nature may also be responsible. But man is a peculiar being in that he is ruled by opinions as well as by nature, and by opinions that can frustrate nature as well as support it. To tell the majority of men that what they had hitherto considered normal is merely statistical destroys their confidence in normality and stimulates the growth of abnormality or "deviations." To encourage deviants to form their own "groups" or "communities" is to strengthen them in their deviancy and hence to weaken the normal majority. Since no one can predict how far this may go, the ultimate effect is to threaten society at its core. Society becomes a mere congeries of groups each with its own ideas, tastes, and way of life, and each equally to be accepted as good.

But Douglas does not exhaust the list of possible groups, even by the addition of sadism. There are the strong-hearted and the weak-hearted, the lazy and the vigorous, the intemperate and the temperate, the freedom-loving and the servile—some of which dispositions, incidentally, have a stronger basis in natural human differences than sexual deviations. If "man was not made in a fixed mould," all such differences should receive equal status and protection. Society, as such, should not place its stamp of approval or disapproval on any. It should have no common goals, no common ideals, no common virtues to be aspired to or vices to be scorned. The only bond remaining among individuals would be the natural desire on the part of all—their shared interest—to preserve themselves, for even a common love of liberty cannot be presumed to have a naturally effective root, as most of human history testifies. We have reverted herewith not to the philosophy of the Constitution or the Declaration of Independence, not to Locke, or even to Mill, but to something like the philosophy of Thomas Hobbes, kept from its demand for absolute sovereignty (including government authority over opinions as well as conduct) only by Justice Douglas's supposition that self-interested human behavior is innocuous.[18]

Returning to Locke, liberalism does make a greater allowance for human differences, for individuality, than any other political philosophy, but it begins by establishing the fundamental interests all men can be expected to share, and for the sake of which they can act together in building political society. They share an interest in safeguarding their basic rights, but once society comes into existence, and in order for it to endure, it develops its own shared morality, rules, institutions, and loyalties. Within civil society, individuals must also think of themselves as members of families, local communities, and society as a whole, and the life they continue to lead as individuals must not be inconsistent with the common life they share. Differences will remain wider than in any other form of republic and almost every other form of society, but if these differences grow too wide, or too deep, the sense of sharing common objectives and a common destiny will be damaged or destroyed, and therewith the society itself.

In 1966, Justice Douglas's oracular utterances represented the greatest headway a philosophy promoting such a fracturing of common ties and national disintegration had made at the highest governmental levels, and wholly inconsistently with the Constitution and our predominant political tradition. On those holding such a philosophy the claims of virtue, morality, society, and human nature itself are lost: the claims of human differences, freely expressed, rise superior to all. But the result will not be to their liking. The various deviants they encourage will not all be devotees of free society, loving the liberty under law that protects them, working for it, or sacrificing for it. Nor will they be happy with themselves or grateful to those who urged them to follow their untutored desires. More likely, a sense of rootlessness and aimlessness will pervade society, and the stage will be set not for further advances toward freedom but for the combination of personal despotism, overarching discipline, and barbaric violence typical of many twentieth-century political movements.

Judicial Progress and Regress in 1973

FOR SEVEN YEARS AFTER THE 1966 CASES, the purveyors of lewdness, vulgarity, perversity, and brutality felt they were no longer bound by law. The assault they launched on the civilized sense of morality, decency, and rationality has had no parallels in history. Then in 1973, with a much-changed Court, the cases of *Paris Adult Theater v. Slaton* and *Miller v. California* brought an unexpected advance in the judicial understanding of obscenity and its harms. Yet a small improvement in the test for obscenity was coupled with what proved a much more important, and much less favorable, practical result. In *Paris*, Chief Justice Burger, speaking for a majority of five, presented a broad understanding of the states' interest in regulating obscenity. In *Miller*, speaking for the same majority, Burger dropped the "no social value" test that had been added in *Fanny Hill*, insisting now that only "serious" value could legally redeem a work otherwise found both prurient and patently offensive. Unfortunately, by retaining the test of "patent offensiveness" and in fact narrowing its field of application, the majority seemed for the first time to restrict the meaning of obscenity explicitly to pornography. Thus, not only did the Court modify and narrow

Roth further still, but in doing so it created a glaring inconsistency with the new defense of the constitutionality of anti-obscenity legislation it had just set forth in *Paris Adult Theater*.

OBSCENITY AND PORNOGRAPHY

To understand these issues, a quick review of judicial events between 1957 and 1966 is necessary. The text of *Roth*, in which the Court formulated the comprehensive "prurient interest" rule, contains no mention of "patent offensiveness." But in his footnote in *Roth* explaining the meaning of prurience, Justice Brennan cited the definition found in the American Legal Institute's Model Penal Code, commenting that "We perceive no significant difference between the Court's definition and the one in the Code." Yet the Code had spoken of obscene works not only as appealing to prurient interest but also going "substantially beyond customary limits of candor in description or representation of such matters."[1]

Five years after *Roth*, Justice Harlan, speaking for the Court in *Manual Enterprises, Inc. v. Day* (1962), centered his opinion on the addition to prurient appeal of something called "patent offensiveness," citing the A.L.I.'s "thoughtful studies." At the same time, Harlan and the majority stipulated that the standards of decency affronted by such offensiveness had to be (in this federal case involving a postal statute) that of the national community—"a national standard of decency." Two years later, in *Jacobellis v. Ohio*, the same additional test and the same *national* community were said to apply in connection with *state* obscenity statutes, so that by 1966 and *Fanny Hill*, "patent offensiveness" so understood had become an accepted, independent, and necessary test of obscenity in state and federal cases.

This test reappears and assumes even greater prominence in *Miller*, but with a subtle modification Justice Harlan did not have in mind when he first formulated it. As Burger puts it in *Miller*, the test must be "whether the work depicts or describes, in a patently offensive way, sexual conduct specifically defined by the applicable State law." And to clarify the point, he takes the unusual step of providing "a few plain examples" of what a state could legitimately prohibit by specification. These are "a) Patently offensive representations or descriptions of ultimate sex acts, normal or perverted, actual or simulated; b) Patently offensive representations or descriptions of masturbation, excretory functions, and lewd exhibition of genitals."[2]

What the general rule refers to as "sexual conduct" is therefore narrowed, in the specific illustrations, to *ultimate* sex *acts* or sex *organs*, thereby suggesting that all words, gestures, expressions, and actions falling short of these cannot constitutionally be prohibited, however powerful or obvious their prurient appeal. In short, only hard-core pornography is now open to regulation—a conclusion that Burger verifies: "Under the holdings announced today, no one will be subject to prosecution for the sale or exposure of obscene materials unless these materials depict or describe patently offensive 'hard core' sexual conduct specifically defined by the regulating state law, as written or construed."[3] In so writing, Burger and the majority presume such material will, in almost all cases, be lacking in that "serious value" of a "literary, artistic, political or scientific" kind by which alone it could be saved from the law. While there was doubt on the Court before *Miller* as to whether only hard-core pornography would be prohibited by the "patent offensiveness" test as such (expressed by Harlan in his opinion in *Manual Enterprises*), that doubt had now been explicitly removed.

By replacing "no social value," in effect, with "no serious social value" (and also, we must note, by retreating from the need for applying a national rather than a local standard of patent offensiveness), the Burger Court had indeed broadened the scope for obscenity prosecutions. But the Court giveth to the press as well as taketh away, for by narrowing the meaning of "patent offensiveness" and confining it to hard-core pornography, the Court effectively placed a tighter restriction on prosecutions. Now only hard-core pornography could be outlawed and prosecuted, and only that lacking in serious value could ultimately be prohibited. Whether a work like *Fanny Hill* itself might continue to elude the law under the new dispensation would depend primarily on the latitude judges and juries gave to that singularly unlegal term "serious." Certainly, the kind of obscenity to which most are regularly exposed through movies, printed materials, shows, and, increasingly, television—the kind which is *not* hard-core pornography—was thenceforth to be completely free of the law, and could therefore be expected to multiply promiscuously.

This conclusion would have been easy enough to accept from the Warren Court—not because of its correctness as constitutional doctrine or wisdom as policy but simply because that Court's majority seemed unaware of any alternative to its libertarianism. The Burger Court, however, grasps the alternative and announces it both in sections of *Miller* itself and *Paris Adult Theater.* In the fourth part of *Miller*, for example, the Chief Justice rejects the alarm of repression sounded by dissenting justices: "[I]n our view, to equate the free and robust exchange of ideas and political debate with commercial exploitation of obscene material demeans the grand conception of the First Amendment and its high purpose in the historic struggle for freedom. It is a '. . . misuse of the great guarantees of free speech and free press. . . .' *Beard v. Alexandria*."[4] That Burger has in mind in this passage the broader, traditional notion of obscenity rather than its new (with *Miller*) restriction to hard-core pornography is revealed in the very next paragraph: "There is no evidence, empirical or historical, that the stern 19th century American censorship of public distribution and display of material relating to sex, see *Roth v. United States*, in any way limited expression of serious literary, artistic, political or scientific ideas. On the contrary, it is beyond any question that the era following Thomas

Jefferson to Theodore Roosevelt was an 'extraordinarily vigorous period' not just in economics and politics, but in belles lettres and in 'the out-lying fields of social and political philosophies.'"

This is an amazing admission on Burger's part, and it compels the reader to wonder why the standards for judging obscenity throughout the nineteenth and first half of the twentieth centuries have, with his own Court's blessing, now been so drastically lowered. Were the standards of that era (that is, by far the largest portion of our history as a nation) constitutionally unsound then? He does not say so. If they were not, and if they had no discernibly bad effects on the intellectual and political life of the country (as he insists), why are they now abandoned? Has obscenity become less of a problem in our time, so that it can be safely ignored? One could truthfully maintain that never before in human history had such a volume and intensity of obscene materials been loosed upon the world as has inundated our citizenry, through the mass media, starting about 1960. Or are we better protected from its ravages by the strength of our moral beliefs and customs—our education—than past generations? Again, the contrary is the case: our citizens are much more susceptible to its blandishments than they were in the nineteenth century, when religion and some sense of the need for republican sobriety were still strong, and when the difficulties born of opulence and bad education were still quite limited.[5]

THE SOCIAL INTEREST

Perhaps Americans prior to 1950 exaggerated the evils that could come from legalized obscenity. Had they expended a considerable effort in suppressing that which was essentially harmless, or at least of little and tolerable harm? For Burger's answer to this question we must turn to *Paris Adult Theater*, where for the first time, in a case involving pornographic movies for consenting adults only, the Court gave voice to a rationale or public philosophy that would justify free societies in suppressing obscenity as publicly noxious. Burger begins his argument, in the second part of his opinion, by taking the unusual step of quoting at length from Alexander Bickel's defense of a legitimate public interest in sustaining "the quality of life." According to Bickel, granting to individuals a right of public access to obscenity (in theaters, for instance) would, by necessity, "affect the world about the rest of us" and "impinge on other privacies"—an impact that the majority has a right to frustrate through legislation.

This point of Bickel's and Burger's is both too weak and too strong. It is too weak because it fails to claim any greater dignity or value for a quality of life free from obscenity than for one pervaded by it. In fact, by speaking of an individual gathering together with those "who share his tastes"—in this case for obscenity—and of the impact such gatherings and their after-effects would have on "other privacies," Bickel (and hence Burger) seems to let the matter rest at protecting majority *tastes* against minority *tastes*, rather than protecting some objective public good as such.[6] But the argument also goes too far, for are there not large areas of publicly expressed thought and action involving something closer to real tastes different from those of the majority—for example in cars, dress, or hair style—which do not ordinarily involve a vital public interest with which free society can legitimately concern itself? If so, what is there about the spread of obscenity that poses a specific and genuine public problem?

Burger moves closer to the heart of the matter when he addresses the question of whether obscene works can be said to affect men, women, and society adversely. Despite the lack of conclusive empirical proof, he says, legislatures in pursuing the *"social interest in order and morality"* (as reaffirmed by *Roth*, with emphasis added there), can "quite reasonably" determine that a connection between obscene materials and anti-social behavior does or might exist. Such "unprovable assumptions" have guided legislators in all civilized societies and in America as well. The case of education can be adduced in evidence of this fact:

If we accept the unprovable assumption that a complete education requires certain books, and the well-nigh universal belief that good books, plays and art lift the spirit, improve the mind, enrich the human personality and develop character, can we then say that a state legislature may not act on the corollary assumption that commerce in obscene books, or public exhibitions focused on obscene conduct have a tendency to exert a corrupting and debasing impact leading to anti-social behavior? The sum of experience, including that of the past two decades, affords an ample basis for legislatures to conclude that a sensitive, key relationship of human existence, central to family life, community welfare, and the development of human personality, can be debased and distorted by crass commercial exploitation of sex. Nothing in the Constitution prohibits a State from reaching such a conclusion and acting on it legislatively simply because there is no conclusive evidence or empirical data.[7]

Now this is a remarkable paragraph on many counts. First, it rests on an implicit distinction between conclusions based on the "sum of experience" and those resting on scientific or empirical proof—that is, between common, intelligent, pre-scientific observation and judgment, on the one hand, and scientifically precise proof, on the other. Political men—legislators, judges, administrators—must primarily base their conclusions on the former, since the latter is often impossible to obtain in complex human matters. But if this is so— as it most certainly is— Burger should not have conceded to science a monopoly on the acquisition of "empirical proof," since he is thus compelled to speak in a disparaging way of common intelligent conclusions based on ordinary experience (and the word "empirical" refers simply to experience) as "unprovable assumptions." The claim that good education requires good books, for instance, can hardly be called an "unprovable assumption": on the contrary, it is one of the best-proved observations in the world.

While Burger's argument does contain this important defect, its attempt to indicate the public interests threatened by obscenity is judicially unique and impressive. Obscenity is harmful because it tends to "exert a corrupting and debasing impact leading to anti-social behavior." It debases and distorts "a sensitive, key relationship of human existence, central to family life, community welfare, and the development of human personality." Let us amplify upon these sentences to see what they imply or suggest. If books, movies, and music have an educational influence on their readers, viewers or listeners, those that are obscene will dispose them to become certain sorts of human beings, to regard sex in a certain light and only in that light, and thus to behave in ways that endanger social institutions and individuals at one and the same time. Civilized life—a life requiring discipline and dedication to high ideals—is threatened at its root by the caninization obscenity stimulates. Society cannot be decent, responsible, or civilized if such stimulation continues over any long period of time. Slowly but surely its debasing and corrupting effect will be felt, ineluctably transforming the freedom of democracies into license, undermining their moral character and vital social institutions.

Thus, the "anti-social conduct" to which obscenity or the autonomous rule of lust leads includes but goes far beyond "sex crimes." By strengthening random sexual desire, quite apart from considerations of self-control, it may, among other things, serve to weaken and destroy marriage and the family, with untold consequences for the nurture and education of the young. How ironic it is—if we may be permitted a note of irony—that the moral language employed to describe the effects of obscenity, the language of "corruption" and "debasement," should so imperceptibly but justly revive the wording of the old abandoned *Hicklin* rule, with its "deprave (or debase, or debauch) and corrupt." For the somewhat more technical term "prurience," adopted in *Roth* to denote lust, had already lost the connotation capturing the harm involved, which was nothing less than to demean the soul of man and reduce it to the brutish.[8]

Burger proceeds, in *Paris*, to consider and reject the various arguments presented by the petitioning theater. He denies that the right to privacy, which "encompasses and protects the personal intimacies of the home, the family, marriage, motherhood, procreation and child rearing," can be extended to include a right "to watch obscene movies in places of public accommodation." Yet he agrees with the petitioners' claim that "the State has no legitimate interest in controlling '. . . the moral content of a person's thought.'"[9] Through its regulation of obscenity, the State is not deciding what is "wrong" or "sinful" but making "a morally neutral judgment" about the tendency of obscene material "to injure the community as a whole, to endanger the public safety, or to jeopardize, in Chief Justice Warren's words, the States' 'right . . . to maintain a decent society.'"

We can agree with Burger that the regulation of obscenity does not derive, at bottom, from any sense of the "sinful" or from religious morality in general: its basis is rational and secular.[10] But he errs in his claim that it rests on a "morally neutral" political judgment. For what is it, when one talks about the "corrupting and debasing" effect of obscenity, and about the right to maintain a "decent" society, but to make moral judgments? And had not Burger himself quoted approvingly *Roth*'s traditional reassertion of a legislative right to protect "*the social interest in order and morality*"? He cannot pretend that the state has no interest in the moral content of the minds of its citizens, since their morality—their sense of right and wrong, good and bad, noble and ignoble, decent and indecent—is precisely what guides their actions. Through obscenity regulation, the state does not indeed exercise "thought control" in any positive sense, but it does exercise a kind of negative or preventive control of the kind of appeal obscenity contains, which is to irresponsible lust. It is this effect that the state, through its regulations, has a right to prevent, and the means whereby the effect is produced—whether wholly, primarily, or only partly non-intellectual—has no bearing on the state's authority.

Burger falls back on the claim that obscene materials appeal to something other than "reason and intellect" and contribute nothing to the exchange of ideas or to "thought." Hence, controlling them is not to control thought. But the freedoms of speech and press in the First Amendment do not automatically protect every appeal to ideas, as distinguished from emotions or passions. It could be maintained, in fact, that there is no appeal to emotions which is not at the same time, at least indirectly, an appeal to ideas. Thus obscenity, by its naked appeal to lust, either intentionally or unintentionally, constitutes an effort to alter the ideas of sexual right and wrong in the citizens—to liberate them from traditional moral restraints. The state, therefore, must keep its eye on the danger it seeks to avert rather than on the proportion of intellectual and non-intellectual elements in offending materials. [11] This is particularly true of all vehicles for obscenity that go beyond lewd pictures or drawings, such as those that take the form of novels, movies, and musical lyrics.

In the sentence he quotes from his predecessor, Burger speaks of the tendency of obscene materials to injure the community as a whole, endanger public safety, and jeopardize the maintenance of a decent society. States have a right to avert these threats, just as they have a right to sustain the "social interest in order and morality." These rights are a part of the traditional the "police powers" of the states, which were directed at insuring the public health, safety, *morals*, and general welfare. Now according to Justice Brennan's majority opinion in *Roth*, explicating the freedoms of speech and press in the First Amendment, "All ideas having even the slightest redeeming social importance . . . have the full protection of the guarantees, *unless excludable because they encroach upon the limited area of more important interests*" (my emphasis). The "social interest in order and morality" as well as in protecting the community as a whole from injury and providing for the public safety are such interests, and the interest in preserving a "decent society" is part of the interest in "order and morality." It follows directly that even *ideas* may be excluded from First Amendment protection if they threaten vital interests the states have a right and duty to protect.[12]

RETURN TO TRADITION

The Court's efforts after *Roth* to narrow the range of obscenity susceptible to legal limitation, ultimately arriving at *Miller*'s reduction of obscenity to hard-core pornography, have no basis in earlier constitutional law. In principle, even the appeals to "reason and the intellect" from which Burger so sharply distinguishes obscenity's appeal to the passions may have to bow to state authority if they "encroach upon the limited area of more important interests." A treatise defending the murder of blacks, whites, or Jews, or calling for the assassination of public officials or for public bombings in the name of some cause is not in principle protected by the guarantees of the First Amendment. So, too, regarding obscenity, the forms of appeal to animal lust can vary in intellectual content from hard-core pornography to cheap, tawdry, and highly suggestive books and movies to more artistic and "serious" works of literature and film. But the greater the obscene or prurient effect, the greater the encroachment upon a vital public interest, from which it follows that the more serious the obscene work, the greater its liability to public prosecution.

In the logic of the case, there is no stopping at hard-core pornography, though it was tempting to think there was. For if obscenity could be defined with precision and regarded as bereft of "ideas," the First Amendment would remain the guardian of all ideas as such. The Court should not have attempted to save "prurient, patently offensive depictions or descriptions" that might also have "serious" value, for this was to sacrifice the powerful public interest in morality to the much weaker public interest in literature, art, or science, and to do so not only blatantly but without reasoned justification. Moreover, by introducing the notion of "serious value" the Court made the legal standard imprecise once again, for how is "serious" to be defined legally? When a judge applies this word, or explains it to a jury that must apply it, what must he have in mind? The Court does not say. Is the average judge or juror better able to judge "serious value" than the prurience of works that are not strictly pornographic? It would not seem so. We are faced, then, with a greater problem of legal precision than before.[13]

But the main objection to the Court's judgment in *Miller* emerges from a consideration of three points: (1) the Court's own admission in *Miller* that obscenity regulation before *Roth* did not inhibit the free exchange of worthwhile ideas; (2) *Paris Adult Theater*'s argument about the harmfulness of obscenity broadly conceived, and the constitutional right of states to inhibit it; (3) the obvious fact that the production of obscenity of every description short of the Court's narrow ban had become a flourishing industry—one that depends for its profitability much more on the marketing of non-pornographic or semi-pornographic material than on pornography so narrowly defined, and one that at an increasing rate and with broadening scope has been undermining public morality. By now, nothing could be clearer than that. A thirty-year-long judicial effort to expand liberty in the name of intellectual, literary, and artistic progress has resulted not in greater thought, literature, and art but in their obvious degradation and vulgarization. And from this unprecedented assault no nation could avoid suffering a debilitation of its character, a weakening of its social institutions, and a reputation for licentiousness that has come to soil the fair name of liberty throughout the world.

The time is long overdue for a resurgence of constitutional responsibility in this area. We must return to the venerable tradition that prevailed before *Roth*, a tradition that was liberal without being libertarian. Deriving from the founders' understanding of Blackstone, this tradition alone reveals the First Amendment's intended meaning, obliging the courts not to keep expanding individual liberty, but to fix it at a point consistent with the people's remaining unified, dignified, rational, and hence capable of sustaining their liberty over a long period of time. Public morality and moderate liberty are mutually consistent and reinforcing, but extreme liberty undermines the conditions for its own preservation and can lead to nothing but the ruin of free society. Moderation stands very close to justice as the guardian of individual rights—surely a lesson that the justices of our Supreme Court should be able to appreciate.

Nevertheless, it is discouraging to see how much that was known of old has been forgotten. By 1973 a bare majority of the Court— however serious the defects in their reasoning, their inconsistencies, their remaining bias in favor of excessive liberty, and their mistaken way of seeking legal precision—had come to understand the bearing of obscenity on public morality and on such essential social institutions as the family. What would have been readily intelligible to the whole generation of founders, to Lincoln, and to almost all Americans before World War II, however, was hardly so to the minority. Yet the dissenting justices did not all argue in the same way. Justice Douglas held a position apart, while Justice Brennan provided the leadership for the two remaining justices.[14] According to Douglas, the First Amendment did not intend to make obscenity an exception to freedom of speech and press. Obscenity, moreover, is not an objective thing but a matter of subjective taste, offensive to some, but as such within the protection guaranteed to all "offensive ideas" by the First Amendment as a means of stimulating open discussion and debate. And because obscenity involves emotion rather than reason, the Court must forever be in arbitrary disagreement about its definition, as the history after *Roth* demonstrates. The results will always be transient, excessively vague, and therefore inoperable as law.

With much of this analysis Justice Brennan and his followers disagree. They grant that the police powers of the states include providing for the morals of the community, and they are impressed by the legislative history of anti-obscenity legislation that goes back, within the states, to elements existing at the time the Bill of Rights was adopted. They do not contend or suggest, therefore, that the First Amendment then (or the Fourteenth later) intended no exceptions to its seemingly absolute language. And they explicitly and repeatedly want to allow for state authority to legislate on obscenity in connection with juveniles and non-consenting adults.[15] Nevertheless, they insist (as does the majority), following *Stanley*, that there is no legitimate state concern in controlling the moral content of a person's thoughts, and can see no limit to such control if this authority were ever granted. Moreover, they regard the suppression of obscenity as founded on "unprovable assumptions about human behavior, morality, sex and religion,"[16] and are willing to concede not a clear-cut but at best an ill-defined state interest in regulating its influence. Thus, because of obvious difficulty the Court has had in defining an allowable rule on obscenity, and the vagueness attending all such rules, they conclude that the whole field should be vacated insofar as material for consenting adults is concerned.

Both the majority and the minority share the constitutional premise, established by the Court in *Gitlow* (1925), that the speech and press guarantees of the First Amendment against congressional action are included in the liberty guaranteed by the Fourteenth against state action. Generally speaking, no innovation has had greater consequences for the federal structure of the nation, removing from the states whole areas of jurisdiction that formerly belonged to them alone. No innovation has laid a heavier, more dangerous, or more needless burden on the federal judiciary. Under the pre-1925 regime, the states were expected— even by such stalwart lovers of liberty as Jefferson and Madison—to punish abuses of the press in the name of the individual and public good.[17] Ordinary obscenity laws had to meet the test of state constitutions as interpreted by state courts, and that test alone. And it was to accomodation this older arrangement even under the new dispensation (allowing for much variation from state to state) that Justice Harlan had argued for a different First Amendment treatment for federal and state laws dealing with obscenity. As a federal subject the problem would no doubt have arisen anyhow, but only in connection with postal and import statutes, and with far less impact on general civic morality.

That the Supreme Court has struggled with this subject unsuccessfully since *Roth*, amid more variations and changes of standards than have appeared in any other area of the law, is hardly proof of the insolubility of the problem.[18] In 1973 the Court's approach was shaped by an inadequate conception of the importance of public morality and an excessive concern for individual liberty—a concern inconsistent with our historical tradition, with our long-range interests as a free people, and with the true interests of thought, literature, and art as well. It was this concern that led to a misplaced and self-defeating quest for precision. But not all areas of the law can be equally precise: the words "freedom," "fair," "reasonable," "cruel" are not as easily defined as "murder," "assault," and "fraud," but they all have an accepted and necessary place in our legal vocabulary. And so it is with obscenity—a term of ancient derivation, imbedded in the laws of every state and the federal government, and still actively used in everyday life. The real problem with obscenity, however, was never its definition, which diligence and care could have sifted out, smelted, and coined for legislative and judicial use in a free society.[19] This task, incidentally, Justice Brennan and his followers also require, and presume possible when—in flagrant contradiction to their general position—they allow for obscenity regulation in connection with juveniles and non-consenting adults.

The real problem with obscenity has been that its effect, like the importance of public morality generally, has been forgotten, or worse, had been subjected to attack and ridicule as an imposition of arbitrary and pernicious superstition, tradition, or convention on our pristine nature. But societies, particularly civilized and free ones, cannot be constructed out of primitive man: they require a unity, discipline, and dedication, and a cultivation of the soul, learned only over many centuries under fortunate circumstances. Free societies are peculiarly prone to thinking that the individuals composing them spring spontaneously from the womb of nature, whereas they are in fact the result of subtle forces of nurture of which they are hardly aware, and to which they give little heed. They tend to forget that democracies are sustained by citizens and that citizens are made, not born. But they do so at their peril. Democracies that insist on proper nurture and limits for their citizens can survive countless challenges to their survival. Those that do not, bereft of civic spirit, fall apart and become the natural prey of despots abroad or at home.

Regulating Obscenity: Why and How

W E MUST NOW ASK how obscenity and other laws protecting sexual morality should be framed, how the differences among the media should be treated, what provisions should be made for the young especially, and whether negative prohibitions in this area will suffice. Along the way we should consider the more narrowly prudential (rather than constitutional or broadly philosophical) arguments against the regulation of the press, many associated with the illustrious name of John Milton. Let us begin from simple considerations. In its most elementary form, obscenity is nothing but what is usually called pornography—that is, the crude effort to arouse lust through pictures or equally graphic verbal descriptions, using physical conjunctions, real or imagined, that defy moral restraints and responsibilities. This kind of appeal endangers civilized societies in many ways, only one of which is its incitement to actions that might be illegal.

When the appeal is less crude, and complicated by the fact that it forms part of a larger work containing other elements, the problem of judging it becomes more difficult. But here society has the right to insist on the primacy of its own moral needs, and indeed art is well served when it does. If the other elements, aspects, or qualities of a work are such as to change its effect on the reader or viewer, subduing or effacing the appeal to lust, so to speak, the work cannot be called obscene. Nevertheless, if the work as a whole still can be said to have an obscene effect, or if any part of it is so strikingly obscene as to remain, unforgettably, a prominent part of its effect, the work must be called obscene.

THE PROPER LAW

Between 1957 and 1973, the Supreme Court invented many complicated criteria to protect art at the expense of morality and ended by vulgarizing art as well as subverting morality. Thus we have the "average man," "contemporary community standards," "dominant theme," "work as a whole," "patent offensiveness," "graphic depiction of organs or acts," "serious value," etc. Of the many defects inherent in these terms, two deserve special mention. One is the attribution of a changeable nature to sexual standards, which in truth should be regarded as essentially fixed by the fixed needs of free civilized society. The second is the failure to keep in mind the special needs of groups like the young, sacrificing their moral education to the reading, viewing, or listening proclivities of the adult public. This error, at least, the *Hicklin* rule did not commit.

The criteria recently invented by the Supreme Court serve only to confuse and distract. Looking to the moral harm the public has a right to prevent, if a work wholly or substantially appeals to lust in its likely reader, viewer, or listener, it is obscene. It *need not* be patently offensive. It *need not* depict organs or acts (for example, it may concentrate on what leads to intercourse rather than on intercourse itself). It *may* have other elements of value, some of which may indeed serve to enhance its prurient appeal (such as the artist's power of description) and some of which may diminish it. In short, whoever is making the decision, whether judge or jury, must contemplate the effect the work is likely to have on its likely audience. It also follows that society has a clear interest in protecting any sizeable segment of itself from obscenity even if that means keeping the work from those unlikely to be affected by it in a similar way.

While the standard for judging obscenity derives simply and uniformly from its essential idea, the media vary greatly in their capacity to stimulate lust. All have such capacity, but movies are far more powerful than books, and movies in the living room—that is, television—present an even more serious problem than film in theaters. A book must be purchased and then, usually, read in the privacy of one's home, and by oneself. A movie, on the other hand, can be shown simultaneously to hundreds of people in one theater, and in hundreds or even thousands of theaters in a given state, or, by television, to millions. Moreover, the use in movies of visual, life-like, and dramatic portrayals makes its impact—its effect on the emotions, the moral capacity, the sense of the good and noble, bad and shameful—immensely more powerful than that of books (at least in the mass), and much more powerful even than the stage, which by comparison, is subject to severe limitations in the kinds of action it can represent (we do not consider "live sex acts" a form of the stage).

As an instrument of national education, or miseducation, movies have no peer. In their capacity to undo, bit by bit, the attitudes, dispositions, and habits built up over centuries, or even, at an instant, to precipitate social convulsions, they stand to books in something like the relation of atomic weapons to ordinary cannon. Immersed in them, we hardly realize that we are changed and not merely entertained and that recently they have led to a marked deterioration in the national character. The word "brutalized" has been much abused, but it would be entirely accurate as a description of the general effect of the movies on their viewers since the mid-1960s. They have been made perceptibly more brutish.

Because of the peculiar power of movies, the Court has allowed in their case an exception to the Blackstonian view of the freedom of the press. Remember that in *Near v. Minnesota* (1931), speaking for the more liberal part of the Court, Chief Justice Hughes had listed four circumstances in which even *prior* restraint might be constitutional. Two of these involved preventing illegal violence, another preventing interference with legal violence—that is, with the country's waging war. The fourth entailed enforcing "the primary requirements of decency" against obscene publications. In 1952 the Court repeated its adherence to these exceptions, and then in 1961, explicitly found the fourth exception applicable to movies and approved of their being inspected by states and cities beforehand in order to insure that they did not contain unprotected material.[1] But during the same period the Court undermined this approval by insisting, for the sake of First Amendment freedoms, that statutes must specify the immorality they ban, that "ideas" may not be banned, however counter to accepted (and necessary) standards of morality, and that censorship may not place undue burdens of time or procedure on the exhibitor. By 1973 the Court had made it impossible to ban, under obscenity statutes, anything but sheer pornography even from movies.[2]

Now this situation is most unsatisfactory, for the result of these protections to the press has been to make almost everything legally available, even in the movies, regardless of lustful appeal, vulgarity, brutality, or perversion. Add the fact that movie classification is something done by a group representing the producers and that the old censorship this kind of group used to apply to domestic movies is no more, and we can account for the large amount of obnoxious material found at almost all levels of the classification. So the power of this medium is now being applied full-force to the destruction of old moral restraints and sensibilities that used to prevail in all areas of human life and which exercised a vital control over our most powerful and most dangerous passions. If anyone asks, "Why the enormous crime rate, the decreasing respect for law, the increase in drug use, profanity and illiteracy, the multiplication of sexual crimes, teenage pregnancy, wife-battering, divorce, and the brutal and senseless violence in the country at large?"

it would hardly be foolish to answer, "Look at what we permitted the movies to encourage over the last three decades, and look at what is coming increasingly to dominate television and popular music."

If our general approach to these matters is correct, the Court must change its definition of what is legally obscene and grant that themes in movies (and in printed matter as well) may encourage ideas, desires, attitudes, and behavior that together or separately are within the purview of the police power if they run counter to necessary laws, institutions, and moral rules. Moreover, the Court must recognize that the parts of movies may be as important as their dominant theme in determining their overall effect: one gripping scene can leave an indelible imprint on the mind and memory. In fact, because of the power of the movies, and especially in movies shown to children, the Court must allow a state concern for morality that goes far beyond the primal themes of sex and violence. Politeness, respect for parents, the elderly, teachers, women, and the law, and a sense of fairness are elements of good moral character that states will wish to ensure are not flouted in the movies or generally made to seem outdated or undesirable.

ARE MOVIES PART OF THE PRESS?

All this could be done by restoring the relation between the police power and the First Amendment which prevailed before 1957, when the public concern for morality clearly took precedence over the artist's (and merchandiser's) concern for art or money. But another aspect of the matter deserves re-examination, and that is the Court's decision to consider movies part of the press and thus entitled to First (and Fourteenth) Amendment protection. Originally, the Court did not think so. In 1915 it regarded the exhibition of movies as a business, like other spectacles, and not "as part of the press of the country or as organs of public opinion." [3] Thirty-seven years later the Court changed its mind: "It cannot

be doubted that motion pictures are a significant medium for the communication of ideas. They may affect public attitudes and behavior in
a variety of ways, ranging from direct espousal of a political or social
doctrine to the subtle shaping of thought which characterizes all artistic expression. The importance of motion pictures as an organ of public opinion is not lessened by the fact that they are designed to entertain
as well as to inform."[4] The Court denied that a sharp distinction could
be drawn between informing and entertaining. And it responded to
the charge that "motion pictures possess a greater capacity for evil, particularly among the youth of community, than other modes of expression" by conceding this capacity, if it indeed exists, to be *subject to community
control.*

One might ask what difference it makes whether the movies are considered part of the press. If one adopts the libertarian view of the freedom of the press, it makes an enormous difference, since government
would then be hard-pressed to clamp *any* restriction whatsoever on the
content of movies. If one adopts the old pre-libertarian or non-liber-
tarian view, it makes much less difference, since this view is disposed to
give great leeway to government in suppressing abuses of the press and
promoting public morality. Even so, the inclusion of movies gives a
different impression of the meaning of "the press" and "the freedom of
the press." Such meanings are important to republican government, and
must have a broad effect.

In the text of the First Amendment, the freedom of speech and
press are obviously considered in their connection with "peaceable assembly" and petitioning the government "for a redress of grievances."
They are, first and foremost, the means whereby citizens can express
their criticisms of government, their thoughts on public matters, the
grievances they wish government to redress, and the needs they wish
government to satisfy. This is political expression, and it is completely
intra-republican. It is directed by some citizens to other citizens or to

members of the government. The object of such speech is to make sure that the government works for the people, adheres to the Constitution, and does not become oppressive or despotic.

Even so, it is clear from the history of the period, from English history, and from Blackstone that the freedom of the press protected more than political material. Blackstone speaks of it as "indeed essential to the nature of a free state. . . . Every freeman has an undoubted right to lay what sentiments he pleases before the public." This does not limit the free man to politics, and Blackstone specifically mentions the subjects of "learning, religion and government" as previously being the business of the censor to supervise, and now, of course, free. He adds, in justification of subsequent punishment, that "the disseminating or making public of bad sentiments, destructive of the ends of society, is the crime which society corrects." As for the meaning of "press," it seems to refer specifically to that which is printed by the printing press, as distinguished from that which is spoken, written, drawn, or painted. It is through printing that one is able to "lay what sentiments he pleases before the public"—sentiments that could not otherwise be disseminated in a form that combined durability with quantity.

While Blackstone does not explicitly refer to "literature," it was probably part of what he called "learning" and was undoubtedly protected by the freedom of the press. Unfortunately, and most peculiarly, Blackstone, in the course of his very long work, has nothing to say about the laws regulating serious theater. About so-called informal "stage-plays," he indicates only that they were classified as public nuisances, along with disorderly inns, bawdy houses, and stages for rope-dancers, and their suppression was handled under the heading of the "public police" or economy.[5] His silence about serious theater and drama is especially strange since in England they were sharply distinguished from the press. Controls over theaters, acting groups, and the printing and showing of plays went back to the sixteenth century. In 1737 Walpole's Theater Act severely restricted the number of legitimate theaters and legally gave over the censorship of plays, prior to showing, to the lord chamberlain, who kept it, without detailed guidance from statute, until 1968. In fact, the relative monopoly in theaters prevailing in Blackstone's own day was only abolished by the Theaters Act of 1843, with the lord chamberlain now granting licenses as he wished, though required to react to plays submitted to him within seven days. In 1909 a liberal joint committee of Parliament wanted to limit his censoring power by making the submission of plays to him optional, though the police could close the play down on grounds the committee specified. These grounds give a good idea of the evils feared from plays: "[I]ndecency, offensive personalities, the representation in an invidious manner of a living person or a person recently dead, violation of the sentiments of religious reverence, the presence of anything likely to conduce to crime or vice, or to cause a breach with a friendly power, or a breach of the peace."[6]

According to English tradition, the "press" does not include the stage: they are different spheres. The stage involves live presentations before a sizeable assembly of people, with a drama capable of moving the members of this assemblage, individually or collectively, in accordance with the ideas and passions expressed by the actors. Joy, sorrow, terror, anger, love for these, hatred for those, a sense of being oppressed, a will to oppress—all can be conveyed vehemently by the art of the poet and actor combined, and with possible consequences, immediate, in one concerted outburst, or piecemeal, afterwards, that are of serious concern. Thus, theater-viewing is different from reading precisely because: (1) it is done in large groups; (2) its visual and emotional impact is much greater; (3) it can incite the viewing group to passionate action; (4) it can more effectively alter the moral, social, and political dispositions of the viewer.

When the Supreme Court first decided to exclude movies from the press, movies were not talkies. By the time it was called upon to consider the matter again (in 1948 and 1952), movies had been talking for many years and had reached the full extent of the art form short of other, less significant technical advances that came later. Under these circumstances, the Supreme Court (in *Burstyn*) decided they were part of the press because "they are a significant medium for the communication of ideas." It might be admitted, with the Court, that the movies were not mere entertainment, but do they communicate "ideas"? They do indeed "affect public attitudes and behavior in a variety of ways, ranging from direct espousal of a political or social doctrine to the subtle shaping of thought which characterizes all artistic expression." But from the wording of this sentence, one might conclude the movies archetypally communicate "ideas" much in the same way that a book of political or social philosophy, or even a novel, communicates ideas. The Court also considers the viewing of a film in a movie theater by a sizeable number of people not essentially different from each person's taking home the script of the movie and reading it there. Such a description of the effect of movies—of their character as a medium—would be like describing the aftermath of an atomic explosion as "a mushroom-shaped cloud." What is lacking in both descriptions is some sense of the magnitude and power involved, which in the movies comes from a combination of two features: the life-like character of the performance, especially in its emotional impact, and the fact that it is experienced publicly in a group. Both of these features make it less likely, less possible that individual members of the viewing audience *reflect* about the performance, as they might about the script brought home and read individually. Even watching a great actor read lines from Immanuel Kant's *Critique of Practical Reason* as part of a film deriding intellectuals would have a far different effect from reading the same lines at home oneself.

These characteristics of the movies make them purveyors of "ideas" in a most equivocal sense, and seriously exaggerate their similarity to real products of the press, which are printed, and can be carried home and read with reflection. In fact, it would be politically more relevant to stress the *differences* between the real press—that is, printed materials—and movies, since these differences have great practical bearing and point to the great and unique harm movies can do to all elements of political society. This is why the Court has been forced to allow for prior restraint in the case of movies alone as a regular part of "the press": for even a single movie shown a few times can have very harmful effects, and the same movie shown simultaneously in hundreds of theaters in a large city, across a state or throughout the country, can multiply this harm manyfold in the space of a few hours. Had the Court not been influenced by a libertarian philosophy mistakenly granting First Amendment protection to the exchange of all "ideas" as such, it might have made its decision about the movies precisely on the basis of their enormous range of content and their *reduction* of the role of thought, judgment, or "ideas" in any strict sense. The movies are a special and unique mode of influencing, partaking of the character of dramatic performances on the stage, but going far beyond them in possible content, power of impact, and capacity to be performed in many places simultaneously. As such, states and cities should have the power to minimize their harmful influence without constantly worrying about protections falsely attributed to the First Amendment.

MOVIES AND TELEVISON

Correcting the Court's imprudent decision to designate movies as part of the press and returning to the rule which had prevailed earlier, on the grounds just provided, would have many advantages. First, it would preserve a true sense of what was originally meant by "the press" and what the framers wanted most to protect. To them the word especially denoted newspapers, pamphlets, and books—things that many people could individually produce, and many more read. It suggested a process of reading and critical evaluation at home, by oneself—even in the case of literature. And in politics it suggested the possibility of reading other pamphlets, seeking other opinions, exchanging views at meetings, and peaceably assembling to express grievances. These are all possible with the press, but not with movies. Second, correcting recent jurisprudence would make it much easier legally to distinguish speech and press not only from movies but from television, recorded music, girlie shows, and other forms of "expression" that have sought (and in some cases been granted) protection under the First Amendment. Third, it would consistently preserve the general understanding of the freedom of the press derived from Blackstone and adopted by the founders and framers, whereby the press is not to be subjected to prior restraint but only to subsequent punishment. This general view was predicated on the minimal risk that was involved in allowing newspapers or books to be published first and suppressed, if necessary, only afterward. With movies this risk is too great to allow—a fact we find it hard to accept only because we have grown insensitive to the harm movies do.

Another advantage of excluding movies from the press and withholding from them whatever advantages are conferred by the First Amendment is that it makes it much easier to treat television in the same way. For two other features distinguish movies from the press, and these are even more pronounced in the case of television. The first is the setting of movie viewing in movie houses out in the public, frequently in impressive buildings, offering access to crowds drawn from the public who do the viewing together. This setting lends an air of public acceptability and approval—a kind of quasi-public status—to movie viewing and to the movies shown that does not equally accrue to newspapers, magazines, or books. The second, at least equally significant, is the oligopolistic structure of the movie-producing industry, which, by its capital demands, makes it all but impossible for outsiders to enter it (in this respect resembling the automobile producers). This leaves the movie-making decisions affecting vital national attitudes in the hands of a tiny minority, responsible to no one but themselves, and motivated primarily not by public-spiritedness or artistic aspiration but by greed. The profit motive, ordinarily sufficient and beyond reproach in other lines of production, is hardly the one to be relied upon for providing the greatest general good and the least general harm of which movies are capable. Instead, it drives the producers (along with the writers, directors, actors, etc.) in the direction of box-office success alone, to be gained by appealing to (and cultivating) the appetites for lust and violence that lie latent in us all and to other dispositions and tastes almost equally dangerous to a free and civilized people.

With the advent of cable, television is much less consolidated an industry than it was. It is viewed in the home, but its quasi-public status comes from everyone's realizing that it addresses all members of the public at once. And it is legally closer to being an arm of the public. The three principal networks still control the lion's share of the industry and in recent decades, very likely through conscious decision, have retreated from their original conception of their role, based on family viewing and a strong sense of moral responsibility in the choice of program materials and advertisements. Instead, they have increasingly modeled themselves on the movies, steadily expanding the role of sex, violence, brutality, terror, vulgarity, and tawdry humor in their shows and utterly destroying the very notion of family-viewing time. Cable has added variety in all directions, including the most extreme, so that today at almost any hour of the day, one can find on television material that even ten years ago would have shocked national sensibilities and provoked a hue and cry for governmental controls.

The legal status of television is markedly different from that of movies, and much more explicitly public. Like radio, television frequencies are allotted by the Federal Communications Commission; first, because they cross state boundaries; second, because without careful allocation by a governmental agency they would overlap and cancel each other out. According to the Federal Communications Act of 1934 establishing the FCC and describing its powers, it is to consult the "public convenience, interest or necessity" in the licensing of stations, but not to censor. Congress explained neither of these injunctions, one positive, the other negative, but it made clear in its debates that the FCC was to examine past or prospective programming in deciding how to allocate station licenses. The air waves were publicly owned and were to be used for the public good and *not* primarily for private profit.

In 1946, the FCC itself made a comprehensive study of radio broadcasting and came up (in the so-called Blue Book) with standards for gauging the "public convenience, interest, or necessity." Some of these recommendations—like balanced programming, and serving the local community—have been actively applied by the FCC to television as well as radio.[7] For a time, the FCC became much more permissive, demanding "balance," but leaving almost entirely to the networks and stations the content of the soap operas, comedies, and other shows that dominate the air waves. Nor was any objection lodged against television fare that gradually came more and more to resemble the average movie. Then, starting in 1987, the FCC expanded its regulation of what it defined as "indecency" on television and radio, allowing it only between midnight and 6 a.m. instead of between 10 p.m. and 6 a.m., but an appeals court threw out the FCC ruling, saying it had not demonstrated such a move was necessary to protect children.[8] In 1988 Congress intervened, ordering the FCC to develop regulations for a twenty-four-hour-a-day ban. In 1989 the appeals court blocked the imposition of the blanket ban mandated by Congress until the FCC produced evidence of a real risk that children were being exposed to late-night programming. In 1990 such evidence, compiled by Arbitron, the ratings service, was supplied by the FCC , along with tens of thousands of complaints from the public.[9] In 1991 the appeals court said the FCC must return to its abandoned rule, allowing "safe harbor" hours during which indecent material can be aired.[10] The following year the Supreme Court let this decision stand, refusing to hear an appeal by the Bush administration which argued that "without a total ban, sexually explicit material would harm children and invade 'the privacy of the home.'"[11] In effect, the highest courts in the land declared that the First Amendment guarantees a right of adults to indecency.

This appears all the more ludicrous when one learns that the FCC had adopted a definition of indecency modeled exactly on the definition of *obscenity* laid down by the Supreme Court itself in *Miller* (1973). The FCC's definition stipulated that indecency consists of "patently offensive" depictions or descriptions of sexual or excretory activities or organs. The only difference between *Miller* and the FCC's definition of indecency was that *Miller* allowed for a defense of otherwise obscene materials through evidence of serious social value. The effect of the courts' interference with the FCC was to keep Congress, a unanimous FCC, and finally the executive branch, from giving expression to the moral fears of the American people, and all in the name of the First Amendment. In the process, what was declared in *Miller* to be *un*protected by the First Amendment (patently offensive representations or descriptions of sexual or excretory acts or organs) was somehow twisted by these later courts into a right of adults to view (or read or hear) precisely such things. Not only had the definition of obscenity in *Miller* been narrowed, not only had the FCC adopted a similarly narrowed definition of indecency in deference to *Miller*, but the courts had reversed the meaning of *Miller* itself and declared a right to view that which had been specifically banned in that decision. No wonder calls for emancipating obscenity and pornography from their traditional First Amendment ban have increased in recent years, and no wonder even intelligent people now assume that the First Amendment actually protects pornography. For at least in some cases, the courts have themselves abandoned the long, consistent tradition they reaffirmed as recently as 1973 in both *Miller* and *Paris Adult Theater*.

In its original debates about the Federal Communications Act, Congress plainly stated "that the Commission's basic responsibility is to see that the licensee puts on the kind of programming that is intended to serve the public interest."[12] This requires not only laying down rules about the balance of different kinds of programming but supplying both positive guidance and negative prohibitions about much of the content within the balance. Nor does this constitute "censorship"—by which Congress may simply have had in mind (per the Blackstonian use of the term) the Commission's demanding to review each program *before* its airing.[13] Moreover, the Commission's general mandate *requires* that it review past programming in reissuing licenses, and may even allow it to notify stations of significant past abuses before their licensing term has run out. Because of its plain legal status, and the legal conditions under which it operates, television (and the same holds for radio) simply cannot be considered part of the "press" and protected by the freedom guaranteed in the First Amendment. On the contrary, it should carry the kinds of programs the FCC deems in the "public interest" and avoid carrying those deemed against the public interest. But for this to happen, Congress must support the FCC in its statutory authority against the influence of networks, station owners, advertisers, and the like.

As for the movies, their Court-granted status since 1952 as part of the press should be withdrawn, and they should be subjected to a most demanding set of prior restraints by the various states and cities. No longer should the entire population fall prey to the mercenary interests, the attempts at moral revolution, the irresponsible artistic creativity of a hidden handful of decision-makers in the studios. Engines of such power can only be permitted to remain in private hands if they are subjected to open public controls that protect the public against the evil they do. Certainly government should not have less authority to protect the public against quasi-monopolistic moral harm than against quasi-monopolistic economic harm: the networks and movie studios are much more dangerous than trusts.

The only way to protect the moral well-being of the young is through a rigorous legal system of classification and segregation. This the public can do in the case of the movies, but in the case of television it is probably impossible. Television will therefore have to cease competing with adult movies and concentrate on programs for the entire family, adding whatever other programs will either fail to interest the young or interest them while transcending their comprehension without harm. But if the movies can be expected to enjoy greater leeway than television (since they can more readily exclude the young), they can scarcely enjoy the irresponsible scope they now possess. On the count of obscenity and encouragement to violence alone, a very high percentage of the movies now shown would not be permitted to young or old by any sensible system of prior restraints. On the other hand, the movies that prevailed up to 1960, like television until more recently, were much less noxious, without being less meritorious.

AGAINST CENSORSHIP

Those who cry "censorship!" should know that the philosophic founders of liberalism were unanimous in rejecting prior restraint of the press— that is, censorship in the strict sense. Nevertheless, like Locke and Montesquieu, they favored punishing abuses subsequent to publication. Were they inconsistent? The best way to pursue this problem is through the defender of freedom of the press with the greatest reputation, John Milton. The arguments usually directed against every kind of prohibitive regulation, prior or subsequent, are largely traceable to Milton's renowned essay *Areopagitica* (1643). The evils of the prior restraint or censorship of books have never been better depicted than in those pages, and yet Milton too maintains that subsequent punishment, susceptible as it is to many of the evils of censorship itself, cannot be dispensed with, even in the case of books. Society has to be protected against religious attacks on other religions and on the government, and also against attacks on the fundamentals of faith and manners which would undermine the rule of law and society itself. [14]

The major arguments against censorship in the strict sense are of two types. The first contends that even a perfect censorship would be harmful, the second that censorship is necessarily imperfect, oppressive, and thus more harmful still. According to the former, man's dignity consists in consciously choosing the good and the true from the variety of possible alternatives and constantly improving his choice. But then the full variety of alternatives, foul and fair, must be made available to everyone. As to the necessary imperfections of any actual censorship, these can be reduced to three points: (1) censorship is arbitrary in application and will curb the beneficial along with the harmful; (2) it defeats itself by encouraging an appetite for what it bans and calling forth subtle techniques of evasion in both the production and distribution of prohibited things; (3) it is insufficient, since it controls only one of the many kinds of influence contributing to the popular ills it seeks to protect against.

These arguments are often applied to subsequent punishment as well, and consistency would therefore seem to require opposition to every form of prohibitive regulation. But Milton, who stated most of them first and best, did retain the safeguard of subsequent punishment, even after demanding for the young a much more thorough moral education than has ever existed in any liberal society—an education without which the citizenry would not, in his judgment, have the capacity to choose virtue over vice. Was he thus inconsistent, or did he see more clearly than we do? Milton seems to admit that citizens should *not* be exposed to all alternatives, that even a well-educated citizenry can be induced to choose vice over virtue, error over truth, in certain important matters. This is the only possible reason for thinking that pernicious writings, while not kept from appearing by prior restraint, should be kept from spreading by subsequent punishment. Why is subsequent punishment less to be feared than prior restraint? How can this be understood?

We return to the passage in Blackstone's *Commentaries* containing the classic definition of the liberty of the press:

To subject the press to the restrictive power of a licenser, as was formerly done, both before and since the revolution, is to subject all freedom of sentiment to the prejudices of one man, and make him the arbitrary and infallible judge of all controverted points in learning, religion and government. But to punish (as the law does at present) any dangerous or offensive writings, which, when published, shall on a fair and impartial trial be adjudged of a pernicious tendency, is necessary for the preservation of peace and good order, of government and religion, the only solid foundations of civil liberty. [15]

Thus, a "fair and impartial trial" in court takes the place of the censor, but the result, some will claim, is still the suppression of part of the press. That, of course, was Blackstone's aim, as it was Milton's. What advantages do the courts have over the censor? It is not simply that the censor is one man: the fault lies in his manner of operating. He does not operate by clear rules to which he can be held; he works in secret, cannot be argued with or appealed from—hence the "infallibility" with which he is in fact invested. But courts are open, a fair trial implies a fair hearing, and appeal can be made to higher courts. Courts attempt to define, before the public, the legal bases for their action; they are guided by precedent. Through them the opportunity for arbitrariness and oppression is much reduced, and the needs of both liberty and society reconciled to the greatest possible degree.

There is nothing in the thought of the first liberal philosophers or Blackstone or the founding fathers that immediately reveals how to cope with movies and television. Just as Blackstone distinguished between the press and the theater, so it is likely that he would have distinguished between the press and movies. Certainly all these men would have been much more concerned about the moral, social, and political effects of the movies than the post-Holmesian Court has been. Can it be doubted that the sight of what Americans are fed daily, and consume, in the movies would have shocked them beyond belief and shaken their confidence in our ability to persevere under republican institutions? It is at least possible, if not highly probable, that these champions of the freedom of the press would be willing to see the system of prior restraint revived if the movies are to be kept at all. Otherwise we would be mechanically assuming that their opposition to censorship of the press also applies to a new and uniquely powerful medium more unlike than like the press they knew. To put such media in the same class with printed material of any kind would be like assimilating tactical nuclear weapons to the type "gun" and issuing licenses for their possession under the law covering guns.

Before the Supreme Court broke with previous constitutional tradition and started on its libertarian crusade against the moral regulation of the press, including movies, many cities and states did have censorship systems for the movies. In case after case between 1952 and 1973, the Court made it increasingly difficult for these systems to work, or for legislatures to devise systems they could be confident the Court would find acceptable. Today, little is heard of such systems, but they must be revived. Those who would protest that no one should tell us what movies we may see should awaken from their naivete and realize that movie and network owners, producers, sponsors, and writers "tell us" what to see right now, and have been doing so for some time. They accept and discard scripts as they wish, keep many a good thing from us, and put many a bad thing before us, leaving us with the illusion that no one is "telling us" what we may see. The real question is whether we will be "told" by a handful of nameless, faceless pelf-seekers, or—in the case of harmful films—by public officials who thoughtfully represent our interests, guided by rules laid down by the legislators we elect?

THE LAW'S SOLE INTEREST

As a general matter, what kind of statutes would have to be written to conform to constitutional protections in the First and Fourteenth

Amendments? If the freedom of the press does not include the freedom to purvey obscenity or to attack essential moral institutions, and
if the police power of the states is given the latitude it had earlier, the
burden placed on government in the framing of such protective statutes is the same as with all ordinary legislation. The role of the courts
then reduces, first, to determining that elements of the press actually
protected by the First and Fourteenth Amendments are not harmed
either by the statutes or by their application; second, to insuring that
the statutes meet with the constitutional requirements placed on all
ordinary legislation—for instance, that they be sufficiently specific, that
the proper trial procedures be used, and so forth. If movies are excluded
from the "press," as they should be, then only the second of these two
requirements applies to legislation concerning movies.

How specific need the statutes be, and once they are framed, do
they allow of objective (rather than subjective) application by judge or
jury? A provision of New York's education law forbade the licensing
of motion pictures "which are immoral in that they portray acts of sexual
immorality . . . as desirable, proper or acceptable patterns of behavior." [16]
The state then forbade the showing of *Lady Chatterley's Lover* on the
grounds that it presents adultery "as being right and desirable for certain people under certain circumstances." This is the least than may be
said about that movie, and the opinion of the censoring body (New
York's Board of Regents) was reinforced by the state's Court of Appeals, only to be reversed by the Supreme Court in 1959 on the grounds
that the advocacy of ideas—of all ideas—is as such protected by the
First Amendment. Justice Stewart, adhering to Holmesian shibboleths,
did not consider whether the advocacy, especially in movies, of child-
molesting, wife-beating, incest, rape, and the like are all similarly protected, as this principle would seem to require. [17] New York forbade
not the mere portrayal of acts of sexual immorality, but their *favorable*
portrayal, and if our analysis has been correct, on very sound grounds,
both constitutionally and prudentially.

In these days of visible and substantial moral decay, when the moral thought and behavior of a very powerful minority has led it to attack our moral tradition, sowing confusion and doubt, can statutes simply assume that "sexual immorality" is a sufficiently clear term? Can they, even more generally, outlaw motion pictures which are "immoral," or which "tend to corrupt morals?" As recently as thirty years ago, the moral ideas of Americans, particularly with regard to sexual matters, were very widely shared. The words "obscenity," "sexual morality," "decency," even "immorality" could be used in statutes with a meaning few would mistake. Then the so-called sexual or cultural revolution took place, mainly solidified through the mass media (with the help of the Court) and demonstrating, for the first time, the vastly accelerated power of modern technology to change moral opinion and behavior.

Given present conditions and the need for re-educating part of the public while confirming and protecting the views of the rest, legislation should provide some additional specifications of what it prohibits, if only by way of example. The term "obscenity" is already a specification with a core meaning that needs no amplification, but "sexual immorality" needs some spelling out, and "immorality" in general even more. On the other hand, the people and their representatives should not have impracticable burdens of specification placed on them; above all, the courts should not substitute their own versions of morality for that protected by the legislators. Their sole task is to support the Constitution and the laws made consistent with it, and while this entails insuring some minimal notion of law in legislation passed, legislative majorities should not be required to explain their meaning in such a way as to convince those opposed to them. The majorities need only sufficiently identify what they are outlawing, and it would be wise to indicate their reasons for doing so in an effort to educate as well as to compel. That education, in fact, is as important as the laws themselves.

The general legislative question in this area of public morality must be, "Does the material in question encourage some manifestly harmful desire, attitude, idea, or action?" Does material charged with obscenity encourage lust per se? Did the movie *Lady Chatterley's Lover* encourage adultery? Does movie x encourage violence, or lawlessness, or cowardice in battle, or fraudulent practices, etc? And since encouragements must work on somebody, the question of the likely readers or audience of the material must be kept in mind from the outset. Now questions stated in this form are not identical with "What do you, the judge or juryman, think of the material in question? What is your personal reaction to it?" However difficult it may be in some cases for judge or jury to separate the two considerations, they are only being asked by the law to assess a likely effect on a likely recipient, and this may or may not be the same as their own reaction to the material. It is possible for an older person to be little affected personally by material that he concludes will have a substantial effect on the young. It is possible for an unusually perceptive person to be much affected by material he thinks will have little effect on its likely recipients, taken generally.

It also follows from the nature of the questions being asked and the materials being pondered that, in some cases, courts in different states may reach different conclusions, and even courts in the same state at different times or in different places. Such difficulties enter other areas of the law as well, where varying popular sentiment colors attitudes toward the enforcement of certain laws (for instance, civil rights legislation in the South, anti-bootlegging legislation in the Tennessee mountains, prohibition legislation in New York City, etc.). These are difficulties that may be reduced in effect, but never totally eliminated, and must be borne with because the protection of morality is so intrinsically important to liberal democracy.

In matters such as these, hewing steadily to a rational, moderate position is what keeps society on an even keel. The Court-abetted period of legal laxity and media corruption through which we are still passing has caused these issues to be injected into national elections, contributed to a strong conservative reaction, and driven many citizens into a religiosity that could in its turn become extreme. For it is possible to want, imprudently, to prohibit too much, losing sight of the fact that certain evils are inseparable from liberty or from life itself, and that other, positive forces, like education, must be called into play as well, wherever possible. Preventing the worst excesses of the movies, television, printed material, and musical lyrics—the mass media—does not ensure their wise and moral conduct. It does not affect certain excesses deriving from unmoderated capitalism or other excesses deriving from the intellectual climate of our time.

Nevertheless, while the regulation of the media must be attended by other improvements, and while there is a limit beyond which one cannot go consistently with the Constitution and the nature of liberal democracy, it is still important to treat the media rigorously. For some time they have been the most obvious center and symbol of moral corruption in our midst, and to shut off one such source of corruption is important in itself. For a man with an illness, it frequently makes a crucial difference if he asserts a strong will to live. Restating and enforcing the old prohibitions would indeed amount to the public admission of a public malady, but it would proclaim, at the same time, a public will to prevail. It would supply, after serious forethought, a standard to which people of public spirit and good sense, regardless of party, religion, race, or economic background, could repair, and at the same time consternate the horde of parasites who thrive solely at the expense of the body politic—or rather, the public soul. And it would allow the public to seek ways, beyond prohibition, of righting itself.

One final argument from Milton must be considered: that truth is the better for grappling openly with falsehood, and virtue for grappling openly with vice.[18] It is interesting that Milton seems to distinguish between these two kinds of struggles, requiring a most complete moral education of the young (modeled on Plato's *Laws*) in preparation for the struggle with vice, but not demanding a similar intellectual education (like that in Plato's *Republic*) in preparation for the struggle with falsehood. Now a moral education, or an education in virtue, does not from the outset give both virtue and vice a fair chance at the young. On the contrary, it is impossible to develop the character traits necessary to virtue without favoring the side of virtue against the side of vice.

While virtue and vice might both have their seat in man's nature, vice has a firm base in his natural self-interest, narrowly understood, and virtue a more tenuous base in his love of honor, his sense of the noble, his conscience, and his affection or sympathy for others. Without the help, over many years, of preachment, habituation, and example, solidly backed by society, virtue could not come to dominate the souls of young men or women. Or if they were equally exposed to vice, even while attempts were made to prejudice the case against vice, virtue could not win out. Thus, exposing the young in the classroom to pornography, or drugstore novels, or to *Lady Chatterley's Lover* will make it exceedingly difficult for virtue to prevail. Only by concealing vice in its fullest and most potent forms can human beings be educated in virtue, and only afterward can they be exposed to the vice that is in the world (unamplified by the mass media) and left to choose, with some hope that most will choose well.

Were this not the case, we would allow our children to mingle with bad as well as good children, expose them constantly to the worst elements in the community, ridden with all the vices one can name, present them with readings, and experiences, that reveal vice in all its attractiveness. They would live the life of gluttony with gluttons, of injustice with thieves and murderers, of drink with drunkards, gambling with gamblers, fornication with lechers. The result would be either vicious or confused young people. Now such are the blandishments of vice that neither age nor virtue is proof against them. Adults can be swayed from their adherence to virtue by repeated exposure to vice, made attractive, bit by bit, so that the sense of shame accompanying virtue is never too strongly shocked. Such in fact has been our manner of retrogression over the past decades, changing from a sense of shame at viewing too lingering a kiss or too close an embrace on the screen to the expectation, without shock, and by adult viewers, of intercourse five minutes after a man and woman meet. And this in the age of AIDS.

Because adults have changed, the young have also changed, since it is the adults who encourage, or allow, what the young experience. As Mill once put it, "The existing generation is master both of the training and the entire circumstances of the generation to come.... If society lets any considerable number of its members grow up mere children, incapable of being acted on by rational consideration of distant motives, society has itself to blame for the consequences."[19] What Mill failed to consider was the degree to which adults themselves could deteriorate morally, even after a decent education, on repeated exposure to immoral opinions and opportunities to do ill. Civilized society is a car that always must be driven on tracks. This Milton seemed to recognize, both by the emphasis he placed on education in virtue and by his insistence on limiting the leeway allowed the press for attacking political, religious, and moral fundamentals. So there cannot be a radical difference in treatment between young and old—a conclusion Milton would no doubt fortify in language only he could summon forth were he so unfortunate as to be exposed to what has become the daily fare in our movie theaters and on television as well.[20]

PART III

DOES THE FIRST AMENDMENT

ERECT A WALL OF SEPARATION BETWEEN

CHURCH AND STATE?

12

The Meaning of the First Amendment

WHEN THE SUPREME COURT, beginning in the 1950s, dismantled *Dennis*'s strong position bit by bit, in effect substituting Holmes's and Brandeis's "clear and danger" rule and granting full legality even to the most hostile political parties, there was little public outcry. And when the Court, starting with its own liberalized view of obscenity in *Roth*, made it almost impossible to prosecute obscenity by 1966, and actually impossible after 1973 to prosecute anything but pornography, the public reaction again was surprisingly weak. Perhaps the people did not sufficiently understand what these decisions entailed; perhaps they were overawed by the Court's great place in our political system. By contrast, two similar innovations of the Court in the same period have precipitated an ongoing furor and fueled strenuous and repeated efforts to amend the Constitution. The one ended prayer in the public schools (1962-63), and the other severely limited state regulation of abortion (1973)—both issues that touched deep religious convictions in a large part of the population. In the former case, an amendment twice came within a hair's breadth of achieving the two-thirds margin needed in the House, suggesting that at least a plain majority of the people favored this extraordinary method of rebuking

the Court. Meanwhile, these and other examples of judicial usurpation and arbitrariness (sometimes benignly called "activism") began to
have a cumulative effect on the mind of the people, arousing a broad
conservative reaction that made itself felt strongly in several presidential elections starting in 1972. By 1980, a group pointedly, if somewhat
boldly, calling itself the Moral Majority sought to reassert the strength
of traditional Americanism and Christianity, joined together, against
the forces of communism, sexual corruption, and secularism. Almost
imperceptibly at first, the innovations of more than two decades—many
engendered or abetted by the Court—aroused widespread resentment
that went far beyond the membership of the Moral Majority and helped
elect three Republican presidents.

SEPARATING RELIGION AND GOVERNMENT

When we examine the Court's treatment of the religious parts of the
First Amendment—its first half, grammatically and thematically—we
find the same errors at work as with freedom of speech and press. The
Court has willfully abandoned constitutional tradition, made erroneous historical claims, substituted its own shallow understanding for that
of the founders and framers, and emerged with a novel view of the place
of religion in American public *and* private life. The Court has mistaken the meaning of "establishment of religion," confused it with "free
exercise of religion," and made dangerous changes in the meaning of
"religion" itself. Along the way it has erroneously read this false interpretation of the religious part of the First Amendment into the "liberty" guaranteed against the states by the Fourteenth Amendment,
claiming that the latter was meant to act upon the states in the very
same way as the former was to act on the federal government.

What do Constitutional innovators mean when they say the religious part of the First Amendment calls for a "wall of separation between church and state"? What would a strict, perfect, unbreached

"wall" (qualities implied by the word "wall" itself) look like? We begin by noting that the exalted phrase—nowhere to be found in the Constitution—represents a Jeffersonian gloss on the first half of the First Amendment. Jefferson coined the phrase in a letter he sent, as president, to a committee of the Danbury, Connecticut, Baptist Association, expressing his agreement that the First Amendment restrained the national legislature with such a wall.[1] Applied to the public schools, the "wall's" adherents on the Court have taken it to forbid any governmental support for, promotion of, or assistance to any and all religions: no opening prayer in the schools written by the New York Board of Regents, however nonsectarian (as in *Engel v. Vitale*, 1962), nor any use of Bible readings, the Lord's Prayer, or religious observances (as in *Abington School District v. Schempp*, 1963). In short, neither sectarian nor nonsectarian religion may be practiced in the public schools: the schools must be neutral to religion, neither favoring nor hindering it in any way.

No one can claim that the public schools, anywhere in the country around 1960, were suffused with sectarian religion. On the contrary, the country had come to accept a largely secular curriculum, supplemented, here and there, by small elements of Biblical or Christian religion—the religion of the vast majority—such as opening prayers, Bible readings, Christmas songs, Christmas and Easter pageants. In removing these, the Court seems to have touched a vital exposed nerve, as if the very slightness of the remaining connections with religion made them all the more dear to the people. The main response to the Court has taken the form of proposing a Constitutional amendment making organized voluntary prayer in school possible—which seems to grant the Court's contention that states ought not to mandate either nonsectarian or sectarian prayers. This proposal grew out of the lone dissent by Justice Potter Stewart in *Engel*,[2] drawing attention to the provisions New York State had made for students to participate in the Regents' prayer only if they wished to.

Justice Stewart was also fearful that the Court's new course would lead inevitably to a complete severing of connections between church and state. To offset such fears, Justice Black, who spoke for five of the six-man Court majority, used his last footnote to deny that reciting the Declaration of Independence (with its "references to the Deity"), singing the national anthem (with its "composer's profession of faith in a Supreme Being"), or the "many manifestations in our public life of belief in God" are inconsistent with the Court's decision. But the hollowness of Black's reassurances is apparent from his peculiar description of Declaration-reciting and anthem-singing. He speaks of the Declaration as an "historical document" used to encourage love for our country, not a statement of perennial American belief; similarly, the anthems are said to contain professions of their composer's faith, not of the faith of Americans today. This implies, simply, that the normal use of the Declaration and anthems—the use that renders them significant expressions of belief for Americans—is in fact unconstitutional, that is, it violates the "wall of separation between church and state." And if Black is forced to express himself so strangely in these matters, how can he support the third element—"manifestations in our public life of belief in God?" Such manifestations are not merely historical: they are direct signs of religious belief constantly employed on the "patriotic or ceremonial occasions" of which he speaks, however short they may fall (as he allows) of "religious exercises" in the strict sense.[3]

It is hard to know whether Justice Black and the four who joined him gave any thought to what their statements imply. Certainly their reassurances must, to any thoughtful person, have precisely the opposite effect. Any principle which would exclude the teaching of the Declaration of Independence, prohibit the singing of any stanza of the "Star-Spangled Banner" or "America the Beautiful" that invokes God's name, or strike "In God We Trust" from the coins and "under God" from the Pledge of Allegiance is certainly radical and far reaching. Openly stated, it would arouse far greater and more irresistible criticism than even the banning of school prayer. Nevertheless, one of the justices, against whom impeachment threats later became vociferous, saw fit to bring it all out into the open. In his concurring opinion, Justice Douglas presented a compendium of those public supports of religion—financial, patriotic, ceremonial—that on principle deserve to be considered unconstitutional: "The point for decision is whether the Government can constitutionally finance a religious exercise. Our system at the federal and state levels is presently honeycombed with such financing. Nevertheless, I think it is an unconstitutional undertaking whatever form it takes." [4]

The following list of practices Douglas would outlaw is representative, though far from complete: (1) chaplains in both Houses of Congress and in the armed forces; (2) compulsory chapel at the service academies; (3) presidential religious proclamations; (4) the use of the Bible for administering oaths; (5) the mention of God in the pledge of allegiance; (6) tax provisions favorable to religion; (7) the opening of any governmental session (as in the Supreme Court itself) with appeals to God; (8) the use of "In God We Trust" as our national motto and in our national anthem; (9) the purchase of community Christmas trees.

While Douglas's opinion is obviously intended to outrage ordinary people and win the plaudits of civil libertarians, it has the distinct merit of presenting the full reach of the "wall of separation" principle. To the extent that the issue is fully joined in *Engel*, it is joined not between Stewart and Black but between Stewart and Douglas. Stewart limits his dissent to the public use of prayer—that is, to the question directly confronting the Court. He cites, among many other illustrations, the invocation of God in presidential addresses—a point omitted in Douglas's compendium but surely covered by his ban. What Stewart and Douglas share is the conviction that the *Engel* ruling must, sooner or later, be extended far beyond the subject to which it immediately applies. Stewart fears this extension; Douglas favors it. Douglas's opinion establishes the fullest extension of the *Engel* principle: logically, there can be no stopping until every vestige of religious belief or aid to religion is extirpated from public affairs. And this contention of Douglas's may possess special significance since only ten years earlier, in the famous *Zorach* case, he had explicitly refused to press the concept of separation of church and state to such extremes, citing as constitutional the prayers of Congress, presidential appeals to God, the oath "so help me God," and "all other references to the Almighty that run though our laws, our public rituals, our ceremonies."[5]

While Douglas seems to star in *Engel* as the radical emancipator from ancient tradition, the principle he employs really derives from a much broader statement of principle by Black fifteen years before. Douglas's new stand appears to be the logical consequence, ruthlessly drawn, of the following well-known and widely accepted passage from Black's majority opinion in *Everson* (1947):

> The "establishment of religion" clause of the First Amendment means at least this: Neither a state nor the Federal Government can set up a church. Neither can pass laws which aid one religion, aid all religions, or prefer one religion over another. Neither can force nor influence a person to go to or remain away from church against his will or force him to profess a belief or disbelief in any religion. No person can be punished for entertaining or professing religious beliefs or disbelief, for church attendance or non-attendance. No tax in any amount, large or small, can be levied to support any religious activities or institutions, whatever they many be called, or whatever form they may adopt to teach or practice religion. Neither a state nor the Federal Government can, openly or secretly, participate in the affairs of any religious organizations or groups and *vice versa*. In the words of Jefferson, the clause against the establishment of religion by law was intended to erect "a wall of separation between church and state."[6]

One might object, somewhat simple-mindedly, that the First Amendment did not itself set limits on the states, and one might wonder what is left for the "free exercise" section of the Amendment if the "establishment" section means all this. Nevertheless, accept this passage as written and one is impelled to reject as unconstitutional every mode, however slight, by which government at any level assists religion. Yesterday it was nonsectarian school prayer; today it is Bible readings and religious observances in the schools; tomorrow it will be religious tax privileges, chaplains in the armed services or Congress, or the mention of God in pledge, anthem, motto, and oath. With what looks like perfect logic, the absurd conclusion will be drawn eventually that it is unconstitutional, under public auspices, to teach or treat as true the claim of the Declaration of Independence that men are endowed by their Creator with certain inalienable rights. Could this have been the intention of the great man, Thomas Jefferson, who gave us both the Declaration and "wall of separation"? Can this be what wisdom, or the Constitution, requires?

JEFFERSON AND THE WALL

Apart from the Declaration of Independence, Jefferson thought his greatest accomplishments were authoring Virginia's statute for religious freedom (adopted in 1786) and founding the University of Virginia (he was also its rector from 1817 until his death in 1826, even though its doors opened only in 1825). Virginia's statute kept the state from both maintaining an establishment of religion and interfering with any religious opinion as such. This makes it a fair approximation, on the state level, to the First Amendment as it was ratified five years later. Thus, whatever "wall of separation" existed nationally because of the First Amendment might equally be said to have existed in the state of Virginia beginning in 1786. Of the requirements of such a "wall" Jefferson must have been quite conscious when he turned his thoughts and energies to public education, and particularly to establishing a state university in Virginia. His views of the role allowed religion in public education should therefore reveal the practices he thought consistent or inconsistent with such a "wall," from which it will be easier to infer his likely attitude toward *Everson, Engel,* and *Schempp.*

The object of primary education, according to Jefferson, was "to instruct the mass of our citizens in . . . their rights, interests and duties, as men and citizens," that of higher education to prepare a more select group for the higher reaches of public service and private happiness, mainly through "moral, political and economical" training.[7] Both parts of public education were meant to enhance public and private good together, and in concerns that were wholly of this life. Within such a framework, religion is not prevented from playing some role, but only when it contributes to natural or secular interests. For this reason, Jefferson's "Act for Establishing Elementary Schools" in Virginia (1817) did not permit ministers of the gospel to serve as "visitors" (overseers), fearing that sectarian jealousy might be awakened if they did. He also provided that the teachers should, "in all things relating to education and the government of their pupils, be under the direction and control of the visitors; but no religious reading, instruction or exercise, shall be prescribed or practiced inconsistent with the tenets of any religious sect or denomination."[8] This last sentence does not mean to ban religious activities, as some have claimed. On the contrary, it seems to take such practices for granted and seeks only to insure their acceptability to all sects, thus moving toward what the sects have in common—that is, toward nonsectarianism. And it is important to note that Jefferson displays solicitude only for "the tenets of any religious sect or denomination," and not for the views of the nonbeliever: to consider nonbelief as having equal rights with belief would nullify any religious activity in the schools whatsoever.

In the following year, 1818, Jefferson submitted his plans for the new state university to the legislature. The teaching of "divinity" or sectarian religion was explicitly excluded, leaving each sect to provide for instruction in its own tenets away from the university. However, there would be a professor of ethics to teach natural theology as well as the obligations "in which all sects agree," and the ancient languages of Hebrew, Greek, and Latin would be taught so that "a basis will be formed common to all sects." In addition, to provide students with the political principles of their state and country, Jefferson went so far as to prescribe the texts to be used in a course of civil polity, among them several (such as Locke's *Treatise*, his own Declaration of Independence, and Washington's Farewell Address) in which philosophical and religious ideas of God are intertwined with moral and political fundamentals.[9]

In another report four years later (1822), Jefferson suggested an important change in the role of sectarian religion at the university:

> It was not, however, to be understood that instruction in religious opinion and duties was meant to be precluded by the public authorities, as indifferent to the interests of society. On the contrary, the relations which exist between man and his Maker, and the duties resulting from those relations, are the most interesting and important to every human being, and the most incumbent on his study and investigation. The want of instruction in the various creeds of religious faith existing among our citizens presents, therefore, a chasm in a general institution of useful sciences. But it was thought that this want, and the entrustment to each society of instruction in its own doctrine, were evils of less danger than a permission to the public authorities to dictate modes or principles of religious instruction, or than opportunities furnished them for giving countenance or ascendancy to any one sect over another.
>
> A remedy, however, has been suggested of promising aspect, which, while it excludes the public authorities from the domain of religious freedom, will give to the sectarian schools of divinity the full benefit of the public provisions made for instruction in the other branches of science. These branches are equally necessary to the divine as to the other professional or civil characters,

to enable them to fulfill the duties of their calling with understanding and usefulness. It has, therefore, been in contemplation,
and suggested by some pious individuals, who perceive the advantages of associating other studies with those of religion, to establish their religious schools on the confines of the University; and
to maintain, by that means, those destined for the religious professions on as high a standing of science, and of personal weight
and respectability, as may be obtained by others from the benefits
of the University. Such establishments would offer the further and
greater advantage of enabling the students of the University to attend religious exercises with the professor of their particular sect,
either in the rooms of the building still to be erected, and destined
to that purpose under impartial regulations, as proposed in the same
report of the commissioners, or in the lecturing room of such professor.

To such propositions the Visitors are disposed to lend a willing ear, and would think it their duty to give every encouragement,
by assuring to those who might choose such a location for their
schools, that the regulations of the University should be so
modified and accommodated as to give every facility of access and
attendance to their students, with such regulated use also as may
be permitted to the other students, of the library which may here-
after be acquired either by public or private munificence. But always understanding that these schools shall be independent of the
University and of each other.

Such arrangement would complete the circle of the useful sciences embraced by this institution and would fill the chasm now
existing, on principles which would leave inviolate the constitutional freedom of religion, the most inalienable and sacred of all
human rights, over which the people and authorities of this state,
individually and publicly, have ever manifested the most watchful
jealousy: and could this jealousy be now alarmed, in the opinion
of the legislature, by what is here suggested, the idea will be relinquished on any surmise of disapprobation which they might
think proper to express.[10]

This proposal ends rather tremulously, almost inviting the disapprobation to which it refers. No doubt it was intended at least as much to enlarge and improve the secular aspects of divinity school training as to facilitate sectarian training and worship. But the seriousness with which Jefferson set it forth is proved by an even more startling accommodation to sectarian religion proposed two years later (1824): "Should the religious sects of this State, or any of them, according to the invitation held out to them, establish within, or adjacent to, the precincts of the University, schools for instruction in the religion of their sect, the students of the University will be free, and expected to attend religious worship at the establishment of their respective sects, in the morning, and in time to meet their school in the University at its stated hour."[11] Not only would this university regulation drafted by Jefferson make it possible for the sects to establish religious schools either near or on state university premises, and invite them to do so, but it would "expect" students to attend daily worship with the sect of their choice—an expression that can only mean it would compel their attendance. Jefferson does not tell us why he was willing to go so far. Anxious for the success of the new university, he may have wished to assure parents that sending their sons to it would not jeopardize their piety. In any case, he did not think a "wall of separation between church and state" prevented his *requiring* the daily "free exercise" of religion at this public university.

Let us sum up Jefferson's understanding of the relation between religion and public education. In the elementary schools, no sectarian "reading, instruction or exercise" was to be required, but those that were nonsectarian could be, and this religion and morality on which all (Christian, or at least Biblical) sects agree was undoubtedly related to the moral aims Jefferson ascribed to elementary education. At the university, the nonsectarian common core would receive further support and amplification from reason in the required disciplines of natural theology, ethics, and politics, and from ancient languages. And the university was also prepared to encourage the various religious sects themselves through a wide range of accommodations, including the use of its own authority to insure the regular attendance of students at worship services. Now, since no man in Virginia can be presumed to have had a better appreciation than Jefferson of Virginia's constitutional ban on religious establishments and guarantee of free exercise, apparently erecting a wall of separation between church and state, we must presume that he did not think his educational policies breached this wall. Or it might be more accurate to say that the word "wall" hardly applies to the connections between government and both nonsectarian and sectarian religion that Jefferson considered perfectly constitutional.

The difference between Jefferson and the absolute separationists who sloganize him is traceable to a different understanding of the needs of republican government—that is, to a purely secular consideration. The various accommodations with religion that Jefferson approved or devised had as their chief objective the avoidance of secular evils and the procuring of secular benefits. In his view, republican government requires a firm foundation in the minds of its citizens, a moral-political education in rights and duties, that at certain points joins with various religions practiced by Americans, beginning with the belief in God. Religious superstition can indeed enslave and divide, but belief in the God of freedom and justice is the very bulwark of republican government, Jefferson believed, and the main obstacle to racial or any other kind of slavery: "And can the liberties of a nation be thought secure when we have removed their only firm basis, a conviction in the minds of the people that these liberties are the gift of God? That they are not to be violated but with his wrath? Indeed I tremble for my country when I reflect that God is just; that his justice cannot sleep forever." [12]

To make use of religious belief and obligation where they support civic responsibility is to strengthen republican freedom, which includes religious freedom itself. This is why nonsectarian religious beliefs and those derived by reason in the areas of theology, ethics, and politics (properly called philosophy rather than religion) can join together to serve a single end. If this same end is also served by equal assistance to the various sectarian religions, government may have recourse to the assistance of religion. Nor by such teachings and such assistance did Jefferson think the rights of atheists and agnostics were being infringed upon. The equality of legal protection and participation afforded believers and nonbelievers alike in a free society depends on anchoring ethics and politics in the belief in God, and hence on government's giving obvious preference to religious belief over disbelief. These observations do not tell us how Jefferson would have voted in *Everson*, *Engel*, and *Schempp*. But they do show that those who invoke his name and words exploit his fame for a dogmatic principle he never accepted. They show that various means of expressing or favoring religion, dogmatically held by libertarians today to be in violation of the First Amendment, were not deemed so by Jefferson, operating under similar restraints (placed there mainly through his own efforts) in the state of Virginia. In short, if Jefferson is the touchstone libertarians claim he is, their libertarianism must be in error.

WHAT DOES "ESTABLISHMENT" MEAN?

If an absolute separation of church and state in American public affairs would be generally untenable, and if Jefferson himself, who coined the expression "wall of separation," was not an absolute separationist, a reconsideration of the religious parts of the First Amendment is in order. Let us examine the famous opening lines of the First Amendment: "Congress shall make no law respecting an establishment of religion, or prohibiting the free exercise thereof; . . . ." The second half of the amendment follows after the semicolon, and adds "or abridging" the freedom of speech or of the press, of peaceable assembly, and of petition for redress of grievances. In the language of that day, and of

Abraham Lincoln, the amendment first guarantees "religious liberty," then certain prerequisites of "civil liberty" and republican government. Overall, the religious half seems to guarantee that Congress shall neither "establish" a religion nor interfere with the freely chosen religious activities of citizens.

What does it mean to "establish" a religion, or to have an "establishment of religion"? From usage outside the Constitution, including the writings of Jefferson, a church or religion was established when the government, through law, gave it a special official status in political society, with authority, privileges and support not shared by other churches or religions. And so there were, in a few states in 1789, established churches, or—as seems to have been true somewhat more often—an established religion like Protestantism, or Christianity in general.[13] Always and everywhere the idea of a religious establishment involved a choice from among two or more religious societies made by the government and embodied in law. Historically, the term as well as the idea arose in the sixteenth century after Protestantism had introduced religious diversity into Europe, with princes "establishing" the religion they preferred, usually with themselves as its head.[14] There was no "religious establishment" in the Catholic Middle Ages, when there was essentially one religion available and it *superior* to, rather than preferred or chosen by, the state. For similar reasons, the religion of ancient Israel could not be called "established." As for the civic religions of the ancient cities, because they were the sole religions in their cities and lacked *any* intrinsic independence from the city, they could hardly have the term "established" applied to them.

The possibility of religious establishments is therefore coeval with the advent of Protestantism, offering a way to preserve an official state connection with a preferred religion or church where already there was Christian diversity. Originally, a particular Protestant church would be singled out by the government for establishment. Much later, as in several

American states, where the feelings of religious kinship might have broadened considerably, establishment could be expanded to include all of Protestantism (but not Catholics, Jews, etc.), or even all of Christianity (but not Jews or infidels). The view taken by the *Encyclopaedia Britannica* in its Thirteenth Edition therefore seems quite accurate: "Perhaps the best definition which can be given, and which will cover all cases, is that establishment implies the existence of some definite and distinctive relation between the state and a religious society (or conceivably more than one) other than that which is shared in by other societies of the same general character. . . . It denotes any special connection with the state, or privileges and responsibilities before the law, possessed by one religious society to the exclusion of others." [15]

If this is what "an establishment of religion" meant to the generation of the founders and framers, it follows that this part of the First Amendment does not forbid Congress to assist or encourage *all* religions—that is, to prefer religion over non-religion. [16] An "establishment of religion" never meant, or could mean, an establishment of religion generally. This becomes apparent in following the various proposals on the subject formulated by the First Congress in 1789. Madison, who initiated the Bill of Rights amendments in the House, put it simply: "nor shall any national religion be established." The Senate, for its part, considered various motions forbidding Congress to establish "one religious sect or society in preference to others," or "any particular denomination of religion in preference to another," or "religion," or "articles of faith or a mode of worship" (the Senate's final version). In all these cases, what the formulators had in mind was singling out a particular church, sect, or religion and giving it legal preference. Forbidding Congress to do this would have been perfectly compatible with allowing it to *assist* religion as such if its delegated constitutional functions made it "necessary and proper" to do so. No doubt this, in fact, was the view of the same First Congress when, in the same year, it reenacted the North-west Ordinance of 1787, by which federal lands were to be set aside for schools that would bring "religion, morality and knowledge" to the youth of the territory.

Despite all the formulations that simply forbade establishing a national religion, or a sect, or a particular mode of religion (as above), the House-Senate Conference Committee finally produced, and Congress accepted, a somewhat mysterious formulation not seen until then, involving the little word "respecting." What is the difference between "Congress shall make no law respecting an establishment of religion" and "Congress shall make no law establishing religion"? The word "respecting," to begin with, simply means "regarding," "concerning," or "with reference to." It is not intended to mean "having respect for or showing deference toward." Restated, then, the amendment reads that "Congress shall make no law concerning an establishment of religion." Obviously a law actually establishing religion would fall within this ban, and Congress may not pass one. But what more is covered by the peculiar term "respecting" (or "concerning")?

To learn the answer, we must remind ourselves of the great differences between the Federalist supporters of the new Constitution and its anti-Federalist opponents, now to be placated or won over by guarantees ensconced in the Bill of Rights. The anti-Federalists feared a central national despotism over the states and the people and wanted their right both as states and as individuals protected in writing. Many states had religious establishments or preferences of one sort or another, and wanted to be sure these would not be subject to modification or abolition by the new Congress on any ground whatsoever. Even some without such institutions might fear any kind of national control in the area. Ultimately, it seems, a group of this persuasion sitting in the First Congress were able to make their view prevail in the Conference Committee and in the Congress itself by using the word "respecting." They could thereby forbid Congress to make laws *concerning* not only a national establishment of religion but an establishment of religion anywhere else, and the anywhere else was in the states. In effect, the amendment now meant that Congress could neither establish a national religion nor alter the establishments of religion in the states. It could make no law "respecting an establishment of religion." [17]

One need not rest at the general meaning of the words themselves or even at the general problem the Bill of Rights was meant to settle in order to arrive at this plausible hypothesis—the *only* plausible hypothesis. Further confirmation is available in the course of proceedings in House and Senate, reported by Thomas Lloyd at the time. Madison's original proposal in the House not only forbade the establishment of "any national religion," as we have seen, but also declared that "No state shall violate the equal rights of conscience or the freedom of the press, or the trial by jury in criminal cases." And it was this latter part that Madison considered "the most important amendment in the whole list"— obviously because it went beyond the body of the Constitution to bind the states on matters of great moment. This part was accepted by the House Committee (on which Madison himself sat) and then by the House, only to be rejected by the Senate and never revived. The Senate, in other words, was a stronger bastion of states rights than the House, and kept Madison from having his way on the part of the Bill of Rights most important to him.

The same sentiment manifested itself at crucial points in the House's own discussion. Its committee, to begin with, dropped the word "national" from Madison's proposal, leaving it to read "No religion shall be established by law." This phrasing introduced a new difficulty, for Madison had not begun his proposal with the phrase "Congress shall make no law," and only by using the term "national religion" had he implied that this was a restraint on Congress' authority. Once the modifier "national" was removed, the ban could be read to cover what the states as well as Congress might do by law to establish religion. The result would be to abolish all state establishments—something Madison himself, as we know from his words and deeds in the state of Virginia, looked upon as a matter of natural right, even though he had not dared introduce it into his own proposals or argue it anywhere in the course of these proceedings.[18]

It may have been this change (dropping the word "national") that first led Sylvester of New York to say, on the House floor, that the committee's words, unintentionally, "might be thought to have a tendency to abolish religion altogether," and then made Huntington of Connecticut express the fear that "the words might be taken in such latitude as to be extremely hurtful to the cause of religion."[19] Madison's response was to state, as the committee's intended meaning, that "Congress should not establish a religion and enforce the legal observation of it by law." Then, showing that he connected Huntington's remarks with the threat to state establishments, he suggested that the word "national" be introduced before the word "religion," so that the text would read: "No national religion shall be established by law."[20] This induced Livermore of New Hampshire to propose that "Congress shall make no laws touching religion"—easily the most extensive ban to reach the floor, since it protected the state establishments from Congress and at the same time kept Congress from legislating on religion (and not merely on an establishment of religion) entirely. By these words, Congress could not even have assisted religion, or all the religions, generally. As it turned out, after having accepted Livermore's motion temporarily, the House ended its deliberations with "Congress shall make no law establishing religion, or to prevent the free exercise thereof, or to infringe the rights of conscience." This version was a compromise between the original committee proposal and Livermore's: it did not directly assault state establishments by making them unconstitutional, but neither did it explicitly exclude a Congressional power to *dis*establish state establishments. The final Senate version was similar: "Congress shall make no law establishing religion, or prohibiting the free exercise thereof."[21] Only in the text propounded by the House-Senate Conference Committee and accepted by the Congress as a whole did the states-righters fully get their way. Earlier in the Senate they had defeated Madison's effort to introduce a compulsion on the states not to violate the equal rights of conscience; now, by introducing the word "respecting," they had protected state religious establishments against congressional interference. Congress could make no law "respecting an establishment of religion," whether on the national or state level.

WHAT DOES "FREE EXERCISE" MEAN?

Turning to the second half of the religious part of the First Amendment, Congress is to make no law "prohibiting the free exercise" of religion, apparently signifying that it must not disallow or forbid the various religious groups to practice their religions as they see fit. And the "exercise" or "practice" of religion apparently refers to the whole content of the religions—to their beliefs, rituals, and prescribed modes of conduct. So interpreted, the free exercise of religion would go far beyond what is guaranteed in the second half of the First Amendment, dealing with free speech and press, for religion involves action as well as thought and communication, and action can directly run afoul of the laws of political society. Does the "free exercise" section of the First Amendment grant to religious groups, in advance, an exemption from the law, and from the Constitution itself—the supreme law—for illegal actions undertaken sincerely in the name of religion?

That it does not can be shown in two ways—one from the logic of the Constitution, the other from the thought of men like Madison and Jefferson, the greatest champions of religious liberty in the founding generation. In the Preamble, the people, ordaining the Constitution, stipulate insuring "domestic tranquillity" as one of their objects, and later empower Congress to make laws on certain subjects and to provide the executive with military power for executing these laws, to the point of suppressing domestic insurrection. The "free exercise" of religion guaranteed in the First Amendment cannot possibly entail a right to violate the laws Congress and the executive have the right, and duty, to enact. Dangerous actions historically associated with almost all Christian churches—for example, refusing obedience to a ruler deposed by the Pope; ignoring the obligations of contract made with heretics; harassing witches, heretics, apostates and other victims of religious hatred—could not be permitted to destroy domestic tranquillity and invite the insurrection government has a clear right to put down. In short, the "free" exercise of religion is only that exercise or practice of religion one is free to undertake consistent with the laws. To grant otherwise is to guarantee the disintegration of the very union formed by the adoption of the Constitution. And this general logic is confirmed by the way the Constitution speaks of itself as "the supreme law of the land," with all government officials bound by oath to uphold it above all else. "Supreme" means supreme for everyone, in fact—a status hardly dependent on the views of this or that sect as to what God requires of them contrary to the Constitution and the laws made in accordance with it.

Those who championed religious liberty in America almost always did so with the explicit reservation that religion not become a ground for lawlessness. The reservation George Mason stipulated was "unless under color of religion any man disturb the peace, the happiness or safety of society." Or as Madison put it at the same time, "unless under color of religion the preservation of equal liberty, and the existence of the State be manifestly endangered." [22] Later, in his Memorial and Remonstrance against religious establishment in Virginia, Madison expressed this somewhat differently: "Such a government (a just one) will be best supported by protecting every citizen in the enjoyment of his Religion with the same equal hand which protects his person and his property; by neither invading the equal rights of any Sect, nor suffering any Sect to invade those of another." And in his Bill for Establishing Religious Freedom in Virginia, Jefferson insisted that "it is time enough for the rightful purposes of civil government for its officers to interfere when (religious) principles break out into overt acts against peace and good order." These examples are adduced not for the specific limitations placed on "free exercise" by this or that writer, but in proof of the point that no person of understanding could claim "free exercise" had no such limitations or abridgements. It is the logic of the Constitution, rather than the words of Madison or Jefferson spoken in other contexts, that must be decisive, and that logic cannot allow a religious right to disobey laws thought to violate religious conscience. Thus, Congress shall make no law forbidding certain religious beliefs, but the laws it passes by constitutional authority will be enforced against all lawbreakers, whether or not acting on religious conscience. In one contemporary state constitution after another, the language guaranteeing religious liberty specifies a similar principle. It could not be prohibited, but—in effect—could be abridged.

The term "religion" itself deserves some clarification. It seems too elementary to mention that the word cannot be thought to include nonreligion and irreligion—that is, belief as such. The freedom of religion is not a freedom of any opinion about religion, including atheism. For a religion is more than a belief or set of beliefs, even about some divinity. Religion presupposes a community of worshipers and a being (or beings) worshiped. Its normal mode of operation includes beliefs, prayers, rituals, and priests or holy men. This conception of religion covers all the examples the founders knew—the religions of the Bible, of pagan antiquity, of the East, and of primitive man.[23] And when the generation of the founders and framers thought about exercising a religion freely, this and this alone is what they had in mind. Deism is a philosophic belief about God, but not a religion. Nor would the premium placed on morality by the Ethical Culture Society have qualified it as a religion. In short, the founders did not identify the free exercise of religion with the free exercise of thought or moral endeavor.

In the original body of the Constitution, religion seemed to have an explicit place only by virtue of a single exclusion—that of *religious* tests for public office.[24] The Preamble and the general spirit of the Constitution as a political instrument of the people are completely secular, completely independent of divine revelation, completely based on a rational understanding of man's interests. Americans constitute a people and are appealed to not as Christians or believers of any persuasion, but as human beings with common natural concerns. By implication, revealed religion does not and cannot form the basis of political society. On the contrary, it is at odds in many ways with man's natural inclinations and hence with any political society constructed to suit those inclinations. Without saying it in so many words, the world the Constitution prepares— with its commerce, enterprise, invention, science, and art—runs counter to the other-worldliness of Christianity by concentrating on civil interests and purposes without mentioning religion, leaving the subject to be cared for at the level of the states or of the people. The First Amendment insures that the national government will not become sectarian. Sectarian religious choices are left to the states and to individuals.

While apparently enhancing the position of religion in American society by extending to it special guarantees, the First Amendment also, of necessity, stresses the variability of both religious establishments and religious exercise generally, thus laying bare a great intrinsic difficulty. For this variability implies that there is no one proper establishment, no one true religion—or perhaps no way of proving the superiority of certain religious claims to others. Not only the superiority of one Christian sect to another, but of Christianity to non-Christianity, of monotheism to polytheism seems beyond demonstration. At the minimum, the harm done to oneself and others by exercising a tolerated false religion seems to be outweighed by the good coming from its being the religion of one's own choice—a somewhat peculiar and paradoxical conclusion. Thus, the First Amendment has the effect of both raising and lowering the dignity of religion—of protecting it from government and at the same time raising suspicions about its intrinsic validity—the former appealing to believers, the latter to skeptics.[25]

On the other hand, nothing in the Amendment compels Congress to treat religion in the same way as non-religion or irreligion. By definition, the ban on Congress's establishing a religion would not prevent it from encouraging or assisting religion generally or all religions equally. Neither would Congress's lack of authority to prohibit the free exercise of religion keep it from encouraging or assisting the free exercise of religion. Thus, the metaphor of a "wall of separation between church and state" articulated by Jefferson hardly does justice to the complexities of the matter, and therefore fails to explain his own practices in Virginia as well. The most important point is that, on the national level, the First Amendment keeps Congress from either establishing a religion or suppressing the various religions. For the rest, Congress is kept neither from assisting religion nor from providing for the enforcement of duly enacted laws against those who violate them in the name of religion.

The greatest error made by liberal interpreters, on and off the Court, is to regard the religious part of the First Amendment as the embodiment of Jefferson's "wall" or Madison's Memorial and Remonstrance, both of which make of religion a completely private matter, unconnected with government by either negative or positive ties.[26] The truth of the matter is that Madison's efforts to bind the states through the federal Constitution failed utterly. His proposal to keep the states from violating the equal rights of conscience was defeated in the Senate; if he favored the House committee's dropping of the word "national" from his own proposed ban on establishments, still he offered in debate to reinsert it; and the absence from his own wording of a ban on Congress' passing laws "respecting" the state establishments was finally supplied by the House-Senate Conference Committee. Judged from the standpoint of the First Amendment, religion could be treated by the

states as they wished—that is, as the people of those states decided to
treat it in their own constitutions. Moreover, even Madison had not
proposed that Congress should give no assistance to religion generally—
or in the words of Livermore, make no law "touching religion." He only
forbade a national establishment of religion, and such an establishment
meant a singling out of some particular religion for official status and
preferential treatment. But on this point, and on a national guarantee
of religious free exercise, all parties were already in agreement. [27]

Looking back at Justice Black's keynote passage from *Everson* (iden-
tifying the establishment part of the First Amendment with a general
wall of separation, state as well as national, between government and
religion), we recognize it as the source of flagrant errors never since completely overcome by the Court, and in some ways (not in all) multi-
plied almost as far as prejudice and judicial activism have allowed. The
first error was to claim that the First Amendment could be applied,
through the Fourteenth Amendment, as a limitation on the states—
when both wording and history combine to show that the First Amendment is meant to leave state establishments and state practices to the
states and their people. The second error was to enlarge the notion of
"establishment" to include all assistance to religion as such, or to all
religions equally. The third error was to read into the "free exercise"
section religious exemptions, by right, from valid laws. The last was to
alter the meaning of "religion" itself, allowing secular or non-religious
equivalents for the belief in a deity, and permitting religion to be
identified with the claimed and highly personalized beliefs of individuals
rather than with membership in some objectively identifiable group
devoted to a common form of worship.[28]

These errors have been costly, both constitutionally and politically.
They have stood in the way of obtainable social benefits, caused avoid-
able social evils, and bred confusion, dismay, and anger. Above all, they
have weakened the notion of objective law, starting with the supreme
law of the Constitution, that judges must understand and apply as in-

tended, in accord with long-standing judicial precedent, rather than constantly reinterpret or create. But fixity has become the fixed enemy of the intellectuals, and it is from them that justices have taken their cue. There has, in addition, been a general loss of understanding of the moral and political contributions religion, and only religion, can make to the well-being of the American commonwealth. It is one thing to know that religion can be constitutionally fostered, another to know why it would be wise to do so.[29] We began to see this aspect of the problem in our discussion of Jefferson; we must now pursue it.

13

American Democracy's
Need for Religion

T HE CASE FOR THE WISDOM of preserving connections between
government and religion begins from our historical tradition,
which is admitted on all sides to sanction a broad range of
such connections—political, ceremonial, educational, economic—at
various levels of government. Justice Douglas himself put it well in
Zorach (1952): "We are a religious people whose institutions presuppose a Supreme Being.... When the state encourages religious instruction or cooperates with religious authorities by adjusting the schedule of public events to sectarian needs, it follows the best of our traditions. For it then respects the religious nature of our people and accommodates the public service to their spiritual needs."[1] Because the American people are religious, and because their institutions presuppose a Supreme Being, it is understandable that they should come to prize the diverse links that have arisen between government and religion, looking upon their undisturbed longevity as obvious proof of their constitutionality. In such circumstances, it is generally imprudent, unjust, and dangerous for the Supreme Court (leaving aside now our view of the constitutional issue) to proclaim or apply novel principles, one hundred and sixty years after the republic's inception, that would

sever all such links in the name of the First Amendment, erecting a "wall of separation" by which religion could no longer be favored over irreligion. In doing so the Court has risked rousing religious passions that had grown quiescent within the constitutional and commercial order the founders had provided, but that now flare up at this sudden, thoroughgoing derogation of religion.

A RELIGIOUS PEOPLE

But it is more than a matter of not shocking a large part, perhaps the large majority, of the American people. When Justice Douglas spoke of our institutions as *presupposing* a Supreme Being, he must have meant that American democracy actually depends on the belief in God. If so, respecting, and not shocking, the "religious nature" of the American people amounts to much more than respecting their private religious beliefs, for those beliefs are intrinsically related to American political institutions, forming part of their foundation. It follows that the strength and vitality of these institutions must partly depend on the strength and vitality of these beliefs. Now Americans can be said to combine two kinds of belief in God, one traceable to the Bible, the other to the Declaration of Independence. Sharing the disposition of all men to link their conception of the highest good to an unchanging being or beings, the American people, from 1776 onward, naturally found ways of bringing together the two greatest goods they knew— the moral-religious truths of Christianity and the political truths of the Declaration—into mutual reinforcement, complementarity, and interconnection. Logically or philosophically, this might not be possible, and the people might well fail to appreciate certain inconsistencies between the two and the need for modifying one or both in order to effect their harmonization. But if Tocqueville understood correctly, the result was most propitious: a modern democracy strengthened by the Christian faith.[2]

The philosophy of liberal democracy expressed in the Declaration is not in fact perfectly consistent with Christianity. Its appeal is to human reason rather than to faith or revelation, and hence to all men on the ground of their natural likeness rather than to a particular set of men chosen by God. Its stress is on natural rights rather than on duties to God and man, on the individual's free pursuit of his interests in this world (including his religious preparation for the next) rather than on a required, immediate, and particular dedication to otherworldly ends. It makes government depend on the consent of the governed, actively demonstrated through participation in a constitutional and republican regime, rather than on unlimited secular obedience to Caesar or the "powers that be." Nevertheless, the Declaration retained a crucial element in common with revealed religion by tracing natural rights to the bounty of a Creator and by acknowledging His active interest in protecting His handiwork. Of the four references to God in the Declaration, the two earlier were introduced by Jefferson in his original draft, the two at the end added by the Continental Congress. Jefferson himself did not go beyond citing the "laws of nature and of nature's God" and the inalienable rights with which men had been endowed by their Creator. It was Congress that added the final references to the "supreme judge of the world" and the "protection of divine providence," insuring that the God who made nature and man would not withdraw from the world, in the manner of deism, but would continue to rule it, in the spirit of monotheism.[3] This brought the Declaration's natural theology into broad correspondence with Biblical religion and the universal inclinations of mankind. Even the new rights the Declaration proclaimed were presented in the form of old truths evident in themselves. Indeed, so powerful has the effect of this presentation been that to this day Americans think of natural rights as an obvious and unquestionable attribute of mankind and as having come from the same Divine hand that imparted the Ten Commandments.

While no doubt anticipating this identification and finding it useful, Jefferson and Madison did not trust much in revealed religion or think it essential to American democracy. From Locke they had imbibed not only the principle of separating church and state, but a deep hostility toward dogmatic Christianity, which they too conceived as fostering fanaticism, tyranny, and passive dependence.[4] Jefferson was willing to accommodate various sects, especially where he could hope to bind them to each other and to the secular goals of the republic. But he tried to make as few concessions to credulous superstition as possible and had great confidence that elementary moral instruction in rights and duties and a higher instruction in natural theology and ethics were enough to satisfy the human mind and perfect man's moral impulses. With the help of required public education, the belief in God would persist and, as in the Declaration, serve to anchor the American system of justice. Yet that belief would, for the most part, be reached through philosophy rather than revealed religion.[5]

Tracing its entirely novel doctrine of individual rights and self-assertion to an ancient belief in God, the Declaration is a subtle blend of sobriety and proud flamboyance. By contrast, the Constitution begins with the purposes of an already existing society or collectivity—"we the people of the United States," making no mention of God or even the rights of man. Neither the purposes, the principles, nor the auspices of the Constitution express, as well they might have, any reference to God. Even the single reference to God in the Articles of Confederation nine years earlier (as having disposed the various state legislatures to accept the Articles) does not reappear.[6] Starkly and almost single-mindedly, the Constitution seems bent on giving the impression that it comprises nothing more than a political instrument devised by men and adopted by the people of the various states for certain limited common purposes. It is not sacrosanct; it may fail of ratification; it can be amended once ratified. The Constitution almost seems, in this respect, to claim a dignity inferior to that of the states themselves, which could individually sustain a direct connection with the God in which they believed.

Why the Constitution was written in this way we can only conjecture. In principle, as the theory of the Declaration makes clear, it *is* only

an instrument of the people, but the Constitution omits making connections with principles of the Declaration, including the existence of
God. It fails to declare explicitly that religion will be cared for by the
states—an omission that might have suited those Federalists who looked
with hostility on revealed religion. Similarly, the omission of any reference to God may have pleased the anti-Federalists, who would not want
even the slightest hint in the document of its having received God's
blessing and thereby having become sacred and unchangeable. Since
that time, of course, a tradition of veneration for the Constitution has
built up and citizens have frequently attributed the enjoyment of its
benefits to a divine dispensation. Nevertheless, they cannot regard it
with religious awe, strictly speaking. Unlike the republics of the ancient world, no direct link between some deity and the life of a particular society could be thought to exist. And from all appearances the
founders consciously wanted it so. Man made rather than divine, the
new union would depend entirely on satisfying the interests of the
people and on their activity in their own behalf: their destiny depended
on themselves, not on the interventions of a transcendent God.

MADISON VERSUS JEFFERSON

An interesting difference of opinion arose between Madison and
Jefferson over the degree to which a self-governing people needed to be
guided by non-rational elements of belief, if not by religion proper. In
The Federalist, Number 49, Madison considers Jefferson's idea that popularly elected constitutional conventions be repeatedly called not only
for amendments to the Constitution but for "correcting breaches of
it." Madison found it neither a matter of right nor prudent for the
people to be appealed to constantly:

> [I]t may be considered as an objection inherent in the principle,
> that as every appeal to the people would carry an implication of
> some defect in the government, frequent appeals would, in a great

measure, deprive the government of that veneration which time bestows on everything, and without which perhaps the wisest and freest governments would not possess the requisite stability. If it be true that all government rests on opinion, it is no less true that the strength of opinion in each individual, and its practical influence on his conduct, depend much on the number which he supposes to have entertained the same opinion. The reason of man, like man himself, is timid and cautious when left alone, and acquires firmness and confidence in proportion to the number with which it is associated. When the examples which fortify opinion are *ancient* as well as *numerous*, they are known to have a double effect. In a nation of philosophers, this consideration ought to be disregarded. A reverence for the laws would be sufficiently inculcated by the voice of an enlightened reason. But a nation of philosophers is as little to be expected as the philosophical race of kings wished for by Plato. And in every other nation, the most rational government will not find it a superfluous advantage to have the prejudices of the community on its side.

While the doctrine of individual rights, popular consent, and rational enlightenment, carried to its fullest, might appear to require what Jefferson proposed, Madison drew back in alarm from this extreme. Government, according to this extraordinary passage, requires characteristics normally associated with religion: "stability," "veneration," "reverence," even "prejudice," understood in its root sense as an opinion formed before judgment. The reason of the individual, or of the people collectively, is not sufficiently strong to serve as the sole foundation of popular government. Now Jefferson, who put more stock in the power of popular enlightenment than Madison, hesitated to accept any large admixture of "prejudice" in the affairs of men. To him, venerable prejudice had overtones of sectarian religion, as opposed to the religion of reason, and he feared, perhaps more than anything else, the darkness and oppression into which the rule of revelation and priests had led mankind.[7]

WASHINGTON AND TOCQUEVILLE

Yet neither Jefferson nor Madison can easily be imagined authoring the direct support for traditional religion placed by Washington in this once-famous passage of his Farewell Address:

> Of all the dispositions and habits, which lead to political prosperity, Religion, and Morality are indispensable supports. In vain would that man claim the tribute of Patriotism, who should labor to subvert these great pillars of human happiness, these firmest props of the duties of Men and Citizens. . . . And let us with caution indulge the supposition, that morality can be maintained without religion. Whatever may be conceded to the influence of refined education on minds of peculiar structure, reason and experience both forbid us to expect that national morality can prevail in exclusion of religious principle. [8]

While conceding that "refined education," without religion, might affect "minds of peculiar structure" in such a way as to bring them to morality, Washington insists that both "reason and experience" prove religion necessary to "national"—that is, public—morality, to inculcating the "duties of men and citizens." Those he opposes might be called the ultra-rationalists, who see no need for anything but reason, and who plan to elicit acceptable conduct from rational self-interest rather than morality. This position Washington rejects, not on religious grounds per se, but on the basis of what reason and experience tell us are necessary to political well-being. And it is noteworthy also that what most needs to be taught, in Washington's view, is a sense of duty, not rights. He seems to have realized that the Declaration's stress on natural rights and rational truths must, within a society dedicated to them, be supplemented and partly submerged by moral education stressing duties and derived from supernatural and suprarational religion—that is, by a moral education that is not "refined."

This point has lost none of its cogency or timeliness, despite its unpopularity with our own ultra-rationalists in and out of the university. Political society, liberal or not, requires that its members be able to restrain selfish passions and subordinate them to higher social and political duties. Without a demanding moral education, this is not likely to occur. But such an education mainly takes place during youth, through habituation rather than rational instruction or discussion, and as an expression of authority—the authority not only of the family and the surrounding community, preserving the ways of its ancestors, but if possible, of those higher beings whose commands are even more absolute. With such backing, various civic duties and virtues can be well taught, but as any component weakens or falls away, significant defects enter the process. In a liberal society that by its nature stresses the rights of the individual, that is new and open to many divisions within the community, the full panoply of revealed religion may be necessary to keep a sense of duty from disappearing completely.

Washington spoke in general terms of popular government's need for religion and for virtue or morality, without considering the peculiar advantages and disadvantages brought by Christianity—in one form or another the religion of almost all Americans—to American democracy. Three decades later, the advantages thus gained became an explicit and major theme of Tocqueville's classic commentary, *Democracy in America*. More vividly perhaps than Washington, Tocqueville makes the same general point about the democratic republic's need for religion and like Washington criticizes the relentless attacks on religion leveled by certain republicans: "Despotism may govern without faith, but liberty cannot. Religion is much more necessary in the republic which they set forth in glowing colors than in the monarchy which they attack; it is more needed in democratic republics than in any others. How is it possible that society should escape destruction if the moral tie is not strengthened in proportion as the political tie is relaxed? And what can be done with a people who are their own masters if they are not submissive to the Deity?"[9] If the people are the rulers as well as the objects of rule, they will be constantly tempted to avoid subjecting themselves to rigors, or to elude those they do resolve upon, unless the moral demands within them—placed there by religion—are insistent and stern.

Religion is the source of discipline, not freedom, in Tocqueville's opinion, but while Christianity did not give Americans their taste for freedom, it enables them to make proper use of it. Tocqueville acknowledges that American Christianity has been compelled to adapt itself to its democratic environment, distinguishing itself in important ways from its European original. In particular, American Christianity could not help but set much greater store on the goods of this life, including material prosperity. Nevertheless, assisted by this accommodation, it still inculcates a strong discipline of the instincts and passions, a concern for the well-being of others, and a dedication to realities and ideals transcending the material world that can serve both to restrain and elevate the citizens of democracy.[10] Without Christianity, in short, American democracy would be more lawless, more turbulent, and more vulgar, not to mention short-lived.

Nor was it only in the home and the church that Christianity was learned. Tocqueville takes note of the "primary instruction" so widely and uniquely available to the people in America, in which are wisely joined together the enlightenment of the understanding and "the moral education which amends the heart." He cites the case of New England, where "every citizen receives the elementary notions of human knowledge; he is taught, moreover, the doctrines and the evidences of his religion, the history of his country, and the leading features of its Constitution."[11] While his remarks do not clearly indicate that public schools were the main vehicles for such instruction, it is the content, more than the auspices, of civic education that interests him. The conveying of skills and information, insufficient by itself, had to be joined with a moral component, associated with if not drawn from religion, and a political component, contributing to republican understanding and allegiance.

LINCOLN

Shortly after Tocqueville's visit to this country, the young Abraham Lincoln devoted some of his gravest, most original, and least-known reflections to the relation between religion and American democracy. These occur in two addresses delivered in Springfield, Illinois, while he served in the state legislature: one on "The Perpetuation of Our Political Institutions," in 1838, the other on the temperance cause, in 1842. The latter deals with the moral fanaticism (shown in compulsory prohibition) toward which certain elements of Christianity may lead. The former, on which we shall dwell, contains Lincoln's analysis of the mob lawlessness and violence that was spreading north and south, most of it connected with the slavery issue. Mob violence involves the refusal of some part of the people to abide by law—a refusal that frequently succeeds because it is difficult, in a democracy, to bring sizeable groups to justice, particularly when their actions have widespread support. And as mob lawlessness spreads, rendering persons and property increasingly insecure, it engenders a condition favorable to the tyrannical striving of the ambitious few, who can find no loftier object of their ambition than the destruction of the republic. Law-abidingness, therefore, is the crucial prerequisite for the "perpetuation of our political institutions." Yet Lincoln does not think it can rest on appeals to the rights or the rational self-interest of the citizens. Nor does he invoke the pious obedience that might be expected from a nation steeped in Christianity. Instead, he is led to the most extraordinary exhortation ever delivered by an American statesman:

> As the patriots of seventy-six did to the support of the Declaration of Independence, so to the support of the Constitution and

laws let every American pledge his life, his property and his sacred honor. Let every man remember that to violate the law is to
trample on the blood of his father, and to tear the charter of his
own and his country's liberty. Let reverence for the laws be breathed
by every American mother to the lisping babe that prattles on her
lap; let it be taught in schools, in seminaries, and in colleges; let it
be written in primers, spelling books, and in almanacs; let it be
preached from the pulpit, proclaimed in legislative halls, and enforced in courts of justice. And, in short, let it become the political religion of the nation.[12]

By calling for this "political religion," and distinguishing the
patriot's support of the Declaration in 1776 from the support of the
Constitution and laws incumbent on "every American," Lincoln suggests a criticism of the Declaration's doctrine of the "rights of man."
The primacy of the individual and his rights (or, collectively, of the
people and their rights) is at odds with the essential citizen duty to
subordinate oneself to the law of the land. Our ancestors raised a "political edifice" of "liberty and equal rights," and all subsequent generations are charged with preserving this inheritance unimpaired: "This
task gratitude to our fathers, justice to ourselves, duty to posterity, and
love for our species in general, all imperatively require us faithfully to
perform."[13] If so, the right of the individual to care for himself during
his own lifetime, above all else, must be subordinated to the necessity
of perpetuating our political inheritance. This necessity derives from
the individual's forming part of both a larger political whole, stretch-
ing back in time to ancestors and forward in time to posterity, and of
another, even larger, transpolitical whole, the species. By introducing
such a perspective, Lincoln shows his awareness of a deep problem in
the Declaration's emphasis on individual rights, which must inevitably
make it more difficult for a society founded on its principles to endure.
    These thoughts of Lincoln clearly represent a profound extension
of Madison's anti-Jeffersonian remarks in *The Federalist*, Number 49.

Both maintain that the republic finds itself in a peculiar and difficult predicament: it must teach the Declaration's doctrine of the rights of man as the source and symbol of its own just origin and intent, but it must also counter this doctrine's anarchic tendencies. It may do so either by not upsetting the natural veneration of this particular Constitution and set of laws that will come with time (Madison), or by positively inculcating such reverence through an all-pervasive moral-political education (Lincoln). Lincoln does not separate formal from informal education in this respect: the mother whispering to her babe, the minister preaching from the pulpit, the teacher addressing her classes (and her textbooks) all contribute to the most important kind of education the citizen can receive, which is to revere the laws.

Lincoln's much more drastic solution to the central problem of the republic is made necessary by his fuller appreciation of the difficulties faced. He shows that the passions strengthening obedience to law at the republic's beginning must weaken, as examples and memories of great sacrifices in the revolution fade, and as the honors to be gained by constructing the republic are no more. He indicates that the great body of those who support the republic as an ongoing institution do so because it protects them, and that only a handful of men befriend it in principle. Similarly, it has two kinds of enemies, both "lawless in spirit": those constantly striving to shake off the yoke of the law because it keeps them from what they most enjoy, which is harming others, and those seekers of the greatest honor who resolve to find their fame in destroying a republic built up by others.[14] Growing lawlessness and violence weaken the forces of those who support the republic, and strengthen the forces of those who would overthrow it.

Having conceived what would be necessary, in principle, to perpetuate our political institutions, Lincoln knows that the "political religion" he recommends lacks even the durability of real religions, and therefore it is strictly impossible to "perpetuate" the republic. By contrast to what he ends by calling the "only greater institution"—the church Christ founded—the republic and its Constitution cannot claim divine origin. They are known by all to be man-made and changeable, and hence remain incapable of winning complete reverence. Yet in this address Lincoln does not turn to Christianity for support. Insuring the "capability of a people to govern themselves," perpetuating "the proud fabric of freedom" are tasks quite distinct from the original mission of Christianity, which views neither self-government nor pride as good in themselves. Lincoln also realizes that absolute obedience to the Christian God can lead to a kind of lawlessness, even to moralizing tyranny, in the name of God's law. Certainly Christians cannot give absolute reverence to the Constitution and laws—a reverence, from the Christian point of view, bordering on idolatry—and will find it difficult to recognize them as the "supreme law of the land."[15]

While beginning from a practical question of great moment— the spreading of mob lawlessness in the 1830s—Lincoln's Perpetuation speech is mainly meant to give theoretical instruction rather than practical guidance. His solution of "political religion" presents an obvious paradox, since enforcing its requirements would require a despotism of the most comprehensive kind. Nor in his day did people need to have their religious beliefs strengthened. Only with the Civil War did Lincoln find an opportunity for repairing some of the defects of the first founding in what amounted to a second, this time under the aegis of a God blending attributes drawn from the Bible with those accorded Him in the more restrained rational monotheism of the Declaration of Independence. Here Lincoln's political art reached its greatest height, for no one knew better how to infuse the sufferings and triumphs of the war with religious meaning, in some measure lending divine support to the true and lasting principles of American democracy. We need only think of the House Divided speech, of the First Inaugural's appeal to the "Almighty ruler of nations" and the "better angels of our nature," of the Gettysburg Address's dedication to "this nation, under God," and its consecration of the Union's cause, of the Second Inaugural's impassioned wonderment at the religious significance of the Civil War, viewed as a terrible punishment for the evil of slavery, and its sublime final plea for "malice toward none, charity for all, and firmness in the right as God gives us to see the right." Through words as memorable as his deeds, Lincoln became not only his country's savior and martyr, but its most profound and best-known educator, fitting its people for a government that "shall not perish from the earth."

MAINSTAY OF DEMOCRACY

We have encountered four related, but distinct, uses of the term "religion." Christianity and the various Christian churches are examples of religion in the strict sense, with its organized worship, beliefs, and practices. The reverence for the Constitution and laws of the country Lincoln calls a "political religion" involves a derivative usage, requiring dispositions, beliefs, and conduct born of habituated veneration, and hence bearing some resemblance to religion proper. The belief in God which undergirds the Declaration of Independence provides another point of similarity with religion proper, though it derives from reason rather than revelation and does not directly involve organized worship. Finally, in what might be called religious exhortation through public discourse, Lincoln blends of the God of the Bible with the God of the Declaration. Strictly speaking, however, despite points of overlap, the second and third meanings of religion are essentially non-religious or secular in nature.

The statesmen and thinkers who found these alternatives useful or necessary to American democracy differed in important ways among themselves, but they shared the conviction that the rights, duties, and aspirations of democratic citizens—the moral foundations of democracy—must be fixed, and must have their source in a being transcending change. They knew that a nation based on freedom and equality must be prepared for ruling and obeying well—for making just laws and being bound by the rule of law. They were sure that rights and the freedom rights impart are not sufficient for this purpose and that the misuse of liberty must spell its doom. None believed men were born good and fit for ruling and obeying by nature. None even believed a combination of enlightened self-interest and properly devised institutions would suffice to keep men acting well. All insisted on the need for some powerful and regular force to be applied toward making good citizens out of mere men, differing only as to whether it could come from the religions of America, from instruction in the schools, from general habituation, or from the educative rhetoric of statesmen. All were well aware of the dangers Christianity had often posed for political life over the centuries, but they differed as to the degree to which dangerous religious opinions could be eliminated and as to the salutary effects of religion. And the strong and unequivocal devotion to religious liberty common to them all led none—not even Jefferson and Madison—to believe the First Amendment precluded all government support of religion or the belief in God.

Concerned as these great men were to establish religious or quasi-religious underpinnings for republican government and the civic virtue appropriate to it, it is hard to believe they would not take alarm at the manifest and abundant signs of ill-used freedom among us today. The willful violation of law by groups and individuals, both well- and ill-intentioned, the incredible crime rate, with its attendant fear and insecurity, the spread of sexual laxity and vulgar hedonism, the morbid fascination with brutality, the decay in the sense of integrity, self-sacrifice, and civic consciousness generally—all bespeak a condition much worse than any known in the founding generation, than any Tocqueville foresaw in 1831, and than any witnessed by Lincoln in 1837, boding ill for the continuation of republican institutions.

In these circumstances a prudent legislator would hardly seek to reduce the resources at his disposal for strengthening the authority of democratic government and inculcating citizen virtue. He would hardly insist on introducing an absolute separation of religion and government. It would little upset him to find the awareness of proceeding under some higher power, with an increased sense of reverence and duty, more widespread at all public functions. He would scarcely bemoan governmental efforts to assist the secular part of education, even if provided in religious schools, or to assist religious education in ways compatible with religious freedom. Realizing that rights cannot stand without duties, that the sense of rights must often be subordinated to the common good, that reverence for law protects justice by binding rulers and ruled, rich and poor, powerful and weak alike, he would, in fact, be prone to seek additional means of fostering these ideas and dispositions. And he would understand the necessity of linking them to fixed principles of philosophy, and better yet of religion, which in the strength of its hold on the human soul can have no rival. By precept and ceremony, by symbol and example, in home and school as well as the halls of government, he would be prepared to encourage moderated freedom, that blend of republican authority with republican freedom, without which government of, by, and for the people must perish from the earth.

These prescriptions, while undoubtedly in keeping with public sentiment, will find little welcome among our constitutional innovators. They will, first of all, be considered antediluvian by those who insist on supplying a new moral basis for democracy other than old philosophical absolutes, whatever place these once had in our founding documents and the thoughts of our great political men, or still have in the hearts and minds of the people. Those who urge such innovations confuse a nation with a graduate seminar, and ruling with inquiry. A nation cannot rest its foundations on ideas that are constantly in flux, in an area where truth—always hard to come by, and as hard to express in politically acceptable form—has been battered almost beyond recognition by modern intellectual prejudice. The principles by which we live must continue to be those that brought us into existence and made us prosper, deriving from a unique amalgam of the Declaration, the

Constitution, and Biblical religion. Looking instead to the transient intellectual tides of the twentieth century is not only to unfix what to be believed and lived by must be fixed, not only to make our destinies depend on theories that are foreign or hostile to the needs of democracy, but to convert the republic into an indirect tyranny of academics and intellectuals totally unaccountable to the people.

There is another opinion according to which democracy and morality have nothing to do with each other, morality being by its nature private, even idiosyncratic, and democracy requiring no common moral beliefs and attitudes. This view of morality presumes either that men are not inclined to harm others, or that they may be, but are sufficiently restrained by laws alone.[16] In the former case criminal laws would not be needed; in the latter they are thought capable of working without the habituated respect for the law, internalized from the earliest age, that has always been present to assist the laws, which even with this help from morality are so imperfectly heeded. But society requires—and morality commands—much more than not harming others. It requires a readiness to assist others, including the society as a whole, and at times with self-sacrificing devotion. It requires the bearing of burdens and the meeting of dangers without which any society, large or small, cannot long survive. These capacities rest on moral dispositions, or traits of character, that may or may not be present in human beings, depending on the kind of moral training they receive. In liberal democracies the moral training is susceptible of being weakened in the name of individual liberty, falsely conceived—as if citizens were born good, or had no need of goodness.

The private view of morality also presumes either that the individual is the best judge of what is good for himself, or that there is no such good, all choices being at bottom subjective and arbitrary. The latter seems to be an invention of theorists, since no one actually lives as if it could be true. Sometimes used as an argument for democracy—

that is, for allowing everyone to live as he pleases—it is at least as suitable to dictatorship, given its denial that choices forced on us can be known to make our lives objectively worse. As to the former alternative, the individual may be the best judge of what is good for himself only if such choices are relatively simple, making little demand on intellect, character, or imagination. Moreover, the "individual" involved is already presumed to live in a liberal democracy, which not only encourages him to be and conceive himself as an "individual," but has also (in the best case) trained and prepared him to take care of himself well. The choices he will have to make do not, therefore, include the system of training that made him an "individual" in the first place. In other words, he can operate well as an individual, and bring good, predominantly, to himself and others, only because of a framework of life that he himself did not bring into existence or choose. Finally, if being an individual includes being a man and citizen as well, simply because the individual must share certain necessary characteristics with others of the same species or nation, then the good for the individual must be a variant on a common natural and political good rather than something unique in all ways.

Moreover, we can hardly believe that human society is compatible with an unlimited variety of individual ways of life. Society requires fundamental likenesses among its members as the basis of mutual trust and sharing in the common good, and this may be particularly true of democracies, where fellow citizens must work together politically at all levels of government. Every political society, in fact, may be viewed as the public favoring of a particular way of life or a limited spectrum of ways of life. Democracy cannot permit individuals to enslave others, to commit crimes, to refuse to bear common burdens, or to violate laws generally. It is incompatible with drastic inequalities of social class or rigid castes. It cannot work well when those directly or indirectly involved in ruling regard each other as members of alien and hostile groups.

Its freedom and its diversity must therefore be moderate, not extreme: it is compelled to blend homogeneity with heterogeneity, and the failure to bear this need constantly in mind prepares it for destruction.[17]

There was a time before and after World War II when supporters of liberal democracy, opposing totalitarianism, proudly claimed that the democracies neither enforced, nor had any need of, common moral beliefs and attitudes. While it is true that liberal democracy makes little effort to indoctrinate in the strict sense, it is of course equally true that it uses both formal and informal education to provide its citizens with some conception of its principles and encourage devotion to them. It does, after all, still teach all school children the Declaration of Independence, the Constitution, and the Gettysburg Address, and it has always paid some heed to the moral qualities that exemplify the best in democracy, drawing inspiration from the example of Washington and Lincoln particularly. It urges its citizens to exercise independence of thought, to treat their fellows considerately and fairly, and to strive for a common good that cannot be conceived as the net outcome of divergent political interests. Its educational system is still predicated on the assumption, however inadequately applied, that citizens have duties as well as rights, that some subordination—to parents, teachers, founders, and the law—is both necessary and proper, and that some uses of freedom are better than others.

To the extent that such teachings are still with us, and very broadly shared, we remain a moderated democracy; to the extent that they have been weakened, or neglected, we move inevitably toward extremes of individual and group alienation, hostility and faction, and with the breakdown of republican authority, toward despotism. Democracies differ from tyrannies, but not in having no need for common ideas and values, or means of inculcating them. The real differences lie in what is taught, how systematically, and the degree to which it remains subject to discussion and control. Democracies inculcate responsible freedom, totalitarian regimes some form of unconditional obedience.

The Case against "Incorporation"

BEFORE DISCUSSING APPLICATIONS of the establishment clause, we must examine the constitutional revolution that began in 1940 with *Cantwell v. Connecticut* and has made the Supreme Court the arbiter of the relation between church and state governments. When the First Amendment was adopted in 1791, it was explicitly intended to bind Congress but not the states: "Congress shall make no law. . . ." This fact was conclusively affirmed for the whole Bill of Rights by Chief Justice John Marshall and the Supreme Court in *Barron v. Baltimore* (1833). But did the Fourteenth Amendment, ratified in 1868, seek to change this situation by incorporating the protections of the Bill of Rights against the states? Not before the next century, in *Gitlow* (1925), did the Court actually incorporate the First Amend-ment's freedom of speech and press into the Fourteenth Amendment. In 1940, *Cantwell* added the free exercise provision of the First Amendment as well, and in 1947 *Everson* did the same for the establishment provision. Ever since, the Court has so read the Fourteenth Amendment as to prevent the states (as well as the federal government) from establishing a religion or prohibiting its free exercise.

Only as late as 1947 did any member of the Supreme Court—it was Justice Black, dissenting in *Adamson v. California*—make a formidable defense of the proposition that the Fourteenth Amendment, right from the beginning, intended to incorporate all the protections of the Bill of Rights against the states.[1] Black argued at great length that the congressional debate over the Fourteenth Amendment proved his point. Did not the two main congressional sponsors of the Amendment—Representative John A. Bingham of Ohio and Senator Jacob M. Howard of Michigan—say as much? Focusing their argument on Section 1 of the Fourteenth Amendment, they claimed that the "privileges and immunities of citizens of the United States" protected against state abridgement included the federal Bill of Rights. *Barron v. Baltimore* notwithstanding, they appeared to presume that such protections already applied against the states and needed only the Fourteenth Amendment's Section 5 guarantee of federal enforcement to become effective.[2]

While Justice Black was never able to win over a majority of the Court to his view, it is still worth considering. There are two lines of argument which affirm that the religious part of the First Amendment is also applicable against the states. One is Black's, involving the Bill of Rights as a whole and connected mainly to the "privileges and immunities" provision in Section 1. The other has been called partial or selective incorporation and is connected with the word "liberty" in the provision immediately following: that no state shall deprive its citizens of "life, liberty or property without due process of law." Must "liberty" be read to include the religious parts of the First Amendment?

THE SLAUGHTERHOUSE CASES

No topic in constitutional law is more hotly disputed than the intended meaning of the Fourteenth Amendment. Everyone grants that it provides federal protection for blacks against discrimination by the states. But which forms of discrimination does it ban? And does it also authorize the federal government to insure that all states come up to a certain standard of civil rights for whites as well as blacks? Judicially, the issue was for a long time decided by the so-called Slaughterhouse Cases of 1873, only seven years after the passage of the Fourteenth Amendment itself. The Lousiana state legislature had granted a butchering monopoly within the city of New Orleans, and the butchers ousted by this action brought suit. They claimed, primarily under the Fourteenth Amendment's "privileges and immunities" provision, that the legislature had abridged their civil rights by preventing them from making a living and interfering with their property.

Writing for a majority of five, Justice Miller insisted that the "privileges and immunities" of citizens of the United States differ from those of citizens of the states and that the Fourteenth Amend-ment protects only the former. Both the majority and minority largely agreed on which "privileges and immunities" citizens of the states might claim, which they traced back to two sources. One was a decision by Justice Bushrod Washington made for the Supreme Court while on circuit (in *Corfield v. Coryell*, 1823). The other was the Civil Rights Bill of 1866. While not always agreeing with each other, these sources tended to emphasize what might be called "civil" rights as distinguished from "political" rights or rights of criminal procedure. They included such rights as the right to be protected by government, to acquire property, to engage in contractual relations, to move from state to state, to enjoy liberty, and to pursue happiness. The minority in the Slaughterhouse Cases thought such civil rights were not only rights of state citizenship but rights of federal citizenship as well. The majority thought these rights did not apply to federal citizenship, claimed that this transfer of jurisdictions would have constituted a veritable revolution in the federal system, and found a different basis entirely for federal privileges and immunities. They decided against the butchers.[3]

Of the nine justices who heard this important case, only one—Joseph P. Bradley—claimed the "privileges and immunities of citizens of the United States" included all rights guaranteed by the original Constitution and the early amendments to it (meaning the Bill of Rights).[4] The other three dissenters did not make this claim—they did not even discuss the Bill of Rights. In the Court's opinion, ironically, Justice Miller did list "the right to peaceably assemble and petition for redress of grievances" among the federal privileges and immunities, but he went no further than this, citing no other part of the First Amendment, any other parts of the Bill of Rights, or the Bill of Rights as a whole. The conclusion to be drawn from the Slaughterhouse Cases, therefore, is that eight of nine justices did not think the Fourteenth Amendment incorporated the Bill of Rights—a possibility of which they were aware, but must have rejected, since it forms no part of their argument. Yet it was mainly in connection with this provision of the Fourteenth Amendment that Representative Bingham and Senator Howard made their case for incorporation.

In his Slaughterhouse opinion, Justice Miller stresses that a revolution would have been effected by taking the rights of state citizenship (civil rights) and making them enforceable by the federal government through section 5 of the Fourteenth Amendment. He thinks this could not have been the intention either of the Congress that proposed it or the state legislatures that ratified it. We do not have to agree with his claim to see that such an issue at least had to be controversial, and once recognized, had to occasion considerable debate. This expectation would have to be magnified if, in addition to those civil rights, it was thought that the federal Bill of Rights was now to be enforceable against the states. With two such innovations at stake, one would have anticipated heated and extended debate in Congress: it did not happen. Most of the discussion centered on the need to end discrimination against blacks, particularly in the south, but in the north as well. Furthermore, this presumed shift in authority from the states to the federal government hardly surfaced as an issue in either the ratifying debates in the state legislatures or the ensuing Congressional elections, thus strengthening Miller's claim.

We are forced to conclude that Bingham and Howard's interpretation of the Fourteenth Amendment was not so plainly expressed in the Amendment as to alarm most of those who considered it. In short, it was generally read as not involving a federal guarantee of civil rights as such in the states (though it would prohibit racial discrimination in civil rights), and as not involving the Bill of Rights at all. Even if we assume, for the sake of argument, that most of Congress agreed with the interpretation of Bingham and Howard, the same certainly could not be said of the ratifiers in the state legislatures, whose silence on so important a matter had to signify their not attributing such a meaning to the Amendment. But if the proposers and ratifiers of an amendment are found to differ in their interpretation of it, can there be any doubt that in a democracy the issue must be resolved in favor of the ratifiers?

At least with respect to the religious provisions of the First Amendment, there are other reasons for thinking our conclusion regarding incorporation correct. In 1875 a constitutional amendment was introduced by Representative James Blaine banning support for sectarian schools by the states. Using language parallel to the First Amendment itself, it began with: "No state shall make any law respecting an establishment of religion or prohibiting the free exercise thereof. . . ." This amendment received the necessary two-thirds vote in the House but failed in the Senate. Between 1876 and 1929, it was introduced another twenty times but never emerged from Congress. Twenty-three members of the Congress that passed the Fourteenth Amendment seven years before were also members of the Congress that first considered the Blaine Amendment. Not one of them claimed that the Fourteenth Amendment had already incorporated the religious provisions of the First Amendment as restrictions on the states, as Representative Bingham and Senator Howard had claimed. Moreover, those who spoke to the

Amendment always assumed that religious matters at the time were still under state control. This must also have been the view of those who kept introducing the amendment, for would it not have been ridiculous to call for something already in existence?[5]

LOGIC AND LANGUAGE

Even were we to presume (as we do not) a need to incorporate some or all of the Bill of Rights as part of the "liberty" guaranteed by the Fourteenth Amendment, the religious part of the First Amendment would still present a difficulty—an absolutely insuperable difficulty—which neither *Cantwell* nor *Everson* ever addressed. It is the same difficulty presented by the Ninth and Tenth Amendments, which speak of unnamed rights retained by the people, and of powers reserved to the states or the people. The Tenth Amendment especially cannot be incorporated into the Fourteenth as a *restraint* on the states because it explicitly involves a vital *reservation* of authority *to* the states. In an exactly parallel way, the first religious section of the First Amendment—dealing with an establishment of religion—is both a guarantee of no Federal religious establishment and a recognition of the power of the states to establish religions. As we have seen, this is the only plausible reason for the somewhat mysterious term "respecting" in the phrase "respecting an establishment of religion." The liberty guaranteed in this part of the First Amendment, therefore, was just as much to have a state establishment in states that so desired as not to have a federal one. By its nature, then, this part of the First Amendment (and hence the First Amendment as a whole) cannot possibly be incorporated into the Fourteenth Amendment as a prohibition on state establishments. It is a matter of simple logic, and illogic has not yet become a judicial virtue.

Historically, the states themselves relinquished whatever religious establishments they possessed decades before the Fourteenth Amendment.[6] By the time the Court decided *Cantwell*, all state constitutions had had both non-establishment and free exercise provisions for at least a century. The Court may therefore have arrived at *Cantwell*'s federal prohibition of state establishments not by any process of constitutional logic but by what it regarded as a clear and powerful mandate in the universal, deep-rooted, and by then, long-standing suspicion of religious establishments among the American people. By reading such a prohibition into the Fourteenth Amendment's guarantee of liberty, the clash of religious majorities and minorities over preferential treatment within the states, and possible changes wrought by religious majorities in state constitutions themselves would be rendered impossible.

Nevertheless, the argument on the other side is more compelling. For if in 1940 all state constitutions *already* contained prohibitions against establishment, and if a universal consensus against establishments *already* existed in all states, whence the necessity to misinterpret the Fourteenth Amendment in order to produce a federal guarantee as well? If permanent national uniformity was so great a desideratum, would it not have been better to allow that step to be taken separately by a new federal amendment? *Cantwell*'s historical errors, however, were immeasurably worsened by the historically false, and harmful, interpretation the Court proceeded to place on the meaning of "establishment," now equally forbidden the national and state governments, in *Everson*. The determination to end sectarian factionalism within the states for all time was at least intelligible on general political grounds, but preserving the historical meaning of "establishment" as the official favoring of one religion or church over others would have entirely sufficed for this purpose. It was not necessary to erect an absolute wall of separation between religion and government, or to deny to the states their original authority to sustain the Declaration's belief in God and certain links with nonsectarian religion or with all religions, so long as free exercise was left inviolate. This at least would have preserved some of the original distinction between the states and the national government, the former able to take a substantial interest, the latter only a peripheral or incidental one, in ties with religion. Because the Court seemed unwilling to maintain the federal division of authority on which the republic was originally founded, and which the Bill of Rights emphatically underlined, and because it seemed to have utterly forgotten the public importance of religion in American democracy, it was led to the mounting constitutional and prudential errors of *Cantwell* and *Everson*.

There is a final, equally conclusive argument against the possibility of incorporating the First into the Fourteenth Amendment through the latter's guarantee of "liberty" and "due process," and it is obvious from the language of the two amendments. The First Amendment begins with the clarion call: "Congress shall make no law"—no law respecting, prohibiting, abridging, etc. But the due process clause proclaims that "no state shall deprive any person of life, liberty, or property without due process of law"—implying that *with* due process of law states *can* deprive persons of life, *liberty* (in this case, religious liberty), and property. The result of some fictitious incorporation would read like this: no state shall make any law respecting an establishment of religion or prohibiting the free exercise thereof, but it may deprive persons of the liberties in question (if establishing a religion may indeed be considered a liberty, like free exercise) *with* due process of law.

While this illustration is drawn from the religious part of the First Amendment, an equally preposterous result occurs when the freedoms of speech, press, etc., of the second part are inserted into the Fourteenth Amendment's language. In the Bill of Rights, the First and the Fifth (in *its* due process section) Amendments were compatible as separate limitations on the federal government, with *different* contents. But even there, were any attempt made (as it was not) to incorporate the language of the First Amendment into the word "liberty" that is part of the "due process" clause in the Fifth, a similar impossibility—a contradiction in terms—would have arisen.

Nor is the reason for this logical impasse difficult to ascertain. The First Amendment stipulates certain limits on the new federal government, while the due process clauses of both the Fifth and Fourteenth

Amendments stipulate a limit (whether on the federal or state governments) that is part of a very general corollary empowerment—an empowerment at the bottom of civil society as such. For civil society *means* limiting each man's right to life, liberty, and property through laws established by government, which to be fair, and therefore obligatory, must have been duly passed and enforced. The "due process" limit, therefore, is a procedural limit practiced as part of an empowerment *to* deprive members of the society of life, liberty, or property when demanded by the common good. Capital punishment, imprisonment, and fines are examples of such legal deprivations, established as penalties for specified crimes. The First Amendment, however, seeks simply to stop the federal government from doing certain things—not from doing those things in a certain way. The things it forbids it regards as unnecessary and dangerous, while there is nothing substantive the due process clauses forbid so long as it is done with "due process."[7]

These are the several irresistible reasons for denying that the Fourteenth Amendment, directly through its language, incorporates the First Amendment as a restriction on the states. Some who admit this conclusion may fear that the Court's position has passed beyond the possibility of recall or serious modification. But the sole alternative to the revisions we suggest is increasingly serious error: error that, apart from its inherent harm, will arouse the abiding, and—let it be said—healthy popular desire to favor religion over irreligion in public life, and that will therefore precipitate increasingly intense public controversy. The Court must soon come to see and admit its errors. Did it not do so in school desegregation, after fifty-eight years of *Plessy v. Ferguson*? Has it not acknowledged that for decades its decisions were excessively favorable to property rights? Do not liberals still call for annulling the Smith Act, going back to 1951? Why, then, does a position on the religious meaning of the First and Fourteenth Amendments, dating essentially to 1940 and 1947, suddenly become fixed and unalterable?

15

The Establishment Clause

ARMED WITH STRONG PRACTICAL REASONS for preserving links between government and religion, let us restate the constitutional limits placed on Congress by the First Amendment and examine how they apply to present problems. The First Amendment keeps Congress from making laws about any establishment—which means principally laws establishing a national religion or interfering with state establishments. Congress is also kept from preventing the free exercise of religion—though the logic of the Constitution clearly requires enforcing valid laws against lawbreakers, religious or not. To establish a religion means to prefer one over others, giving one religion alone official status and special privileges under the government, including financial support. And religion itself involves worshiping a being or beings higher than man, and in association with others, thus forming a sect, cult, church, or religious society. In general the Constitution delegated no power over religion to the national government: religious matters were reserved to the states and the people, but not so rigidly that they might not, in the exercise of some authority delegated to Congress, become the subject of national legislation.

NATIONAL APPLICATIONS

In applying these principles, we shall begin with establishment issues and with the simplest case: the mention of God in our national anthem, pledge, and motto. Congress's constitutional right to provide the country with such accessories cannot be found among its directly delegated powers, and must therefore, to be appropriate, comprise a way of either directly implementing or obliquely applying such a power. Since these accessories are meant to express and encourage patriotism, they may therefore be reasonably associated with Congress's express right to "provide for the common defence and general welfare of the United States," and with its implied right to preserve republican government in the country as a whole. Their nonsectarian appeal to God is consistent with that of the Declaration and the beliefs of the vast majority of Americans. Such an appeal establishes no religion, and in fact encourages rather than prohibits the free exercise of religion.

The invocation of God in presidential addresses and proclamations and the use of prayer or solicitations of God's blessing to open Congress's day, or the Supreme Court's, have similar justification, although they fall strictly within the option of the branches of government involved. In this respect, Congress's formally maintaining only a Protestant chaplaincy may be excused by virtue of both the sectarian alternation that is actually practiced and the nonsectarian character of the prayers employed. And when representatives of the major religious sects (Protestant, Catholic, and Jewish) participate in presidential inaugurals, not only is it a convenient way of asking God's blessing for the new administration, but it has the further advantage of confirming the high and equal status of all religions in the public eye, thus strengthening religious freedom.

The main justification for providing the armed forces with sectarian chaplains, as Justice Brennan explains in *Schempp*,[1] is to enable the soldier to exercise his own religion within the confines of military life.

So far is this from being a religious establishment that its primary intent is to assist religious liberty. The expectation that it might also contribute to military effectiveness is probably the principle reason for another long-standing, but now discarded, practice in the armed forces, whereby officer candidates at the various service academies were required to attend chapel. The religious choice, of course, was left to the candidate himself, but the compulsion to attend—no doubt an abridgement of religious freedom—probably had its basis in the supposition, grounded in the experience of nations, that the moral training and beliefs of religion were an important adjunct to effective and responsible military conduct.[2]

As for Congress's extending exemptions from military service to religious conscientious objectors alone, it is important to note that no constitutional right, deriving from the free exercise of religion, is involved. On the contrary, the right of the country to demand their service, and their bearing arms, is supreme and has never been surrendered by Congress. Their special treatment derives solely from Congress's willingness to respect their objection to war as sincerely based on their holiest belief—normally ascertained by the established traditions of certain sects. In this limited situation, honoring the consciences of objectors and making non-military use of their abilities is deemed preferable to executing them or having them languish in jail. But this privilege can only continue if the number of those receiving it remains small—a result largely achieved by confining it to religious believers, that is, members of organized and recognized sects. This restriction to recognized religious bodies has a double advantage. It extends the privilege only to those likely to fear otherworldly penalties more than those of this world and therefore to persevere in their refusal to fight. At the same time, it affords a sufficient guarantee that the number of objectors will remain relatively small, fixed, and identifiable, unswelled by those who oppose war selectively or by a rising tide of secular pacifism.[3]

We come now to the most difficult category—federal aid to all religions, whether financial or not. But let us first be clear about federal aid to education as it pertains to religious schools and colleges. Constitutionally, education as such is a state, not a national, function, and it became an object of national aid for special, disparate reasons, including the furtherance of national defense, of desegregation, of aid to the disadvantaged, and of education itself. In all these cases, the inclusion of parochial schools is perfectly constitutional. Only incidentally, indirectly, and unintentionally does it also constitute aid to the various religions supporting their own educational institutions. In short, in pursuing proper national objectives, the federal government has the right to insure that it is done in the most comprehensive manner—that is, in *all* schools, colleges, etc. Parochial schools and colleges even have a *right* to partake of such national aid, since, if they have a right to exist, as they do, then refusing to include religious schools in educational aid comprises an unconstitutional mode of discrimination or unequal treatment on the part of the national government. As we shall soon see, the situation with the states is different.[4]

Turning now to the problem of federal aid to religion as such, a distinction must be made between positive and negative forms of aid, the former illustrated by an actual gift of money, the latter by tax exemptions. Beginning with the latter, federal and state tax privileges for religious properties and ministers are sporadically under attack, though the Court has not yet yielded on so powerful and long-standing a tradition. Judged by Justice Black's hallmark passage in *Everson* (1947), however, such privileges are tantamount to increased tax burdens on the rest of the citizenry who thereby help to support the various religions—a clear violation (in Black's terms) of the establishment part of the First Amendment. And this, quite consistently with Black, was the conclusion Justice Douglas had already announced in *Engel*. Moreover, it is worth noting that Justice Brennan's exhaustive attempt in *Schempp* to show which connections between religion and government can constitutionally remain, allows only tax exemptions *not* defined in religious terms. True, when the issue came before the Court in *Walz v. Tax Commission* (1970), the Court took refuge in the distinction between excessive (unconstitutional) and non-excessive (constitutional) entanglement of religion and government, with a positive grant to religions falling within the first category, and religious tax exemptions within the second. This ruling, together with the uniformity of historical tradition and the inclusion of religion as one of many nonprofit organizations so favored, drew an overwhelmingly favorable vote from the Court.[5]

Walz's lone dissenter, Justice Douglas, grounded his objection on Black's opinion in *Everson* and Madison's Memorial and Remonstrance, claiming that the wall of separation between church and state had been obviously and unconstitutionally breached. Religious tax exemptions, Douglas argued, were a form of religious establishment, using tax moneys to assist religion, and at the same time—by not giving exemptions to atheistic organizations—favoring religion over irreligion. Nothing in the Court's opinion meets this objection, or clearly overcomes the principles (attributed to the First Amendment) expressed in the passage from Black's opinion. By our account, equal federal aid to all religions, whether positive or negative in form, violates neither the establishment nor the free exercise prohibitions. By giving equal nonpreferential aid to all religions, it does not constitute part of an establishment of religion. In fact, it can be understood as a means of encouraging the free exercise of religion and favoring religion over irreligion, neither of which is forbidden by the First Amendment.[6]

If aid to the various religions themselves must be equal and nonpreferential to avoid all possible hint of an establishment of religion, how is equality to be measured? Are unequal tax deductions for various religions acceptable? Can positive grants be proportioned to the number and wealth of the members of each sect? In the case of tax exemptions, religions would pay different amounts of taxes depending on their wealth. But to take nothing from them all is to treat them equally. We should also be aware that Congress did not devise the income tax in order to aid religions: on the contrary, it simply allows tax exemptions to prevent religions from being harmed by a general scheme of taxation needed for ordinary non-religious purposes. As in the case of conscientious exemptions from military service, Congress extends a privilege that cannot be claimed by religions as a matter of constitutional right: Congress's right to tax, and to tax religious property and income as well, remains supreme. Through tax exemptions, however, Congress voluntarily abjures the collection of certain tax moneys, which would prove costly, and possibly crippling to some or all religions, thus acting to preserve the free exercise of religion.

Positive grants of money meant to assist religions directly should not be unconstitutional so long as they are linked to some valid secular purpose and so long as they are equal. But here one must be careful, for equality cannot be proportioned to the number of members, of schools, of churches, of wealth, etc. To give more assistance to larger or wealthier churches—when the grant is directly for the support of religion—is to treat religions as numerical or economic entities, and not as religions. It would have the effect of adding, from general state revenues, to the superiority of the larger or wealthier religions, and thus of involving a peculiar form of religious preference. It would mistakenly assume that citizens originally paid into those general revenues as church members rather than as members of the civil society, thus making it seem—but only seem—that they receive back a share proportionate to their numbers, church by church. These considerations should allay the fears of some and chasten the hopes of others: the constitutionality of equal aid to all religions requires a strict view of equality, which both limits the form such aid might take, and is bound to disappoint those who seek superiority.

PRAYER IN SCHOOLS

In no area has the erroneous decision of the Court to apply the establishment clause against the states had graver implications than in public education. It should be clear to us, as it was to those founders of
American public education, Jefferson and Horace Mann,[7] that public
schools have no more important function that the making of good citizens, men and women with the moral and intellectual attributes necessary to preserve democracy. This public function can involve a range
of activities, including the teaching of rights and duties, the study of
the deeds and discourses of our great men, and the practice of civic virtues inside and outside the schools. It requires inculcating the principles of the Declaration of Independence, but strongly emphasizing
the duties corollary to rights that the Declaration implies but does not
spell out, and admonishing the young to revere the Constitution and
laws. It requires conveying some sense of the great challenges of republican self-government and instilling the moral qualities needed for the
citizen to take care of himself, work well with others, and love his country: sturdy independence, sobriety, decency, neighborliness, patriotic
concern for the common good.[8]

Among a people drawing much of its morality from the Bible, such
civic training cannot be accomplished without referring all to a just God
and strengthening rational elements from the Declaration with religious elements from the Bible. When Jefferson designed a system of
public education for Virginia, he spoke of using nonsectarian prayers
drawn from the Bible, teaching the Declaration and the principles of
natural theology and ethics, and even encouraging sectarian education
and worship. In doing so, he laid down the main lines of what the states
can constitutionally and prudentially do in their own interest. In his
view, such practices did not violate the ban on religious establishments
and the guarantee of free exercise found in Virginia's own constitution
(since added in all other state constitutions). And they certainly do not

violate any historically accurate reading of First Amendment liberties into the Fourteenth—supposing such reading necessary.

In *Schempp*, where the Court struck down as an establishment of religion the use of Bible readings and the Lord's Prayer in the public schools, Justice Brennan claimed the practice involved using "religious means to serve secular ends where secular means would suffice." He suggested that such important secular purposes as "fostering harmony and tolerance among the pupils, enhancing the authority of the teacher, and inspiring better discipline"[9] may be served by various secular devices rather than by religion. But these purposes, mainly dealing with conditions that should prevail within the schools, fall far short of what the states intended to accomplish with the help of Bible reading, which was the general training of citizens. And as we have seen, there is good reason to believe that public morality, in a country nourished on the Bible, is best taught by linking its principles to the belief in God. Certainly, a connection Jefferson, Washington, Tocqueville, and Mann all favored should not be subjected to airy dismissal by the Supreme Court, but left to reasonable legislative discretion.

The First Amendment, like its counterparts in state constitutions, forbids establishing any religion but does not forbid teaching the Declaration's teaching about "nature's God" and the rights and duties He supports. Nor does it forbid gathering from the Bible or the holy books of other Americans those passages that would reinforce the moral qualities needed for citizenship in American democracy. In Christian churches the Bible, used for its own sake, can be taken full strength and in all its parts and dimensions, but its place in the public schools is wholly and simply to serve the secular purposes for which the public schools exist. This requires a principled selectivity in finding passages that have the desired effect while avoiding passages that do not, whether because their moral point is unsuitable or their spirit sectarian.[10] No doubt state legislatures or school boards should make clear their secular intent, and assure believing citizens that, in principle, all holy writings may contribute to this common civic purpose. The result will be not only to instill or reinforce the moral qualities citizens need, but to impress Americans with the degree to which the various religions agree on certain moral fundamentals and contribute to the well-being of American society. In short, the public employment of religion will help religion as well as civil society, guaranteeing it a lofty public place in the body politic.

While parts of the Bible and other scriptures may be helpful to American democracy, the backbone of American political belief clearly derives from reason rather than revelation, and displays itself for all to see in the Declaration of Independence. What the Declaration conveys, strictly speaking, is not a religion at all, but a set of beliefs, anchored in the existence of God, the Creator of the natural world. It calls for no common worship, no rituals, no priesthood; it has nothing to say about the various experiences of bliss or woe, from cradle to grave, around which religions build their most impressive ceremonies; it does not instruct us how to pursue happiness but concerns itself solely with the preservation of our rights. Thus, the public schools can and should teach the Declaration's rational core, supplemented by a stress on civic duties that are also known through reason to be such, but are better illustrated and more strikingly enjoined by various religions than by the Declaration itself. States that convey such necessary beliefs through their public schools, even with prayers, found or devised, which testify to them, are hardly establishing a religion; they are neither preferring one of the existing religions, nor creating a new one. What they are doing, or should be doing, is teaching the civic morality without which their form of government cannot endure.

Before it was struck down as an establishment of religion in *Engel*, the following prayer, composed by the State Board of Regents, was recited in New York's public schools: "Almighty God, we acknowledge our dependence upon Thee, and we beg Thy blessings upon us, our parents, our teachers and our country." The Regents had taken pains to write a nonsectarian prayer to which all believers could conscientiously subscribe, and had even gone so far as to allow students who could not— on whatever ground, religious or irreligious—to abstain from the proceeding.[11] It was part of what they called "Moral and Spiritual Training in the Schools." The Court, through Justice Black, argued that prayer was a religious activity, and an official prayer the beginning of a religious establishment. Quoting copiously from Madison's Memorial and Remonstrance, as if the First Amendment were simply an excerpt from that document, Black conjured up all the dangers of sectarian faction that the framers sought to prevent. A footnote toward the end of the opinion, we should recall, maintains that the Declaration's references to the Deity should not keep it from being recited as an "historical document, and that school children can also be asked to sing official anthems (such as the "Star-Spangled Banner") which include "the composer's professions of faith in a Supreme Being."[12]

There are several errors in Black's reasoning. The first is his failure to recognize that some references to God derive from philosophy and not from religion—as in the Declaration itself—and that therefore some form of prayer, directed at such a God, may conform to philosophy rather than religion. Consider the Declaration's references to "nature's God," to the "Creator," to the "Supreme Judge of the world," and to the "Protection of Divine Providence": would prayer to such a Being be inappropriate? Black's second error is to assume that a religious activity—supposing prayer to be such—implies a particular religion of which it is an activity. The Board of Regents tried to formulate, for school use, a prayer religious believers could agree upon generally. Thus, having school children express this prayer is not to form a new religion, but to ask them to avow for public purposes, in the classroom together, part of what they would express separately within their own churches and temples, or in the home. Precisely the same is true of the prayers opening daily sessions of Congress and the state legislatures, as well as the countless invocations of God's help and blessing found in presidential addresses. (Justice Stewart, in his lone dissent, quotes such passages from Washington, Adams, Jefferson, Madison, Lincoln, Cleveland, Wilson, Roosevelt, Eisenhower, and Kennedy.) Even supposing these to be rooted in religious rather than philosophical beliefs, they certainly form no part of a particular organized religion, do not prefer one religion over another, and hence fail to constitute an establishment of religion. Or are presidents employing such invocations in their official utterances to be impeached for violating the Constitution?

The reasons which moved the Board of Regents to introduce such a prayer in the first place receive utterly no attention in the Court's opinion (or Justice Douglas's concurrence). The Regents were not being frivolous or light-headed, though the wording of their prayer might well have been more copious and dignified, and better connected with historical precedent. They wanted students to sense a dependence on Almighty God, and to think of the benefits they should want to see brought not only to themselves but to parents, teachers, and country—that is, to those in whose debt they remain. They were intent on overcoming, in other words, the growing sense among the young that they are subject to no higher law, have no superior obligations, may act as they please, and think solely of themselves. In the name of civic education and morality, they were contradicting a dangerous egoism. Unfortunately, they were themselves contradicted by a Supreme Court that had nothing in its lexicon but the word "liberty," making it increasingly difficult for public authorities to inculcate that sense of duty and discipline without which liberty becomes a dangerous threat to others and oneself. Only recently, since the 1960s, has it become possible to call the public schools "godless" with any accuracy, a change concurrent with a precipitous decline in the teaching of citizenship and its demands, generally abetted by a Court that stripped school authorities of essential powers in order to magnify student rights. Thus has the Court contributed to the widespread spirit of laxity and lawlessness, aroused deep resentment within much of the population, and engendered a mounting conservative (and religious) reaction to its own "liberal" recasting of the Constitution.[13]

But the term "liberal" should not be conceded to those who are fanatics in the name of liberty, and who invoke the names of Madison and Jefferson without studying the fullness of their thought. These great men realized that the Declaration, anchored in monotheism, would itself anchor the American people's belief in inalienable rights, with the right of religious freedom included within the right to the pursuit of happiness. However paradoxical in appearance, the right to be different—in religion and other matters—depends for its effective continuance on the general public's not markedly differing about the right itself—that is, on a very widespread agreement concerning the right itself. The same is true of equality: no stronger basis can exist for the equal rights of all men, regardless of race, religion, sex, or ethnic background, than the teaching of the Declaration of Independence. To assure the most widespread conviction in connection with these rights, and at the same time in connection with the duties that alone can make the rights lastingly effective, is certainly a vital part of each state's authority, and the most important object of its educational system. This entails teaching the monotheism inherent in the Declaration, and against this imperious need no plea of individual rights should be permitted to prevail. Jefferson had no hesitation to require the study of the Declaration, as well as courses in natural theology and ethics, at the University of Virginia. Nothing in the First or Fourteenth Amendments keeps us from doing something similar today.

STATE AID TO RELIGION

Let us look somewhat more briefly now at problems involving state encouragement of the various religions, first within public schools, then in parochial schools. We take it for granted that public schools are not churches, and would, moreover, be barred by anti-establishment clauses

in state constitutions themselves from putting on certain sectarian pageants to the exclusion of others. Whatever sectarian pageants or observances they do permit for the whole school would therefore have to take
the form of educational presentations, or exercises in mutual understanding, rather than religious practices as such, and would have to be
non-preferential as well. Within these limitations they would not constitute establishments, but even so, much discretion is called for, since
the greater the involuntary exposure of one individual to the religious
practices of another, the greater the possibility of infringing on the
former's free exercise of religion.

The problem presented by "released" or "dismissed" time is different.
Here the avowed purpose is to encourage the free exercise of religion
by permitting public school students to avail themselves of instruction
in (and provided by) their own religion either on school premises ("released") or off school premises ("dismissed") during one part of the school
week. We may recall Jefferson's willingness, at the state University of
Virginia, to "expect" students to attend daily services of their own religions, and in buildings erected on publicly donated land near or on
campus. Jefferson may have been willing to compel student worship to
assure parents that their sons' religious needs would be met at the distant university. In any case, this compulsion was somewhat mitigated
by the voluntary nature of university matriculation itself.

Both released and dismissed time in the public schools properly
avoid legal compulsion: the student and his parents are given the choice
of deciding whether he is to receive sectarian religious instruction. Nor
can the activity's taking place on school property, as with released time,
make a difference if the state has a right (unimpaired, at least, by either
state or federal non-establishment provisions) to help all religions equally,
or better, to encourage religious belief. It has been argued that informal coercion from the compulsory school setting remains, but such
"social" pressure falls far short of Jefferson's "expecting," and is hardly
irresistible. On both sides, however, there are prudential considerations.

These programs require that students be visibly separated by differences of religious affiliation, in a setting where their fellowship as American citizens should be stressed. On the other hand, such differences do receive an open and respectful acknowledgment and encouragement from the public, promoting religious toleration and connecting the schools, at least in some important way, with the belief in God and moral training that undergird republican citizenship.

From what we have said before regarding federal aid to education, it is also clear that religious schools and institutions of higher learning are not barred by the Fourteenth Amendment from receiving state assistance designed to improve the "secular" components of education throughout the state. Not that these educational facilities have a right to such aid, for they are by their nature consciously endowed with an existence and a means of control separate from and independent of the state's authority and educational system. From the beginning, and by common and mutual understanding, the responsibility for their support lay with those setting them up. But while they are not "entitled" to public assistance, it may be in the public's interest to assist them in various ways, and there is no constitutional bar (deriving from nonestablishment provisions in either state or federal constitutions) to the public's doing so.[14] The matter is therefore prudential, and state legislators must weigh both the dangers to the public school system, whether by supporting or not supporting religious schools, and the educational advantages to be procured for those of its citizens who have chosen (with the Supreme Court's blessing) this educational route. Again, the fact that the sectarian and religious elements of these schools will benefit indirectly from aid to their secular elements is not a constitutional deterrent, though it may certainly figure in the prudential considerations involved.

The case of state aid to the religious components of religiously sponsored education (like that of federal aid, discussed above) is different. Even here, if we are correct, equal aid is not barred by any federal or state constitutional requirement of non-establishment. But it must be equal among the various religions, and not proportioned to the number of their schools or of students within their schools. Large and small religions must be treated with perfect equality, and those possessing their own religious schools must not be favored above those that do not. The assistance, in short, must be to religions as a whole, and not to any part of some religions (for example, schools) which may not be present in all. This prime requisite of direct and positive state aid is bound to set drastic limits on its practicability, and thus for the most part confine financial aid to tax exemptions.

Since the position we are advancing sanctions an unequal treatment of religious belief and unbelief, we should show how it escapes the Fourteenth Amendment's prohibition on state action denying "to any person within its jurisdiction the equal protection of the laws," and any implied restriction of the same kind (there is no explicit one) on federal action. We take it for granted here that the religious parts of the First Amendment do not protect the free exercise of atheism. The sole, but sufficient, safeguards for the non-believer are found in the guarantees of freedom of speech and press. As for "equal protection" by state laws, the common good may require that certain beliefs be promulgated through public education—which necessarily works to the disfavor of opposite views. By teaching the desirability of democracy, liberty, and equality in the public schools, the public necessarily treats unequally the belief in dictatorship, slavery, and the master race undoubtedly held by some of its citizens. Similarly, the public has good reason for concluding that the perseverance of our society depends on citizens' believing in God-given rights and duties, and can therefore make use of public instrumentalities to further that belief. This in no way detracts from the "equal protection of the laws" intended by the Fourteenth Amendment—laws to protect the atheist along with everyone else, but without guaranteeing equal public status to his views.

16

"Free Exercise" and "Religion"
in the Modern Court

THE EARLIEST SUPREME COURT CASES involving the religious part of the First Amendment grew out of massive federal efforts to suppress polygamy among the Mormons in the Idaho Territory. Bigamy and polygamy were made felonies; the right to vote depended on abjuring such practices (which Mormons could not conscientiously do); the charter of the Mormon Church was removed, and most of its property declared forfeit.[1] The Court voted 9 to 0 against Mormon claims that their polygamy was an integral part of their religion and hence not subject to these laws. It did so on the basis of the following interpretation of the "free exercise" clause: "With man's relations to his Maker and the obligations he may think they impose, and the manner in which an expression shall be made by him of his belief on those subjects, no interference can be permitted, provided always the laws of society, designed to secure its peace and prosperity, and the morals of its people are not interfered with. . . ."[2] Starting in 1940, the modern Court, in making the religious clauses of the First Amendment part of the "liberty" protected by the "due process" clause of the Fourteenth, also introduced new views of "free exercise" and "religion." It did not completely abandon the rule proclaimed by Justice Field in

the Mormon case, but it modified it so as to allow more readily for religious exemptions to valid laws, making itself the arbiter of when such
exemptions are to be granted. Along the way it began to loosen the
meaning of "religion" itself.

HOW THE CHANGES BEGAN

To see the Court's innovations at work, let us examine a few landmark
cases. First the father of them all, *Cantwell v. Connecticut*, decided by
a full and unanimous Court for Cantwell and against Connecticut in
1940. Could reasoning so flimsy have had such far-reaching effects?
Without the slightest effort to show why, the Court begins its holding
with the flat assertion (concerning the Fourteenth Amendment) that
"The fundamental concept of liberty embodied in that Amendment
embraces the liberties guaranteed by the First Amendment. The First
Amendment declares that Congress shall make no law respecting an
establishment of religion or prohibiting the free exercise thereof. The
Fourteenth Amendment has rendered the legislatures of the states as
incompetent as Congress to enact such laws."[3] Here, by sheer judicial
fiat, the Court avoids all the complications presented by its own argument in the Slaughterhouse Cases, by the historical circumstances of
1868, and by the inconsistencies of wording between the two amendments. But the logic the Court then uses to reverse Connecticut's supreme court is almost as startling. The Cantwells, proselytizing on
behalf of Jehovah's Witnesses, had been found guilty on two counts.
The first involved violating a state statute requiring prospective solici-
tors to apply to a public official for permission, empowering that official
to grant permission only after determining that their cause was religious. The second involved the common law offense of inciting a breach
of the peace.

In connection with the first count, the Court granted that the two
parts of "free exercise"—the "freedom to believe and freedom to act"—

were not equally protected: "The first is absolute but, in the nature of things, the second cannot be. Conduct remains subject to regulation for the protection of society. The freedom to act must have appropriate definition to preserve the enforcement of that protection. In every case the power to regulate must be so exercised as not, in attaining a permissible end, unduly to infringe the protected freedom."[4] The "protected freedom" means the freedom to believe, and the Court found Connecticut's arrangement an "undue" infringement on it, since the public official granting permission exercises a "censorship of religion" by his power to withhold permission from causes he does not deem religious. The Cantwells, of course, had denied they were soliciting in the first place—a claim shown to be manifestly untrue by the facts the Court itself cites. But they had also solicited without first asking official permission, as required, so that there was no evidence indicating that the law had been prejudicially applied against them. Instead, they simply argued against any official having the right to determine, before granting them permission to solicit, whether or not they were doing so for a religious cause. Why this constitutes "censorship of religion" is beyond comprehension. The statute clearly *reserves* the freedom to solicit for religious groups, and the official determination of whether groups are religious is made in other ways as well, some necessitated by the safeguards the First Amendment extends to religion and only to religion. It should be added that this particular public official's determinations were reviewable in court and not final.

As to Cantwell's inciting a breach of the peace by others, the Court claims that "There is no showing that his deportment was noisy, truculent, overbearing or offensive," yet it also concedes the record he played "singles out the Roman Catholic church for strictures couched in terms which naturally would offend not only persons of that persuasion, but all others who respect the honestly held religious faith of their fellows."[5] The Court goes on to say that Cantwell had admittedly asked permission to play the record, and that both religious and political pleaders sometimes resort "to exaggeration, to vilification of men who have been, or are, prominent in church or state, and even to false statement."[6] But, the Court concludes, "the people of this nation have ordained in the light of history, that, in spite of the probability of excesses and abuses, these liberties are, in the long view, essential to enlightened opinion and right conduct on the part of the citizens of a democracy."[7] For this reason, only a statute written in "clear and present danger" terms and thus carefully defining "breach of the peace" would satisfy First Amendment requirements here.

This argument contains many defects, one of them being its insistence on "clear and present danger" statutory language in such situations—despite the long precedent giving greater leeway to authorities in determining a "breach of the peace." Moreover, it speaks as if slander and sedition were no longer criminal, and as if "the people of this nation" had ordained as much in the First Amendment itself—both of which are certainly untrue. Finally, it gives encouragement to the excesses of religious and political fanaticism by treating them as a normal part of religious or political persuasion. What the Court forgot was that both religious and political liberty depend on setting limits to what may be in contention and to the manner of contention as well. By justifying religious (or political) offensiveness within the process of persuasion or conversion, the Court made it more likely various groups would drop the considerateness, the decency of address enabling them to get along and work together as fellow citizens of one democracy, despite important differences. In sum, whether considering the Court's case on the second count, on the first, or on the absorption of the First into the Fourteenth Amendment, it seems an extremely flimsy basis for overturning the decision of a state supreme court. Clearly the judicial innovation Holmes and Brandeis first injected into the Court's understanding of liberty had won out. The result was an enormous expansion of federal judicial hegemony and individual liberty combined, both working to the detriment of a moderate federal republic.

THE FLAG SALUTE CASES

A similar tendency is shown in the flag salute cases, again involving members of Jehovah's Witnesses. Their refusal, on religious grounds, to salute the flag and recite the Pledge of Allegiance in public school was condemned by an eight to one vote of the Court in 1940, and then, in a complete reversal, supported by a six to three vote in 1943. Speaking for the majority in the earlier case (*Minersville School District v. Gobitis*), Justice Frankfurter already took it for granted that the First Amendment had been absorbed into the Fourteenth. But compelling the flag salute—a vital part of civic or patriotic training—did not violate religious liberty: it constituted a reasonable exercise of state authority to which religious conscience had to bend. In his dissent, Justice Stone maintained that the "very essence of the liberty" guaranteed by the First Amendment "is the freedom of the individual from compulsion as to what he shall think and what he shall say, at least where the compulsion is to bear false witness to his religion. If these guarantees are to have any meaning they must, I think, be deemed to withhold from the state any authority to compel belief or the expression of it where that expression violates religious convictions, whatever may be the legislative view of the desirability of such compulsion."[8] This passage introduces a novel interpretation of the religious and non-religious parts of the First Amendment, likening free speech (and thought) to the free exercise of religion—free from governmental control. Together they form something like "freedom of belief"—a right evidently as much possessed by school children as by adults. Yet Justice Stone's position needlessly stresses the role of religious convictions if *no one* can be compelled to believe or say *anything* against his will. Applied to school children, this principle would call into question all efforts to teach right beliefs, moral and political, through compulsory programs in the public schools. In other words, much more than flag saluting must fall, given Stone's wholly novel interpretation of the First Amendment.

Three years later, speaking for a majority now opposed to compulsory flag saluting (again Jehovah's Witnesses were involved, this time in West Virginia), Justice Jackson gave Stone's errors this memorable formulation: "If there is any fixed star in our constitutional constellation, it is that no official, high or petty, can prescribe what shall be orthodox in politics, nationalism, religion or other matters of opinion or force citizens to confess by word or act their faith therein. If there are any circumstances which permit an exception, they do not now occur to us."[9] This fixed star is said to be located in the First Amendment, but it is the First Amendment read in the light of John Stuart Mill's *On Liberty* rather than the framers' intentions. Just as Mill inconsistently claimed to set forth an absolute principle regarding liberty while denying that any principles can be known infallibly, Jackson inconsistently proclaims the orthodoxy —the one absolute principle—of no orthodoxy. Nor does he seem to realize how devastating its consequences would be for public education generally. Here is his own description of the general program West Virginia had established, of which flag saluting and the pledge together were but one part: "Following the decision by this Court on June 3, 1940, in *Minersville School District v. Gobitis* . . . , the West Virginia legislature amended its statutes to require all schools therein to conduct courses of instruction in history, civics and in the Constitution of the United States and of the State 'for the purpose of teaching, fostering and perpetuating the ideals, principles and spirit of Americanism, and increasing the knowledge of the organization and machinery of the government.'"[10] As West Virginia (and all other states) see it, there *is* an American orthodoxy, consisting in the belief that the principles underlying our government, principles like those in the Declaration of Independence and those set into the Constitution, are true, right, and good. Can this orthodoxy, so crucial to the training of good citizens, be taught in the public schools? Can the courses be made compulsory? Can the manner of conducting the courses, and judging student performance, oral and written, require that these principles be memorized, understood, and repeated? If so, not only is there an American orthodoxy, but it can be compelled, even to the utterance, in the public schools. In short, underlying American liberty, with all its diversity, is the homogeneous belief in American liberty. This was obvious to Thomas Jefferson, who did more for public education than any other member of the founding generation. And it means that the compulsion involved in flag saluting and pledging allegiance is only part of a more general compulsory inculcation essential to the training of citizens. If one part goes, the whole must go.

The founders and framers did not relegate the question of "what shall be orthodox in politics" to the realm of "matters of opinion," as Justice Jackson does in this famous passage. They thought the principles of politics derived from reason or philosophy, and were therefore matters of knowledge rather than opinion. The freedoms of the First Amendment drew their importance and dignity from the place they occupied within a particular political philosophy. Those who understand this philosophy can hardly be said, in the strict sense, to have embraced an orthodoxy. For Jefferson, the Declaration would hardly have been the expression of an orthodoxy. But for young minds, even rational truths must first be presented in forms that fall short of demonstration and that therefore partake of orthodoxy or belief simply. Programs in Americanism, as practiced by every state in the Union, are of this kind, combining history and civics with ideals and principles, in a manner suitable to the political and moral instruction of the young.

The First Amendment was intended to apply against Congress alone explicitly, and the Fourteenth Amendment, generally, was not intended to apply the First Amendment against the states, where civic training has its proper locus. Even so, Stone and Jackson to the contrary notwithstanding, the First Amendment does not protect some "freedom of belief" for young *or* old. It included a right of the states to have religious establishments free from federal control; the free exercise of religion it protected had to be subordinated to the needs of civil society.

The freedoms of speech and press it protected did not include a freedom to call and work for an end to liberty, equality and republican government. On the contrary, they were the necessary means of making republican government work. Thus, both Justices Stone and Jackson are mistaken in regarding the amendment, from one end to the other, as a safeguard against governmental coercion for the individual to think or speak as he pleases.

This kind of safeguard was generally thought to be associated with republican government as such, but without guaranteeing that under no circumstances, or in connection with no part of the population (especially the young), could thought or speech ever be coerced. Political education might necessarily involve a form of coercion—that is, coercion not only in the requirement of receiving an education but in the content of certain beliefs necessary to good citizenship. Moreover, in the political philosophy of the Declaration and the founding generation, citizenship as such is always, strictly speaking, voluntary, and it would hardly be unconstitutional to ask of citizens, even to make it a requirement of voting as well as holding office, that they swear their freely-chosen allegiance to the Constitution and laws, much in the manner prescribed by the Constitution itself for federal and state officials. What is the "pledge of allegiance" but a habituated preparation for voluntarily assuming the rights and obligations of citizenship? Certainly nothing in the First or Fourteenth Amendments, as originally intended, forbids such a preparation.[11]

Nor does practical wisdom counsel against it. Justice Frankfurter, now dissenting rather than expressing the view of eight of the nine justices, as he had three years earlier in *Gobitis*, presses the distinction between judging and legislating, between the proper function of the Court and the proper function of democratically elected legislatures. He reminds the Court of the principle of civil supremacy to which religious conscience must bow. He insists that the adequacy or necessity of flag saluting as an instrument of civic training is not for the Court to decide. He reviews the Court's record throughout the flag-salute controversy: "That which three years ago had seemed to five successive Courts to lie within permissible areas of legislation is now outlawed by the deciding shift of opinion of two Justices."[12]

Frankfurter concludes that the one proper test of unconstitutionality—"the absence of a rational justification for the legislation"—can hardly be found to apply here. His call for judicial self-restraint is, of course, well taken, but he does not seem to have penetrated to the root of the Court's error. Misreading the First and Fourteenth Amendments, the Court arrogated to itself the right to decide the substantive content of the term "liberty" in the Fourteenth, and then—quite contrary to the words of the Amendment—to declare what part of liberty *no amount of "due process" could remove*. Having vested in itself the supreme right to philosophize about the constitutionally sacrosanct, unguided by any explicit words in the Constitution, any historical record, or any binding hold of precedent, the Court could then feel free *not* to be bound by the sole test of unconstitutionality Frankfurter claimed to exist—that is, by whether a legislature defied rationality in its acts of legislation. This is why Justice Jackson's opinion in *Barnette* actually reads like an essay by Mill rather than a statement of law, based on the careful weighing of the words, intentions and precedents of the law. Emancipating themselves from the tight hold of original meaning, evidenced in constitutional words and history, the justices invested the words with meanings drawn from the intellectual world of the twentieth century and not from the founders or framers of the amendments. Without opposing this trend root and branch, Frankfurter's pleas for judicial self-restraint were bound to fail, the Court's usurpations and contraventions of perfectly valid legislation bound to burgeon, the division of opinion on the Court bound to increase, and policy views of the Court bound to assume greater importance.

OATHS

Another case that reveals the extent and depth of the Court's errors was *Torcaso v. Watkins*, decided unanimously in 1961. At issue was a requirement of Maryland's constitution that state officers declare a belief in the existence of God. Justice Black begins the Court's opinion with a disquisition on the part "test oaths" played in the experience of American colonists, culminating in the federal Constitution's ban (in Article VI) on religious tests as prerequisites to federal office. To this ban were added, almost immediately, the special religious protections of the First Amendment.

Black recapitulates the elements of *Cantwell* and *Everson* in which the Court claimed that the First Amendment calls for a complete separation between the state and religion—with the Fourteenth extending the same prohibition to the states. He quotes extensively from his own famous passage in *Everson* defining "establishment of religion." It then seems a simple matter to fit the Maryland test oath into this framework, since it requires professing a belief in a religion, and favors religion over non-religion. Yet even on the surface certain complications show themselves. The most obvious is that the Court finally charges Maryland with invading Torcaso's "freedom of belief and religion" rather than establishing a religion, as it seems to be arguing all along.

Of course Black's definition (of establishment) in *Everson* always suffered from this defect: it left nothing to the "free exercise" clause; or, put another way, it swallowed up "free exercise" within the ban on establishment—much as Madison had coalesced the two in his Memorial and Remonstrance, but reversing their priority in favor of free exercise. Black's difficulty also shows itself quite visibly in his reference to a "freedom of belief and religion" that as such is present neither in the First Amendment nor anywhere else in the Constitution. Thinking that the Amendment allows no preference for religion over non-religion any more than for one kind of religion over another, he expresses this in such a way as to make it look like a phrase from the Amendment itself. In fact, he finds that Maryland's requirement of a testimonial to the existence of God favors religions believing in God over religions that do not, explaining, in a note, that "Among religions in this country which do not teach what would generally be considered a belief in God are Buddhism, Taoism, Ethical Culture, Secular Humanism and others."[13] But if all these are religions, the free exercise of which is protected by the First Amendment, why add the word "belief" and create a "freedom of belief and religion"? Either Black wants to find a rubric for protecting religions that do not believe in God, calling this "belief," or—more likely, since he clearly calls these religions, too—he wants to find a direct way of protecting not only those non-believers organized into groups like the Ethical Culture Society but all shades of irreligious opinion, organized or not. And for this the notion of a "freedom of belief" as well as a "freedom of religion" (or better, the "free exercise of belief and religion") seems perfectly designed. The only trouble is that it forms no part of the text of the First Amendment, which never required an equal treatment of religion and irreligion.

Black's statements also prompt us to ask, as he does not, how the Supreme Court should go about defining religion. Its options are to use the meaning the founders and framers used, the meaning generally attached to the word currently, or the meaning adopted by any claimant wishing to be considered a religion. If it treated the First Amendment as a fundamental law passed in 1790, constantly bearing the meaning then attached to it, some of the non-theistic groups Black instances would qualify and some would not. Buddhism and Taoism share enough of the then commonly accepted traits of religions to be legally recognized as such. They do have organized worship, a set of beliefs, practices and rituals, a priesthood—in fact, after a certain point in their history, both incorporated celestial beings into their system of belief (the name Buddhism suggests that to some extent the Buddha himself became treated as such a being). Moreover, both draw their essential teaching from the nature of the universe, viewed as a permanent super-sensory structure. On the other hand, Ethical Culture and Secular Humanism would unquestionably have to be denied the legal status of religions on the founders' basis—unless organizations for fraternal and educational purposes like the Rotarians and Boy Scouts are to be included as well.

Of course, the Court cannot afford—in the name of progress—to adopt the definition of religion current in the intellectual circles of the country or the world at a given time, any more than it can allow claimant groups to define religion as they please. Not only are such views notoriously superficial, variable, and self-serving, but their currency is likely to be inversely related to their political practicability. For the key question must be the degree to which a given definition makes the First Amendment and our republican system as a whole workable. If governmental assistance is to be given to "religions" or, as with the modern Court, privileges extended to them, it is vital that the word "religion" be kept very restrictive and anchored in beings or realities that are permanent, transcending ordinary experience. Otherwise, the aspect of religions most useful to American democracy will be forgotten, and the ever-widening application of either assistance or privileges will vitiate the intent of the First Amendment, causing these to be extended to everybody, or, more likely, to be withdrawn from everybody at some point. Unfortunately, such considerations did not occur to Justice Black and the entirety of the Court for which he spoke, proving that it is not enough to claim fidelity to the exact words of the Constitution if the research and reasoning applied to the words are warped by libertarian inclinations not shared by the founders and framers.

It is remarkable how little attention the Court as a whole, acting *unanimously*, gives to the history and intention of Maryland's constitutional requirement in *Torcaso*. Armed with a simplistic interpretation of the First and Fourteenth Amendments together, the Court feels itself justified in striking down even provisions of state constitutions enacted long before by the people of those states. In determining the liberties on which no state may infringe, the Court lets itself be guided not by the founders and framers but by Jefferson and Madison, and by these only to the extent that they are closer to John Stuart Mill—their own stripped-down version of Mill—who has replaced the founders as their guide in expanding individual liberties and extirpating the limits or conditions that had previously qualified those liberties.

This is why the Court pays so little attention in *Torcaso* to the provision the people of Maryland placed in their state constitution—a provision they must have thought consistent with both the ban on establishment and the guarantee of free exercise also written into that constitution. Nor had their own highest court said anything to dispute this assumption. As to the people's motive, they may have thought the belief in God would make office-holders more likely to adhere to their required oath of office, more likely to adhere, through thick and thin, to the notion of divinely-derived rights and duties found in the Declaration of Independence and presumed by our entire political system. Such a view would not be irrational and undoubtedly, as they saw it, fell short of being a religious establishment since it did not favor one religion over the others.

The problem involved here may be traced back as far as John Locke himself, the founder of liberalism. According to Locke, civil society is entirely separate from religion—from which it follows that there can be no religious requirements for civil rights of any kind. Yet this same John Locke was of the opinion that civil society could not function well without a widespread belief in God, for, as he put it, "Promises, covenants and oaths, which are the bonds of human society, can have no hold upon an atheist." He was therefore willing to prohibit the public expression of atheism, but did not take the further step of demanding that citizens positively attest to their belief in God in order to hold office.[14] Still, the fear of atheism he expressed might lead some of his followers to support a provision like that included in Maryland's constitution. Originally, we may recall, the First Amendment was intended not to eliminate the state establishments but to leave such matters to the states themselves. Seen in this light, Maryland's keeping the provision to which Torcaso objected was well within its authority. By adding this to a ban on establishments and a guarantee of free exercise, Maryland could even be understood as combining all three components of Locke's teaching.

Clearly the federal union itself was not founded on this quasi-religious variant of Lockean liberalism. Not only did the Constitution omit all references to God and bar religious tests for public office, but the oaths it does require of the president and other federal officers are not explicitly religious in character. It might have been expected that, in practice, the taking of these oaths would become occasions for the public display of religious belief (by adding the presence of the Bible and the words "so help me God"), as they actually have. Nevertheless, the oaths (or affirmations) do not contain such words. On the other hand, several of the states, in 1789, expressed religious preferences of a sort and had religious prerequisites for office-holding in their constitutions. When these were abolished by the states themselves, what remained in some, like Maryland, Arkansas, Pennsylvania, and Tennessee, was the kind of broad oath requirement Torcaso refused to meet.[15] The people of these states wanted to combine two purposes: the achievement of the modern liberal republic, with its religious liberty, and the support of this republic by upholding, through its officers, the example of a belief in God. The view of these states had to be sacrificed when the Supreme Court, misusing the First and Fourteenth Amendments, forced the federal view of citizenship on the states in 1961, though the two views had lived side by side for more than a century.

PARAMOUNT INTERESTS

That same year the Court also decided several cases dealing with Sunday closing laws. By lopsided votes (eight to one, seven to two), in most of them, but amid a plethora of opinions, it held such laws constitutional. Even though Sunday was the Christian day of rest, said Chief Justice Warren for the majority, states neither established the Christian religion nor deprived others (Saturday sabbatarians in particular) of the free exercise of religion by requiring most businesses to be closed on Sunday. Had they done so for the purpose of encouraging religion, Sunday closing laws would indeed violate the First Amendment. But their purpose (he said) is wholly secular—the provision of a common day of rest by virtue of state police powers, with the choice of a particular day being left to legislative discretion. To Justice Douglas, however, the choice of Sunday, the Christian Sabbath, constituted both a form of establishment, by showing religious preference, and an infringement on free exercise, since it forced some people to observe the Sabbath of others. It also inflicted particular hardship on those who observed another Sabbath day and were kept from doing business on Sunday.

Two years afterward, in *Sherbert v. Verner*, the Court voted seven to two that South Carolina could not refuse to pay unemployment insurance to persons who refused to accept (or were not permitted to remain in) any job that included work on Saturday, the day they considered their Sabbath (Sherbert was a Seventh-Day Adventist). The Court maintained that the burden thereby placed on Sherbert's free exercise of her religion was hardly outweighed by any "compelling" state interest. As Justice Brennan said for the majority: "It is basic that no showing merely of a rational relationship to some colorable state interest would suffice; in this highly sensitive constitutional area, 'only the gravest abuses, endangering paramount interests, give occasion for permissible limitation.'"[16] From this view, only Justice Harlan, joined by Justice White, dissented: "I cannot subscribe to the conclusion that the State is constitutionally compelled to carve out an exception to its general rule of eligibility in the present case. Those situations in which the Constitution may require special treatment on account of religion are, in my view, few and far between, and this view is amply supported by the course of constitutional litigation in this area."[17]

More astonishing and confusing still is the Court's decision nine years later in *Wisconsin v. Yoder* (1972), where it forced Wisconsin to grant the Amish an exemption from its compulsory education law. All seven members of the Court participating favored this exemption, Douglas's dissent being only a more radical extension of the majority's view. In other words, absolutely no one on the Court remembered Frankfurter's dissent in *Barnette*, some thirty years before, counseling judicial self-restraint. In weighing (as Frankfurter agreed they must) the value to the state of required formal education against the value to the Amish of the free exercise of their religion, *all* justices found the state's interest insufficiently compelling. To arrive at this conclusion, they had to substitute their own view of the goal of education for the state of Wisconsin's: "It is one thing to say that compulsory education for a year or two beyond the eighth grade may be necessary when its goal is the preparation of the child for life in modern society as the majority live, but it is quite another if the goal of education be viewed as the preparation of the child for life in the agrarian community that is the keystone of the Amish faith."[18]

In *Yoder*, the full implication of the new principle relating valid secular laws and religious interests became all too clear. The older principle—it has been called the "secular regulation" rule—had accorded such laws priority over any and all religious practices violating them. But now the Court considers that rule insufficiently sensitive to religious imperatives, and hence violative of "free exercise." It takes upon itself the right to determine whether "paramount interests" of the state are at stake or not, making the constitutionality of the law depend on this finding. But what does "paramount" mean, and why should the courts rather than the people's legislatures define and apply it? Did the framers of the First Amendment originally intend such special protection for religions? Did the Fourteenth Amendment intend their adoption against the states?

The Court's record in these cases confirms what should have been known from the outset: by explicitly making itself a weigher of values, the Court has entered a field that by its nature is not judicial at all, and can never be. For to be a judge means to apply a law, standard, or rule known beforehand or capable of being known beforehand. But in this weighing of values and this determination of what state interests are paramount, the Court is not applying any standard known, or capable of being known, beforehand. The state, by passing such laws through its duly elected legislators, has expressed the judgment that the law is needed. But the Court has no law derived from the Constitution (which the people approved) that it can apply to the state laws. The word "liberty" in the Fourteenth Amendment does not explain itself, and there is no way for a judiciary to determine what it must mean, as an abstract matter, apart from the meaning it had in the minds of those who passed it. Otherwise, the Court has set itself afloat on an unfathomable sea. Its verdicts become arbitrary, inconsistent, splintered, changeable, and unintelligible—the imposition of the justices' policy views or wishes rather than of the Constitution and objective law.

The main motive animating libertarian support for the Court's interventions is anti-majoritarianism—a fear of legislation legally passed by popular majorities but unjust to the interest of minorities, particularly in the area of "beliefs." What concerns them may be subsumed under the general problem of majority rule discussed by Madison in *The Federalist*, Number 10, and they are not satisfied with the solution Madison propounds to the possibility of "majority factions" passing self-interested and unjust legislation. This solution depended on a combination of great diversity of viewpoints in any given field of legislation and the moderating effect of representative government as such. For example, in the area of religion, encouraged by the general principle of liberty, one would expect there to be many sects that could not easily or steadily combine against others. This effect would then be compounded by representative government, which removed political decisions from the more impassioned hands of the people and also beset it with complicated internal checks and balances. The result, Madison felt, while not eliminating injustice to minorities, would make it more infrequent and less severe.

Madison's prediction has probably been borne out by the facts, particularly with the added protection of the First Amendment and similar clauses in state constitutions—and before the judicial revolution introduced by *Cantwell*. There has been remarkably little religious oppression in this country, particularly after the inner logic of the Declaration of Independence and the general spirit of liberty it engendered brought the states, one by one, to retract any religious establishments that remained and to guarantee religious liberty. Few if any countries in the world as various in their populations can boast of a record so little sullied by religious oppression. This massive fact libertarians especially tend to forget as they concentrate on lesser ways in which laws sometimes hurt minorities. Within the novel ambit of American liberty, the Jehovah's Witnesses, Jews, and Amish who figure in many of the cases just treated are perfectly free to practice their own religion in all essentials that do not touch on secular interests, can even form whole communities of their own, and are not barred from occupying the highest offices in the land. This is the salient feature of our constitutions, whatever currents may occasionally run counter to it, and it was all accomplished straightforwardly, without the judicial legerdemain of *Cantwell* and its successors.

Since 1940 and *Cantwell*, however, libertarians on and off the Court have been pleased by numerous decisions that have struck down state laws preferring religion over irreligion, offending a fictitious "freedom of belief," or failing to make exceptions for religious minorities. Many of their supporters are willing to have the Court wield something like royal prerogative and intervene on the side of the "oppressed," even where the rule being applied by the Court is unsusceptible of rational explication or defense. Some would like to pick and choose even among the Court's more liberal decisions, wondering whether it did not give too much state authority away in *Yoder*, or whether the same principle making an exception to the law for Sherbert should not have been applied to the Sunday-closing cases as well.

What these people do not realize—like the old supporters of royal prerogative—is that constant interventions by one branch of government, when unguided by clear principles, can readily lead to a usurpation of the authority of the other branches. Here and there, some greater immediate justice may be done than would be the case in trusting to the ordinary legislative and judicial processes of the state and federal governments. Yet elsewhere much harm is done to public authority and the long-range public good. Compared with this, the harm done to the various plaintiffs, however palpable, is surely of a different magnitude and reach. Like some of the merchants who close on both Saturdays and Sundays, Mrs. Sherbert would have found a way to survive, much as the Amish would have survived without the Court's exempting them from two years of compulsory education. But the republic may not survive such decisions continued and expanded into the future.[19] This is not to say that Mrs. Sherbert and the Amish did not deserve—from their respective state legislatures—the relief they requested. In a diverse society like ours, the ruling majority should be sensitive to the special needs of minorities and act to alleviate the hardships caused by general laws wherever possible.

Intellectuals in our country may be persuaded to accept arbitrary government in the name of social justice, even as the common people are alienated from the judiciary. Nevertheless, we should return to the situation prevailing before *Cantwell*. Otherwise, the Court's arbitrariness will help destroy the ballast of our society, which is the conviction that we all live under the rule of law and, nationally, under the rule of the same law. This belief in an objective, over-arching supreme law, subject to judicial explication and application but not creation, to reasoning but not to will, holds a diverse and changing society within one generally accepted, stable framework. Without it, society is apt to divide into hostile groups claiming gross abuse of the law, growing more used to arbitrariness, and increasingly hoping for an end to republican government.

This eventuality should be acknowledged on all sides as the worst possible evil. Compared with it, the minor injustices done here and there to religious or other minorities fade into insignificance, since the collapse of the republic might well entail the end of the great amount of justice that we take for granted as its regular intrinsic accomplishment. The Court must begin to understand that its exercise of judicial prerogative, unstated and unstatable in clearly defined legal terms, is the bane, not the salvation, of the republic, and the evil it must avoid above all else. At the same time, religious minorities and their allies must seek to strengthen the bonds of friendship with their fellow citizens and persuade them to grant needed exemptions from ordinary laws wherever practicable. This is the only way to expand religious liberty in a manner consistent with the rule of law.

DEFINING RELIGION

To appreciate how casual the Court has become in its extreme presumption—that is, how regal—let us take a brief final look at two cases dealing with exemptions under the Draft Act, where it decided explicitly to redefine "religion" and thereby reverse the meaning of a federal statute. In *United States v. Seeger* (1965), by a vote of 9 to 0, the Court found for Seeger's claim to conscientious objector status, and in *Welsh v. United States* (1970), by a vote of 5 to 3 for Welsh. In the law, Congress had exempted from combatant training and service in the armed forces any persons "who by reason of their religious training and belief are conscientiously opposed to participation in war in any form." Religious training and belief in this connection means "an individual's belief in a relation to a Supreme Being involving duties superior to those arising from any human relation, but does not include essentially political, sociological or philosophical views or a merely personal moral code."[20] Seeger declared his opposition to war came from his religious belief. While preferring to leave the question of his relation to a Supreme Being open, he nevertheless spoke of his skepticism or disbelief in the existence of God. He claimed to believe in goodness or virtue for their own sakes and thus to have "a religious faith in a purely ethical creed."[21]

How could these admissions be saved from the obvious conclusion that Seeger was precisely the sort of person Congress did not wish to exempt? The Court unanimously declared its belief that "the test of belief 'in a relation to a Supreme Being' is whether a given belief that is sincere and meaningful occupies a place in the life of its possessor parallel to that filled by the orthodox belief in God of one who clearly qualifies for the exemption. Where such beliefs have parallel positions in the lives of their respective holders we cannot say that one is 'in a relation to a Supreme Being' and the other is not."[22] In short, what the Court said in this ridiculous and disgraceful passage is that a relation to a Supreme Being can be of two kinds: a relation to a Supreme Being and a relation *like* that to a Supreme Being, but without such a Being. Five years later, this "constructive" doctoring of the plain words of Congress for the sake of an effect contrary to that intended by Congress was carried to even more absurd lengths, but this time under bitter attack by the minority as arbitrary judicial legislation—a charge not a single member of the Court had seen fit to level in *Seeger*. Welsh actually *denied* having any kind of religious training and belief, but still the Court found that the historical, philosophical, and sociological views on which he based his opposition to war warranted exemption rather than the refusal of exemption Congress had so specifically demanded.

Speaking for himself and three others, Justice Black maintained that such views can be held "so firmly" as to be "religious" within the meaning of Congress's law.[23] The fifth vote came from Justice Harlan, who saw in the law an unconstitutional religious establishment favoring religion over non-religion—a mistaken view on his part, but of an entirely different sort from the meddling usurpation engaged in by the other four. These men, in the short run, managed to frustrate Congress's will and obstruct the draft—both tangible harms to the republic. But it is the penumbra of harm and the long range harm that arouse the most concern. For the Court has jeopardized the constitutional protection given "religion" by making that term unintelligible and impracticable. At the same time it has further lowered its own stature and added to doubts about its place in a system of republican government. Bound always by the intention of the lawmaker and by precedent—as Hamilton presumed it would be in famous defense of judicial review in *The Federalist*, Number 78—the judiciary provides constitutional democracy with vital stability. Unrestrained and on its own, the judiciary proves to be not the least dangerous branch of government, as Hamilton thought, but the most dangerous.

CONCLUSION

Regaining the Past
for the Present

A FEW YEARS BEFORE MADISON proposed the Bill of Rights in Congress, Hamilton (in *The Federalist*, Number 84) had expressed his skepticism about the need for such a bill. In particular, he was fearful that a provision guaranteeing the "liberty of the press" would prove impossible to define with precision. This fear the judicial experience of our time shows to have had some merit. Hamilton could not have been ignorant of the Blackstonian meaning the phrase "liberty of the press" had always had: he knew that meaning as well as any founder. But he must have wondered how its intricacies could be expressed in a simple phrase like "liberty of the press." Once the Supreme Court began to exercise the power of judicial review Hamilton himself favored, it might be in a position to pour into the abstract word "liberty" any meaning it chose.

Strange as it seems to us, the Court made no effort to do this for a very long time. On both state and national levels the old Blackstonian meaning persisted unchallenged for a century and a quarter. Only toward the end of World War 1, with Oliver Wendell Holmes Jr., did departures from it begin, and it took almost another half century for Holmes's new version to prevail completely. Today, after several decades of Holmesian orthodoxy on the bench and in the law schools, it is hard to remember any other state of affairs or to think of any alternative. Whatever the individual variations on the bench today, the Court has generally forgotten that most of our national history was conducted under such an alternative.

As a democracy, we might have been tempted to move toward extremes of liberty and equality from the very beginning. Had not Aristotle noted that the immoderate partisans of democracy (like those in oligarchy) tend to push the principles of their regime to extremes? But, in the area of civil liberties at least, this did not happen. The great impetus for movement in the direction of extreme liberty came not from within the system but from new philosophies and theories, mostly imported from abroad. These were thought to be truer than the philosophy of divinely bestowed and inalienable rights explicitly stated in our Declaration of Independence and underlying the Constitution.

The nineteenth century witnessed powerful utilitarian, historical and evolutionary attacks on old absolutes, including our own. Just after the middle of the century, John Stuart Mill supplied a new theoretical foundation for liberty, calling for its vast expansion in the name of freedom of thought. In the first half of the twentieth century, Freudian psychology, a new cosmology, the sciences of sociology and anthropology, and the philosophy of logical positivism all spread their unsettling influence among the educated. By the middle of the twentieth century, those end-products of modern thought—relativism and subjectivism—surged out of the graduate schools and colleges to affect Americans generally, including judges and lawyers.

It is hard to chart the judicial effects of these changes with precision, but we have already seen telltale marks of many of them. Holmes's reading John Stuart Mill into the First Amendment is perhaps the foremost. Justice Jackson's denial of an American orthodoxy in *West Virginia v. Barnette* is another. Then there is Justice Douglas's overt relativism in *Fanny Hill*, and the Court's extension of the meaning of "religion" to include atheistic beliefs operating in a manner similar to religion. Or think of the Court's decision to consider flag burning part of some "freedom of expression" guaranteed by the First Amendment—a decision that could not have been made without relativizing and subjectivizing the "freedom of speech and press."

These intellectual changes took many decades to affect daily life in this country. They could also be dressed out in American garb, as was the case with the idea of a "living" (and changing) Constitution that became so popular on and off the bench. Since they were taken to constitute great progress over the benighted views that preceded them, their growing influence made it easier for the Court to start discarding traditions and distinctions transmitted from the past. Nor, as the case of Holmes shows, was it always considered necessary to refute, or even take note of, precedents: Holmes created his "clear and present danger" principle without doing either. Decades later, precedent, far from being the constitutional mooring and ballast Hamilton expected in *The Federalist*, Number 78, often became a target for suspicion and rejection. After all, if progress was the rule, how could the old still be the good? Judges began to think of themselves as free to make law rather than submit to the "dead hand" of the founding fathers or precedent. Lawyers, with this vast opportunity opening before them, lost no time in concluding that it was their duty to challenge old precedents—at least when it suited their clients. It is in the midst of a hodgepodge of innovations and shredded remnants of old laws that we live today.

All three First Amendment areas we have studied show the effects of unwarranted and unwise judicial innovation, stimulated not by a change in the problems the nation faced—as is usually contended—but by a new way of thinking about old problems. Openness to revolutionary organizations, often paramilitary, with even explicit threats to the government and other citizens; allowance of obscenity and violence in the mass media, with their crude appeals to unbridled passion; reduction of the role of religion in public life—these have been with us for several decades now. Is their effect not obvious? Has so high an organ of government in any society ever done so much to prepare for the collapse and overthrow of that society—and all in the name of an abstract doctrine of freedom not derived from the founders at all? How long can we go on with policies that simultaneously corrupt our inner character and weaken our defenses?

In cases involving the First and Fourteenth Amendments together a double mistake was made: first the Court assumed a jurisdiction it did not rightly possess, then decided the issue wrongly as well. The incorporation of the First Amendment into the Fourteenth began as early as the *Gitlow* case (1925), with Justice Sanford, otherwise very traditional, simply assuming that the freedom of speech and press were so incorporated. But the argument on the other side has always been powerful—much more powerful. Ohio's statutes regarding criminal advocacy should not have been within the Court's jurisdiction, but given that jurisdiction, the Court (in *Brandenburg v. Ohio*) should not have forbidden Ohio to make the advocacy of "crime, sabotage or unlawful methods of terrorism" criminal. The burning of a flag in Texas should never have come before a federal court, but once it did (in *Texas v. Johnson*), burning the flag should not have had the mantle of First Amendment protection thrown over it through something called the "freedom of expression." The film *Carnal Knowledge* should have been subject to the jurisdiction of Georgia alone, but the Supreme Court then used the mistaken standards of *Miller* to find it not obscene. The Court had no business telling Rhode Island how to conduct its commencement exercises, but even so the decision banning a rabbi from offering nonsectarian prayers at graduation ceremonies (in *Lee v. Weisman*) rested on a false view of the establishment clause.

The Court has grown used to reading its own philosophy into the First and Fourteenth Amendments and enjoying its vastly expanded power. In fact, the judiciary generally has assumed so influential, so pervasive, and so dominant a position in American life as to affect significantly our form of government. By its interpretation of the Fourteenth Amendment it has swept a host of state and local matters within the orbit of its authority. And by magnifying the range of issues it is willing to consider, at the same time that it reduced the authority of precedent, it has made itself not only the court of last appeal but often the court of first appeal at every level. "Let the courts decide," "Flout the law and bring it to the courts" have become maxims not only of daily existence but of legal training as well. This significant alteration of our affairs is now an accepted, and usually unremarked, fact of life, but it should not be welcomed. Its effect—sometimes abetted by the other branches themselves—is to remove matters from democratic decision-making and bend the government toward arbitrary oligarchy. The people become less responsible for solving their own problems, the courts more overbearing. But the courts have become more easily targeted too since they now frustrate the will of the people over a much larger range of issues. This problem is compounded by the sense the public is beginning to gather from the experts that there are only partisan, not objective, interpretations of the Constitution. The reasons for establishing an independent judiciary, armed with judicial review, start to dwindle and disappear.

The cure is not to eliminate the independent judiciary. It certainly is not to abandon liberal democracy itself. A nation that could win the love and admiration of Washington and Lincoln, Hamilton, Madison and Jefferson, that could produce so much virtue in its leaders and citizens, and so many outstanding men and women in almost every field of endeavor, that could endure a civil war and end slavery in its own midst, that could for so long offer liberty, equality, security, and opportunity to oppressed peoples everywhere, that could undertake to save Europe and the world twice, once from unspeakable barbarism, is no ordinary nation. It has taken some wrong and dangerous turns—not by malice, but by superficial thinking that on the Court could merge with a quite ordinary love of power. Believing themselves superior to the founders, certain justices became eager to invest the old texts with their own superior meanings. They failed to realize that our foundations in the Declaration of Independence and the Constitution must be preserved in their original form, that we are not free to abandon or replace them, that we cannot change horses—or societies—in midstream.

It also turns out that the principles we have been asked to switch to are not only alien to what the founders—all the founders—thought and wanted, but greatly inferior as well. So powerful has the founders' idea of human rights proved itself, that it became and still remains—if in somewhat attenuated form—the world's dominant political principle. It may even be said that Thomas Jefferson and the Continental Congress gave this idea not only its earliest but its most perfect expression, beyond what Mill or anyone else could provide for practical political guidance. Thus, in clinging to our tradition we cling to something good as well as old, something that does not deserve to be—any more than it can successfully be—abandoned. Supplementing it, even modifying or adjusting it, may be necessary, much in the manner of Lincoln, but only after accepting it in its own terms.

If we retrace our steps and find where we went wrong, the Courts can be brought back to their essential but more restricted role in American life. If they understand the situation, they themselves should have the strongest motives for doing this. The arguments for judicial review in our constitutional system are sound, but only in areas properly subject to judicial authority. Hamilton (in *The Federalist*, Number 78) argued that the courts had to have the power of declaring laws unconstitutional in cases where there was a manifest inconsistency between the Constitution and the laws. The word "manifest" that he first uses there suggests a trait obvious to all or most people who look. This makes it possible for the decision of a few judges appointed for life to receive a kind of democratic approval from the nation at large. As the Court stretches its review into areas less manifest, however, and also becomes more divided within itself, its rightful authority to decide constitutionality becomes correspondingly less clear. When the Court struck down national and state legislation directed against the Communist Party, state laws suppressing obscenity, state provisions for nonsectarian school prayer—all on interpretations of the First Amendment that were hardly manifest—it began to undermine its own authority. To regain the confidence of the American people, it must systematically retrench its powers and return to that limited sphere in which its powers are undeniably proper, and with a better understanding of the First Amendment itself.

The First Amendment is not difficult to interpret. It was not intended to change the body of the Constitution but to stipulate expressly certain limitations on the national government in the name of republican government. It has two main parts, one religious, the other political, reminiscent of the distinction in John Locke's writings (the Locke from whom they drew their fundamental political principles) between his *Letter on Toleration* and his *Second Treatise of Government*. In the former work the religious question is settled in favor of religious liberty; in the latter, the role of government in civil society can be concentrated on with hardly a mention of religion, since it is at that point assumed to be a simply private affair. Locke's approach seems to have been adopted in the First Amendment too. Its framers must have taken it for granted that they could deal with civil or political questions only after the religious question is removed from contention. This explains why the amendment begins by preventing a national religious establishment (while also keeping Congress from interfering with state establishments), and protects the private practice of all religions. That accomplished, it turns its attention to the means whereby the new national government can be kept responsive to the people. The freedom of speech and press is linked with the right to assemble peaceably and petition the government because all are necessary, together, for sustaining the public and open criticism essential to republican government. Given this simple reading, the idea that the First Amendment was meant to protect the propagating of ideas and the building of organizations for the purpose of destroying republican government collapses instantly. This idea, unchallenged on the Court for some time, came from John Stuart Mill, not the framers.

This general understanding of the nature of the First Amendment is the most important step necessary to appreciating what it meant to its framers, and what it must mean for us. By sticking to this plain and direct reading, without importing latter-day philosophies, we have a sure guideline to follow. All that has to be added is the meaning of the individual elements of the statement—of "establishment of religion" and "freedom of speech and press" particularly. This we have attempted to do in considerable detail and need not repeat here. Despite the chorus of nay-sayers on the other side, it *is* possible to discover original meanings. Even in this difficult case, we are perfectly capable of ascertaining and understanding the meaning of the framers. And as Blackstone maintained, to be guided by a law is first and foremost to be guided by the intention the lawgiver expressed in the words of the law itself. Whether the law was passed by Congress yesterday or by the First Congress in combination with the states in 1791 is irrelevant: the same principle holds in both cases. The First Amendment must mean for us what the framers and ratifiers took it to mean when they passed it. Any other view not only violates the very notion of what a law is but can only lead to chaos, since it will have removed the sole element giving a law its objective fixity.

It is vital that the Court be made to withdraw its claim to incorporate the First Amendment into the Fourteenth. This would free the states to follow their own constitutions and signal a return to the federal structure set up by the post–Civil War Amendments. Understood in this way, the prime object of the Fourteenth Amendment was not to guarantee liberties to whites but to guarantee that the states granted the same liberties to blacks that they did to whites. It would then be up to the states to handle the local dimension of revolutionary parties, obscenity, and religion, as well as a host of other issues, in their own way. Nothing is better calculated to revive the self-reliance of the states, which in most of this century has been so worn down that the states themselves, losing the very sense of it, have been content to do nothing to regain the powers taken from them. It would also clear the Supreme Court's calendar of many an issue into which its intrusion was a source of embarrassment (for example, by its having to watch movies charged with obscenity), at the same time making way for issues of greater national importance. The excessive crowding of its calendar about which the Court has been complaining for some time—a crowding entirely of its own making—would be drastically reduced if not eliminated.

Even more important than correcting the Court's misinterpretation of the Fourteenth Amendment is correcting its misreading of the First. It should not be impossible for the Court to give up the "clear and present danger" requirement, returning to the principle that preceded it. This principle, expressed so well by Justice Sanford in his much-reviled *Gitlow* opinion, looks to the threat of criminal dangers without insisting on their imminence. While modernizing intellectuals will not easily surrender their Holmesian and Millian corruption of the First Amendment, the return to the original would be welcomed by the public and its representative bodies as we begin to face dangers of unknown magnitude from paramilitary groups and international terrorists. It will have the additional benefit of rendering more secure those citizens singled out by such groups for disenfranchisement or extermination. Protected from the outset by both state and national governments, these citizens will no longer feel that they must face such threats alone, thus adding considerably to the internal solidarity of the citizen body as a whole.

The various biases inherent in the Court's treatment of religion could also be corrected without very great difficulty: the First Amendment does not require the government to have nothing to do with religion or to be neutral between believers and non-believers. That said, it is still true that the Constitution established a government that in its essential ends is based on reason, not faith, thus providing the basis for uniting people of all faiths and beliefs behind it. By this Constitution, along with the First Amendment, they are all protected in what they deem most valuable. If they fully understood the importance of religion in sustaining American democracy, they would not begrudge the mild favoritism the First Amendment allows religion over irreligion, where appropriate.

Obscenity is the one area I have treated in this book in which the First Amendment's support for our earlier constitutional tradition would face enormous obstacles. There is no question that every last one of the founders and framers would be shocked and deeply alarmed by what has for some time been the nation's daily fare in movies, television, recordings, books and magazines. In fact, the whole country, as late as 1960, would have been shocked by what a large number acquiesce in or dote on forty years later. One does not have to be a member of the religious right to realize that what we are facing is a very grave threat to society as a whole and to it members as individuals. When the founders envisaged the kind of human being they were seeking to form, they pictured traits deserving of respect and admiration. American democracy was to elevate the average man, encourage his independent self-care and prosperity, release his potential for improvement, cultivate his devotion to principles of justice and human welfare generally. But under the Court's new dispensation, the mass media have been free to appeal to lower and lower elements of our nature, and especially to encourage passions of lust and violence that make civilized life impossible. The founders wanted to make everyone gentlemen; the mass media are trying to make everyone brutes, lechers, and slobs.

Our first tendency with respect to the mass media is to regard them, in their most recent forms, as great technological advances over what preceded them. And our general and natural tendency, in a society which in its very Constitution encourages the arts and sciences, is to let technology alone. This would especially be appropriate if it were thought that the mass media have only an enlightening or entertaining effect—they would then seem on a par with all the other technological advances we celebrate, like the electric light, the car, and the airplane. But what if their effect is mixed, or largely bad? As a nation we are not used to judging the effects of technology on character and taste, but that issue has been thrust on us by what the individual owners of the mass media have seen fit to incorporate in their products. While we still possess enough of our moral capacity, whether derived from religious or rational sources, we can sense the danger we are in and think about the best course to take. How much of the old American character remains, hidden from the limelight provided by reporters and talk-show pundits, nobody knows. If a good deal remains, we can still right ourselves, refusing to be deterred by the screams of the networks, studios, advertisers, and producers or First Amendment extremists. The parallel example is air pollution. The mass media are the pollutants of the soul, having it in their power to do gradual, often invisible, but definite harm by degrading our thinking, our ideals, our character, taste, and conduct. No democracy worthy of the name can permit itself to be destroyed by this kind of internal force.

The main difficulty here is not protecting children alone: it is protecting everybody from a subtle assault on the sensibilities that over a period of time will leave few unaffected. The thought that the products older people enjoy can be kept from affecting the young, one way or another, is entirely baseless. Again, the parallel with air pollution holds true. What is in the air for adults will be in the air for children. Clearing the moral atmosphere in which we unthinkingly permit ourselves to breathe will therefore require across-the-board solutions in some cases. Especially worrisome are the movies, television shows, recordings, videos, and sleazy books and magazines. Those that can affect large numbers of people all at once may need to be examined prior to publication; it may suffice to hold the others legally responsible after publication.

The relevant parts of our Blackstonian tradition are there to be revived in this hour of need. Remember the way Chief Justice Hughes listed the exceptions to the freedom of the press in *Near v. Minnesota* (1931). Among the areas requiring prior rather than subsequent restraint, he included, as a matter of course, enforcing "the primary requirements of decency" against obscene publications. Nor is it only our own nation that the actions we undertake would serve. We are still the beacon for democracies everywhere, and the standard by which they often judge themselves. They are more likely to tolerate Communist and Nazi parties if we do. They will be more open to obscenity and violence in the mass media if we are, and if we stand ready to export our pernicious products for their consumption. If we give religion a more prominent position in public life, they are likely to do so too. This may not hold in every case, but the more impressive our character as a nation, the more democracies, especially the younger and newer ones, will admire our accomplishments and look upon our longevity as assured.

We have lived, and are still living, through a period of unprecedented license. Nowhere on the face of the globe, at any time in history, has such a massive experiment with standards of good and evil been attempted. We have been like alcoholics or drug addicts, pulled ever more deeply into our habit, apparently enjoying this new freedom from traditional restraints, and utterly unable to comprehend just how sick we are. The violence portrayed becomes ever more barbaric, the sex more tawdry, the boorishness more general, the ugly and menacing more unforgettable. It is impossible to believe that these have no relation to the fact that crime and drugs are rampant, the illegitimacy rate unbelievable, the family in tatters, the young often ungovernable. Our music and literature have all but disappeared. Even those popular songs that kept poetry alive in the soul of the average man have given way to the most primitive chants and rhythms. If this descent has taken place in only a few decades, what can we expect in a few more? Will the moral characteristics necessary to sustaining a democracy survive this onslaught? Did we beat down barbarism abroad only to find ourselves breeding it at home?

The renewal we need must be moral, rational, and spiritual all at once. The incentive for it can be furnished not by some artificial vision of America's future but by the memory of her past. We have allowed ourselves to be pulled from our natural moorings and now live immersed in a world artificially molded by technological advances and the mass media. A Sierra Club that brings us back occasionally to the natural wilds is not enough. It is in the texture of our everyday lives that we must attempt to regain the marvelous simplicity that was ours for so long. It is in cultivating the memory of our past—our great accomplishments as a nation, our outstanding individuals, our pious, sober, and loving families, our great authors and artists, our active industries, our music, folk and popular—that we can best keep from being engulfed by the present and renew our democratic humanity in the highest sense. Whether or not this can be done we do not know, but whoever finds practical ways of doing it will earn the eternal gratitude of his countrymen, and of the world besides. We have perhaps been the world's most forward-looking nation: now we must look backward, regaining the past for the present, in order to be able to look forward well again.

A Glossary of
Supreme Court Decisions

PART I

REVOLUTIONARY GROUPS

1   1919 *Schenck v. United States* (249 U.S. 47): In a 9 to o decision, the Court upheld the Espionage Act of 1917 against Schenck's mailings to draftees urging them to resist the draft. Holmes made the first explicit statement of the "clear and present danger" rule in the opinion he wrote for the Court.

2   1919 *Frohwerk v. United States* (249 U.S. 204): In a 9 to o decision, the Court upheld the Espionage Act of 1917 against Frohwerk's newspaper articles attacking the war and the draft. Holmes wrote the opinion for the Court.

3   1919 *Abrams v. United States* (250 U.S. 616): By a 7 to 2 vote, the Court upheld Abrams's conviction under the Sedition Act for urging workers to resist the Allied military intervention against the Bolsheviks in Russia. Holmes was joined by Brandeis in dissent.

4   1925 *Gitlow v. New York* (268 U.S. 652): By a vote of 7 to 2, the Court upheld New York's Criminal Anarchy Act against Gitlow's "Left-Wing Manifesto." Holmes and Brandeis dissented in the name of the "clear and present danger" rule, which Sanford, writing for the majority, rejected.

5   1927 *Whitney v. California* (274 U.S. 357): The Court, by a vote of 9 to 0, upheld Whitney's conviction under California's Criminal Syndicalism Act, which made it a crime to advocate, and organize to advocate, the commission of crime, sabotage, etc. In a separate opinion, Brandeis, joined by Holmes, concurred.

6   1951 *Dennis v. United States* (341 U.S. 494): Speaking through Chief Justice Vinson (with concurrences by Frankfurter and Jackson), the Court, by a 6 to 2 vote, upheld the conviction of eleven leaders of the American Communist Party under the Smith Act. This Act made it a crime to advocate, and organize to advocate, the overthrow of the government by force or violence, or by assassinating any officer of the government. Black and Douglas dissented.

7   1952 *Beauharnais v. Illinois* (343 U.S. 250): By a 5 to 4 vote, the Court upheld the conviction of Beauharnais, under Illinois's "group libel" law, for publicly exhibiting attacks on the Negro race. Dissenting were Douglas, Black, Jackson, and Reed.

8   1969 *Brandenburg v. Ohio* (395 U.S. 44): By a 9 to 0 vote the Court struck down the conviction of a KKK leader and the Ohio statute under which he was convicted making it a crime to advocate "crime, sabotage or unlawful methods of terrorism."

PART II

OBSCENITY

1   1931 *Near v. Minnesota* (283 U.S. 697): By a 5 to 4 decision, the Court struck down the Minnesota statute applied against Near, finding it in violation of the freedom of the press as guaranteed by the Fourteenth Amendment against the states. Chief Justice Hughes spoke for the Court and presented an important summary of the meaning of the freedom of the press. He even conceded that four specific abuses of the press deserved *prior* restraint, including one by which "the primary requirements of decency may be enforced against obscene publications."

2   1952 *Burstyn v. Wilson* (343 U.S. 495): The Court unanimously declared (9

to o) the movies to be part of the press and then found the banning of *The Miracle* as "sacrilegious" a violation of the freedom of the press guaranteed by the Fourteenth Amendment.

3   1957 *Roth v. United States* (also *Alberts v. California*) (354 U.S. 476): These were the opening cases on obscenity, and were decided by 6 to 3 and 7 to 2 votes. In them the Court upheld Roth's conviction and the federal obscenity statute dealing with the mails, while giving obscenity a new legal definition in terms of appeal to prurient interest.

4   1959 *Kingsley International Picture Corporation v. Regents* (360 U.S. 684): With many variant concurrences, the Court unanimously struck down New York's refusal to allow the showing of *Lady Chatterley's Lover* because of its "portrayal of acts of sexual immorality as desirable." This, the Court maintained, was to obstruct the advocacy of ideas and hence to violate the First Amendment.

5   1962 *Manual Enterprises v. Day* (371 U.S. 478): By a vote of 6 to 1, the Court reversed the banning from the mails of magazines featuring pictures of nude males. It emphasized "patent offensiveness" as well as appeal to prurient interest (from *Roth*) for a finding of obscenity.

6   1964 *Jacobellis v. Ohio* (378 U.S. 184): By a 6 to 3 vote, the Court reversed Ohio's banning as obscene a French motion picture called *Les Amants*. It insisted that only something utterly lacking in social value could be considered legally obscene, and also required that the item in question be found to offend a national standard of decency.

7   1966 *A Book Named "John Cleland's Memoirs of a Woman of Pleasure" v. Attorney General of Massachusetts* (383 U.S. 413): By a vote of 6 to 3, the Court reversed the conviction of this erstwhile classic of pornography, better known as *Fanny Hill*, finding that it had some literary and historical value and could therefore not be considered obscene.

8   1966 *Ginzburg v. United States* (383 U.S. 463): Voting 5 to 4, the Court affirmed Ginzburg's conviction for mailing obscene erotic materials, using Ginzburg's own advertising as evidence against him.

9   1966 *Mishkin v. New York* (383 U.S. 502): Voting 6 to 3, the Court affirmed Mishkin's conviction for producing and selling books that appealed to the prurient interest of the deviant group for which they were written.

10   1973 *Miller v. California* (413 U.S. 15): Speaking for a majority of five, Chief Justice Burger upheld Miller's conviction for sending obscene literature through the mails, while reviewing the Court's understanding of obscenity and the tests for it. The "no social value" requirement was changed to a "no serious value" requirement. At the same time, the obscenity unprotected by the First Amendment was further reduced to hardcore pornography.

11   1973 *Paris Adult Theater v. Slaton* (413 U.S. 502): Also by 5 to 4, Chief Justice Burger remitted a film found obscene in Georgia for reconsideration in the light of the tests laid down in *Miller.*

12   1974 *Jenkins v. Georgia* (418 U.S. 153): By 9 to 0, the Court decided that the film *Carnal Knowledge* could not be found obscene by the standards laid down in *Miller.*

PART III
CHURCH AND STATE

1   1873   The Slaughterhouse Cases (16 Wallace 36): By a vote of 5 to 4, the Court denied that the virtual monopoly of slaughtering in New Orleans granted by the legislature violated the first section of the Fourteenth Amendment. The majority and minority interpreted its "privileges and immunities" provision very differently.

2   1940   *Cantwell v. Connecticut* (310 U.S. 296): A unanimous Court overturned Cantwell's conviction for soliciting funds for religious purposes without a license and inciting a breach of the peace, all in the course of missionary work for Jehovah's Witnesses. The Court expressly took for granted that the freedoms of the First Amendment were guaranteed against the states by the Fourteenth Amendment.

3   1940 *Minersville School District v. Gobitis* (310 U.S. 586): With only Stone

dissenting, Frankfurter spoke for the remaining eight justices in affirming Pennsylvania's right to expel the children of Jehovah's Witnesses from public school for refusing, on religious grounds, to salute the flag and pledge allegiance.

4   1943   *West Virginia Board of Education v. Barnette* (319 U.S. 624): With Frankfurter among the three dissenters, Jackson spoke for six justices in reversing *Gobitis* and siding with Barnette. In an oft-quoted passage, Jackson denied that a national orthodoxy can rightfully be forced on school children through such things as salutes and pledges.

5   1947   *Everson v. Board of Education* (330 U.S. 1): By a vote of 5 to 4, the Court, speaking through Black, affirmed New Jersey's right to fund transportation for parochial as well as public school pupils. The highlight of the case is Black's statement about the meaning of the establishment clause.

6   1948   *Illinois ex. rel. McCollum v. Board of Education* (333 U.S. 203): Voting 8 to 1, the Court struck down Illinois's "released time" program allowing religious instruction in the public schools as a violation of the establishment clause.

7   1952   *Zorach v. Clauson* (343 U.S. 306): Speaking through Douglas, the Court voted 6 to 3 to allow New York's "dismissed time" program for religious instruction off school grounds.

8   1961   *Torcaso v. Watkins* (367 U.S. 488): All nine justices voted to strike down Maryland's constitutional provision requiring all public officials to swear to a belief in God. The provision was considered violative of the establishment clause in the First Amendment, made applicable against the states by the Fourteenth.

9   1962   *Engel v. Vitale* (370 U.S. 421): Speaking for six justices with only one dissenting, Black denied the constitutionality of a nonsectarian prayer prepared for the public schools by New York's Board of Regents.

10   1963   *Abington School District v. Schempp* (374 U.S. 203): Voting 8 to 1, the Court struck down as an unconstitutional establishment Pennsylvania's re-

quiring the reading of Bible verses at the beginning of each school day. Government must neither help nor hinder religion, said the Court.

11 1963 *Sherbert v. Verner* (374 U.S. 398): By a vote of 7 to 2, the Court ruled that only the existence of a compelling state interest can require a person to obey a valid secular law that violates his religious conscience.

12 1965 *United States v. Seeger* (380 U.S. 163): By a vote of 9 to 0, the Court upheld Seeger's claim to conscientious objector status despite its not being based on the belief in God required by federal law.

13 1968 *Board of Education v. Allen* (392 U.S. 236): Voting 6 to 3, the Court affirmed a New York state law compelling local public schools to lend textbooks to students free of charge, including students in parochial schools.

14 1970 *Walz v. Tax Commission* (397 U.S. 664): By a vote of 7 to 1, the Court affirmed the constitutionality of New York tax exemptions for religious organizations on property used solely for religious purposes. Maintaining that religion is not thereby established, the Court added that the effect to be avoided is "excessive government entanglement with religion."

15 1970 *Welsh v. United States* (398 U.S. 333): By a vote of 5 to 3, Welsh's claim to draft exemption was granted on grounds similar to Seeger's. The three dissenters thought the majority construed the federal legislation in a manner that went far beyond its language and intention.

16 1971 *Lemon v. Kurtzman* (403 U.S. 602): Speaking for varying majorities of seven and six, Burger denied the constitutionality of state funding of those teaching secular subjects in church-related schools, formulating a three-part test: a statute must have a secular purpose, a principal effect that neither helps nor harms religion, and must not lead to excessive government entanglement with religion.

17 1972 *Wisconsin v. Yoder* (406 U.S. 205): By a vote of 6 to 1, the Court made it impossible for Wisconsin to compel Amish students to remain in school till age 16. The public interest in their doing so was ruled not compelling.

18   1983   *Marsh v. Chambers* (463 U.S. 783): By a vote of 6 to 3, the Court upheld the right of the Nebraska legislature to sponsor a chaplaincy.

19   1985   *Wallace v. Jaffree* (472 U.S. 38): By a 6 to 3 vote, the Court decided that Alabama could not authorize its public schools to observe a moment of silence. Rehnquist's dissent argued that the establishment clause was directed solely against the preference for one religion over the others.

20   1990   *Employment Division, Department of Human Resources of Oregon v. Smith* (494 U.S. 827): By a vote of 5 to 3, the Court decided that the free exercise clause did not compel Oregon to exempt members of the peyote-using Native American Church from its anti-drug laws.

21   1992   *Lee v. Weisman* (505 U.S. 577): By a vote of 5 to 4, the Court held it unconstitutional for Rhode Island to have a clergyman (in this case a rabbi) give nonsectarian prayers at middle and high school graduation ceremonies. Souter's concurrence examined the origin of the establishment clause and opposed Rehnquist's conclusions in *Wallace v. Jaffree*.

Notes

1 *Present Dangers*

1   The tendency in western and western-style democracies after World War II to ban totalitarian parties of both right and left, or severely restrict them (unless, of course, they were already too big, as in France and Italy), has given way to an almost universal tendency to treat Communists at least as legal equals. In Germany both Communist and Nazi parties used to be illegal, then only the Nazi. And when the new Spanish and Portuguese democracies were formed, they made no attempt to inhibit their Communist parties.

2   Some relevant cases are: *Yates v. United States* (1957), *Baggett v. Bullitt* (1964), *Elfbrandt v. Russell* (1966), *Keyishian v. Board of Regents of New York* (1967), *Baird v. State Bar* (1971).

3   395 U.S. 44 (1969). This is the view espoused by Brandeis and Holmes in *Whitney* (1927), shorn of some of its more eccentric features.

4   *Communist Party of Indiana v. Whitcomb* (1974).

2 *Interpreting the Constitution*

1   After *Dennis v. United States*, 341 U.S. 494 (1951), Justices Black and Douglas abandoned the "clear and present danger" rule they had hitherto accepted from Holmes and Brandeis, and tried to tie punishable speech or press to that which is coupled with immediate criminal action. See their brief concurrence in *Brandenburg*. The rarely held absolute interpretation of the First Amendment received some prominence from Alexander Meiklejohn in *Free Speech and Its Relation to Self-Govern-*

ment (New York: Harper, 1948). It was also defended by Thomas I. Emerson in his *The System of Freedom of Expression* (New York: Random House, 1969).

2   William Blackstone, *Commentaries on the Laws of England*, 4 vols. (London, 1765-69), vol. I, p. 59.

3   Ibid., vol. IV, pp. 152-53.

4   Ibid., pp. 150-51, for the definitions of libels. See also note 2 to chapter 5, for the higher crimes involving words.

5   *The Constitution of the United States of America: Analysis and Interpretation*, for the year 1952 (edited by Edward S. Corwin), pp. 769-70. Frankfurter's opinion is in *Dennis v. United States*, 341 U.S. at 524.

6   Leonard Levy, *Legacy of Suppression* (Cambridge, Mass.: Harvard University Press, 1960), pp. 237, 247-48. The title expresses Levy's disapproval of Blackstone, the framers of the First Amendment, and the Adams Federalists. But his own libertarianism makes him critical of the Jeffersonians too for leaving Blackstonian powers of suppression to the states. His conclusion destroys a similar historical claim Justice Black took for granted in *Bridges*, 314 U.S. 252, 264 (1941): "To assume that English common law in this field became ours is to deny the generally accepted historical belief that 'one object of the Revolution was to get rid of the English common law on liberty of speech and the press.' More specifically, it is to forget the environment in which the First Amendment was ratified."

7   Terrence Murphy says the Pennsylvania Constitution of 1790 was the first to add to its guarantee of the freedom of speech and press an express statement of the legal liability for abusing that freedom. Thereafter, the phrase "being responsible for the abuse of that liberty" became a standard part of state constitutions, with at least forty-three of them containing such a phrase by the time he wrote (1963). See his *Censorship: Government and Obscenity*, pp. 111-12. This demonstrates the degree to which the prevailing view of speech and press remained Blackstonian from the very creation of the Bill of Rights onward. Many excerpts from these constitutions can be found in Theodore Schroeder, *Obscene Literature and Constitutional Law* (private, N.Y., 1911), ch. 10.

8   See *The Mind of the Founder: Sources of the Political Thought of James Madison*, edited by Marvin Meyers (Indianapolis: Bobbs-Merrill, 1973), pp. 297-352.

9   The report, called the Address of the Minority, appeared in the *Journal of the Virginia House of Delegates*, Dec. 1798, pp. 88-90, and also as a pamphlet published in Richmond that same year. It can be found, slightly cut, in John Roche's edition of *John Marshall: Major Opinions and Other Writings* (Indianapolis: Bobbs-Merrill, 1967), pp. 32-48.

10   Quoted in Robert K. Faulkner's *The Jurisprudence of John Marshall* (Princeton, N.J.: Princeton University Press, 1968), p. 88, note. Faulkner joins Albert Beveridge, Marshall's best-known biographer, in recognizing the Minority Report as

Marshall's and approving its logic. Roche, in his edition of Marshall's writings, does so as well, calling Marshall's reasoning from the powers of the national government "ingenious." See Beveridge, *Life of Marshall* (Boston: Houghton Mifflin, 1916), vol. II, pp. 404-405, 388-89, 451-52; also Roche, pp. 32-48. Irving Brant makes an extensive effort to rebut this argument of Marshall's in *The Bill of Rights: Its Origin and Meaning* (New York: Mentor, 1967), ch. 24. But Marshall's report and its argument go unmentioned in Leonard Levy's *Legacy* and also in his essay, "Liberty and the First Amendment: 1790-1800," in *Origins of American Political Thought*, edited by John Roche for Harper Torchbooks (1967). This causes Levy to present a very one-sided view of the Alien and Sedition Acts. We should add that some doubt about Marshall's authorship of the Minority Report has been raised by the editors of his papers.

11　Meyers, pp. 342-45.

12　Ibid., p. 336.

13　Quoted from his letter to Abigail Adams in Walter Berns's *The First Amendment and the Future of Democracy* (New York: Basic Books, 1976), pp. 82, 111. My emphasis.

14　Corwin, pp. 770-71.

15　The common law origin of this principle is given by Rollin M. Perkins in *Criminal Law and Procedure* (Brooklyn, N.Y.: Foundation Press, 1952), p. 243: "At common law, it is a misdemeanor for one to counsel, incite or solicit another to commit either a felony or a misdemeanor, certainly so if the misdemeanor is of an aggravated character, *even though the solicitation is of no effect, and the crime counseled is not in fact committed.*" My emphasis.

16　Quoted in Samuel Konefsky, *The Legacy of Holmes and Brandeis* (New York: Collier Books, 1961), p. 180. The passage is from *Masses Publishing Co. v. Patten*. For the role of majority rule and the obligation to obey duly constituted law, see Locke's discussion in his *Second Treatise*, sections 95-97 and 134. Concerning this obligation he says: "And thus every man, by consenting with others to make one body politic under one government, puts himself under an obligation to every one of that society to submit to the determination of the majority, and to be concluded by it; or else this original compact, whereby he with others incorporates into one society, would signify noth-ing. . . ."

17　In the Constitution: I, 8: 15; IV, 4; III, 3; VI, 2, 3; II, 1: 8. A strange position is taken by George Anastaplo on this issue of using words to stimulate federal crimes. Treason, sabotage and espionage number among such crimes, he admits, since they form no part of "the ordinary process of self-government." Yet he fails to cite overthrow of the government as an action the federal government can rightly make criminal. In addition, he argues, with the "absolutists," that words can be made criminal only if they incite to immediate criminal acts—a rule he establishes by fiat rather than by constitutional argument, and one running counter to his own view that the First Amendment leaves all authority over speech and press to the states. See *The Constitutionalist: Notes on the First Amendment* (Dallas: Southern Methodist Univ. Press, 1971), 112, 120, 124, 127, 543 (note 121), and 520 (note 66).

18 In his massive work, Thomas I. Emerson begins his treatment of "solicitation to crime" by defining it comprehensively, accurately, and very traditionally: "The offense of solicitation to crime includes, broadly speaking, not only the common law crime of solicitation, but various statutory provisions making it an offence to solicit, advise, counsel, aid, abet, or otherwise induce a crime." Perfect. Then, using his own "theory of expression," distinguishing expression, which as such is totally protected, from action, which is not, he reduces criminal solicitation to using words to incite to, or as part of, an immediate criminal action. For consistency, Emerson should at that point have gone back and rewritten, along these wholly untraditional lines, the original definition of solicitation from which he began. For he has utterly gutted it by his own "theory." And in so doing he has added to a demonstrably false view of the original meaning of the First Amendment an even more imprudent view of both federal and state authority than the "clear and present danger" rule itself. See Emerson, p. 403.

19 The Supreme Court vindicated state "group libel" laws in *Beauharnais v. Illinois*, 343 U.S. 250 (1952).

20 See Hamilton's description in *The Federalist*, Number 1.

21 See the beginning of Madison's *The Federalist*, Number 10.

22 The new libertarianism of 1800, which Levy himself favors, claimed the utmost latitude under the First Amendment, he tells us, for even the most radical political criticism in order ". . . to keep the electorate free, informed, and capable of making intelligent choices." But Levy fails to show—using twentieth-century examples—whether this would necessitate tolerating a Communist Party, Nazi Party, or KKK, for it is hardly clear how doing so might assist in keeping the electorate "free, informed, and capable of making intelligent choices." That it would have the opposite effect is much clearer. Furthermore, Levy ignores the obvious fact that this so-called libertarianism presumes, in its very statement, that what the people want above all is republican government and nothing but republican government. It is still founded on the "rights of man," and hence hardly has that openness to nonrepublican popular choices found in Holmes and Brandeis. It is certainly not "libertarianism" in their sense. See Levy's aforementioned essay in Roche's *Origins of American Political Thought*, p. 271.

23 Even by 1800, the new libertarianism was represented by only a very small, if vocal, minority of men like Tunis Wortman and St. George Tucker. See Levy, ch. 6.

3 *The Constitutional Revolution of Holmes and Brandeis*

1   Quoted by the dissenters in *Near v. Minnesota* 283 U.S. 697, 732-33 (1931), from the fifth edition of Story's work.

2   Cited in Corwin, pp. 772-73 (133 U.S. 333, 341-42).

3   See note 16, p. 22.

4   Corwin, p. 773 (236 U.S. 273).

5   Quoted in Konefsky, p. 173 (205 U.S. 454, at 462).

6   *Frohwerk v. United States*, 249 U.S. 204 (1919).

7   *Schenck v. United States*, 249 U.S. 47, 51-52 (1919).

8   *Abrams v. United States*, 250 U.S. 616, 627 (1919).

9   See note 6, p. 13.

10 *Gitlow v. New York*, 268 U.S. 652, 673 (1925).

11 *Whitney v. California* (274 U.S. 357), end of fifth paragraph.

12 Ibid., end of ninth paragraph.

13 Zachariah Chafee, *Free Speech in the United States* (New York: Harcourt Brace, 1920), p. 23.

14 Emerson explicitly criticizes the "clear and present danger" rule and even the dichotomy between advocacy and incitement as too vague, useless in practice, and improperly restrictive of expression protected by the First Amendment. Emerson, p. 124.

15 Compare, for example, Brandeis's statement with Madison's much more famous statement in *The Federalist*, Number 10, that the protection of the "faculties of men" from which the rights of property originate is "the first object of government." In Locke's *Second Treatise* individuals consent to join together in political society and to establish government solely to secure their inalienable rights to "life, liberty and property"—which together are later summed up in the one word "property" as everything that is one's own.

16 From the very end of Lincoln's Sub-Treasury speech in the Illinois House, Dec. 26, 1839. See Basler's edition of Lincoln's *Works* (New Brunswick, N.J.: Rutgers University Press, 1953), vol. i, pp. 178-79.

17 *The Complete Jefferson*, edited by Saul Padover (New York: Duell, Sloan and Pearce, 1943), p. 947.

18 Ibid., p. 675.

19 See the discussion of this political creed in Berns, p. 83, and in Meyers's *Madison*, pp. 442-46.

4 *The New Founding Father*

1   Mill's illustration of the limits that must be placed on freedom of speech and press

is better than Holmes's example (in *Schenck*) of falsely shouting "fire" in a crowded theater. Mill distinguishes between the use of press, speech, and placards: "An opinion that corn-dealers are starvers of the poor, or that private property is robbery, ought to be unmolested when simply circulated through the press, but may justly incur punishment when delivered orally to an excited mob assembled before the house of a corn-dealer, or when handed about among the same mob in the form of a placard" (beginning of ch. 3 of *On Liberty*). Mill does not take up the case of calls in the press for specified acts of violence to specified groups, including corn-dealers or wealthy property owners (to follow his examples), or for the violation of particular laws. He would allow the press to call private property robbery: would he allow it to call for the violent seizure of some or all such property?

2 For a much broader survey of Holmes's thought than is attempted here, and a comparison with John Marshall's, see Faulkner, Appendix I. According to Faulkner, "Holmes went so far as to speak of his 'ideal' as a 'commonwealth where science is everywhere supreme.'"

3 Holmes's tendency to lay down constitutional interpretation *ex cathedra*, without even the attempt at inference from the written Constitution, was noted by early critics like Corwin and Powell: see Konefsky, pp. 190, 193. Critics also took note of the inconsistency between his defiance of the legislative branch in regulating speech and press, and his having become "the chief exponent of deference to legislative choice" in matters of economic regulation: Konefsky again, pp. 213–215.

4 Even the right to "the pursuit of happiness" that Jefferson substituted, in the Declaration, for Locke's right to "property" has a clear basis in Locke's more theoretical writing, the *Essay Concerning Human Understanding*. There Locke uses the phrase "pursuit of happiness" to cover the great diversity of objects different men consider essential to their happiness and pursue accordingly. See *Essay*, II.21.51–59. Like Hobbes before him, Locke rejects the ancient idea of a *summum bonum*—i.e., a single complete good or happiness for men as men, a supreme good by nature. Both are much more realistic and permissive in allowing these divergences among the human passions than were either the ancient Socratics or the ancient materialists like Epicurus. *Cf.* Hobbes, *Leviathan*, ch. 11.

5 See Tocqueville, *Democracy in America*, for the two well-known chapters on the omnipotence and tyranny of the majority in vol. I, and the two less-known but equally important chapters in vol. II (book 4, chs. 2, 6) on the kind of concentration of power and ultimate despotism democracies have to fear. In the introductory chapter of *On Liberty* (New York: Crofts Classics, 1947), p. 4. Mill prepares the way for his own principle of liberty by referring explicitly to the fearful "tyranny of the majority." Back in 1835 and 1840, he had written lengthy reviews of the Tocqueville volumes as they appeared. These can be found in his *Essays on*

Politics and Culture, edited by Gertrude Himmelfarb (New York: Doubleday Anchor, 1963), chs. V and VI.

6   *On Liberty*, p. 10.

7   Ibid., p. 9. Mill actually calls it a "very simple principle."

8   Ibid., p. 83: "The existing generation is master both of the training and the entire circumstances of the generation to come. . . ." For the other qualifications of this "very simple principle," see pp. 75 and 82 in ch. 4.

9   In that work, see ch. 2, "What Utilitarianism Is." Mill thought this qualitative understanding of pleasure a great improvement over the sheerly quantitative view of it in Bentham and others: it gives his ethics a distinctly Aristotelian cast, with its repeated references to higher faculties, virtue, nobility, worth, etc. These can also be found in chs. 3 and 4 of *On Liberty*, but are somewhat overshadowed there by the stress on individuality and liberty. See pp. 59-62 in the former and pp. 76-79 in the latter. He speaks of "perfecting and beautifying" man himself, of "the most passionate love of virtue," of making human beings "a noble and beautiful object of contemplation," etc. These common and higher goals to which individuals are expected to make their own way, and which ultimately justify the regime of liberty itself, are either drastically underplayed or completely ignored by libertarians today. They accept his fear—majority domination—and the way he proposes to offset it, which is the principle of liberty. But they reject the end this principle is intended to reach, which is human perfection, understood in utilitarian terms. Far from being an admirer of the vulgar uses of liberty, Mill despised them; the same cannot be said for those who still invoke his name. Something like Mill's view of liberal democracy is presumed in the very first paragraph of Thomas Emerson's *The System of Freedom of Expression*.

10 *On Liberty*, p. 13. Ten years before, Marx and Engels had already ended the *Manifesto* with this warning: "The Communists disdain to conceal their views and aims. They openly declare that their ends can be attained only by the forcible overthrow of all existing social conditions. Let the ruling classes tremble at a Communist revolution." Evidently Mill gave little attention to this kind of anti-liberal counterrevolution and the ideological hostilities it portended. For his faith in the rational improvement of mankind knew almost no bounds. In *On Liberty* he says: "As mankind improve, the number of doctrines which are no longer disputed or doubted will be constantly on the increase: and the well-being of mankind may almost be measured by the number and gravity of the truths which have reached the point of being uncontested" (p. 43). Or from *Utilitarianism*: "Yet no one whose opinion deserves a moment's consideration can doubt that most of the great positive evils of the world are themselves removable, and will, if human affairs continue to improve, be in the end reduced within narrow limits" (in the Everyman's Library of that and other essays, London: J.M. Dent, 1925), ch. 2, p. 14.

11 In the first note on the first page of ch. 2. As we shall soon see, Mill did not always hold this view, and, in fact, nineteen years earlier, had held opposite and deeper views.

12 Ibid., p. 17.

13 Ibid., last few pages of ch. 2.

14 Mill, *Essays on Politics and Culture*, p. 135.

15 Ibid., pp. 136-37.

16 Ibid., pp. 137-38. My emphasis.

17 Ibid., p. 139.

18 In his dissent in *Lochner v. New York* (198 U.S. 45, at 75-76).

19 Blackstone, Introduction, at 69.

20 Martin Shapiro, *Freedom of Speech: The Supreme Court and Judicial Review* (Englewood Cliffs, N.J.: Prentice-Hall, Spectrum Books, 1966), p. 93. The next, briefer quotation is to be found on p. 121. A similar view about our relation to the framers of the First Amendment is expressed in the very last line of Levy's *Legacy:* "That they were Blackstonians does not mean that we cannot be Brandeisians."

21 This theme is developed in Faulkner, pp. 196-99. It also forms the basis of Lord Bryce's distinction between modern written constitutions and flexible older ones like Great Britain's. As he says in *Studies in History and Jurisprudence*, "Even forty years ago it was the Flexibility of the historical British Constitution that was its glory in the eyes of the admirers of the British system, its Rigidity that was the glory of the American Constitution in the eyes of fervent democrats" (New York: Oxford University Press, 1901), p. 204. This connection between a fixed constitution and the guarantee of democracy is often obscured by judicial activists. They claim to speak in behalf of the people, but their activist opinions transform the original Constitution away from what the people originally agreed upon (in 1789) and precedent continued—and not only without consulting the people but often in ways the people manifestly detest.

22 Tocqueville had this to say about the accepted rule of precedent in American jurisprudence: "The English and the Americans have retained the law of precedents; that is to say, they continue to found their legal opinions and the decisions of their courts upon the opinions and decisions of their predecessors. In the mind of an English or American lawyer, a taste and reverence for what is old is almost always united with a love of regular and lawful proceedings" (*Democracy in America*, vol. 1, pp. 286-87). The principle of judicial review is essentially founded on this very conservative proclivity of lawyers and judges, but their "taste and reverence for what is old" was changed by the new historical and scientific ideas, favoring adaption and change, that came to dominate Western thought by the end of the nineteenth century. These ideas gradually replaced the thought of the founding fathers as the first principle of American jurisprudence—witness the innovations

of Holmes and Brandeis. Thus began that judicial activism now so widely rampant in the country as to render any law challengeable, and precedent—even clear and long-lasting precedent—almost an assured basis for losing cases. Lawyers and judges began to look forward to the renown that came, not from preserving the old, but from shattering the old and introducing the new. And the way was open to the covert reading of partisan bias, via supposedly impartial judicial review, into the Constitution itself.

23 Ever since Holmes and Brandeis, the Court has in fact fallen prey to just such dissensions and not merely to the natural differences of interpretative opinion that might always exist. Ideology in its various forms was bound to inject itself once a good part of the Court abandoned the idea of being bound by the objectively discoverable meaning of the founders and framers. *Their* policy preferences, and hence *their* philosophies or ideologies, came in to replace the philosophy that inspired the Constitution originally.

5 *The Dangers of Anti-Democratic Conspiracy*

1 Sir James Stephen, *History of the Criminal Law of England* (London: Macmillan, 1883), vol. 2, p. 298.

2 Ibid., p. 377. In Blackstone's classification, treasonable libel and seditious libel are different crimes, with the former obviously more serious. Elsewhere in his *Commentaries* he describes other crimes involving the use of words and writings against the government, and these go much beyond seditious libel, which he understands as involving the defamation of subordinate government officials. These crimes come under various headings: treason, felonies against the king's prerogative, praemunire (i.e., derogations of legitimate political authority in favor of some foreign source of authority), and contempts: see vol. IV at 79-80, 98, 117, 123-26.

3 Stephen., pp. 377-78.

4 *Dennis* at 572.

5 Ibid. at 574. Jackson is quoting from a standard work on criminal law by Miller. A conspiracy, in criminal law, is a combination of two or more people to do some unlawful thing, either as an end or a means to an end.

6 Ibid. at 575.

7 Ibid. at 566-70, 577. Justice Jackson also had a long analysis of the nature of the American Communist Party in *American Communications Association v. Douds*, 390 U.S. 382 (1950). At the beginning of Section II he remarks, caustically: "I cannot believe that Congress has less power to protect a labor union from Communist Party domination than it has from employer domination."

8 Ibid. at 574.

9   Robert H. Jackson, *The Supreme Court in the American System of Government* (Cambridge, Mass.: Harvard University Press, 1955), p. 4.
10   Tocqueville, vol. I, p. 200. Compare our situation in the twentieth century with his observation, from 1832, that in America there are no political conspiracies! See p. 203, top and bottom, and Berns, pp. 169-71.
11   Berns, pp. 174-78.
12   Ibid., pp. 83-84, 109-10.
13   See Chapter 4, note 1, *supra*.
14   Padover's *Jefferson*, p. 384. It is also true that this supreme qualification of popular sovereignty was not always made explicit, or even remembered. But, in logic, a believer in the principles of the Declaration of Independence must be a liberal—a believer in the rights of man—even before he is a democrat: he cannot be both equally, and certainly cannot reverse the priorities, and be a democrat first, a liberal second. This is because, in the Declaration, individuals are in possession of inalienable rights before they join together to form a people and a government. Locke's view of this is in the *Second Treatise*, ch. VIII, "Of the Beginning of Political Societies," sects. 109-112. In Query XVII of Jefferson's *Notes on Virginia* we find this statement: "This is a summary view of that religious slavery under which a people have been willing to remain, who have lavished their lives and fortunes for the establishment of their civil freedom." See Padover, pp. 675, 285, 1048.

6 *The Imprudence of the "Clear and Present Danger" Rule*

1   This attempt to combine in one society would-be oppressors with their intended victims calls to mind Locke's great line: "Who would not think it an admirable peace betwixt the mighty and the mean when the lamb without resistance yielded his throat to be torn by the imperious wolf?" (*Second Treatise*, sect. 227).
2   See Chapter 2, note 16.
3   Ibid.
4   From the majority opinion in *Gitlow v. New York* (268 U.S. 652).

7 *Liberty without Morality?*

1   Tocqueville, vol. II, bk. 3, ch. 11, p. 215.
2   Jefferson, pp. 1056, 286.
3   Ibid., pp. 1097, 1098.
4   In *American Historical Documents* (Harvard Classics no. 43, 1910), p. 260, paragraph 16.

5   Montesquieu, *Spirit of the Laws*, bk. 3, ch. 3.

6   *American Historical Documents*, p. 260.

7   John Marshall, *Life of George Washington* (Philadelphia: C.P. Wayne, 1804), p. 877.

8   *A Book Named "John Cleland's Memoirs of a Woman of Pleasure" v. Massachusetts*, 383 U.S. 413, 431.

9   In his *Kingsley International Pictures Corporation v. Regents of the State of New York*, 360 U.S. 684, concurrence at 698 (1959). Douglas's earlier conformity to constitutional tradition is shown in *Berman v. Parker* (1954) and in *Dennis v. United States* (1951), where he states that "the teaching of methods of terror and other seditious conduct should be beyond the pale along with obscenity and immorality." See his dissent at 581. Chief Justice Hughes's statement in *Near v. Minnesota* is at 716.

10 Blackstone, vol. IV, at 150–53.

11 See Morris L. Ernst and Alan U. Schwartz, *Censorship: The Search for the Obscene* (New York: Macmillan, 1964), pp. 12–13, 15, 18.

12 Blackstone, vol. IV, p. 162.

13 In *Brown v. Maryland*, 12 Wheat. 419, as pertaining to the state power to provide for the public health and safety, in this case by directing the removal of gunpowder.

14 *Stone v. Mississippi*, 101 U.S. 814, quoted in Corwin, *op.cit.*, p. 351.

15 *C. B. and Q. Ry. Co. v. Illinois*, 200 U.S. 561, quoted in Pritchett, p.567.

16 *West Coast Hotel Co. v. Parrish*, 300 U.S. 379, quoted in Noel T. Dowling and Gerald Gunther, *Cases and Materials in Constitutional Law* (Brooklyn, N.Y.: Foundation Press, 1965), 7th edition, p. 878.

17 *Berman v. Parker*, 348 U.S. 26, quoted in Pritchett, *op.cit.*, p. 569.

18 *Lochner v. New York*, 198 U.S. 45.

19 Quoted in Noel T. Dowling, *Cases and Materials in Constitutional Law* (Brooklyn, N.Y.: Foundation Press, 1965), 5th edition, p. 345.

20 Ernst and Schwartz, p. 12.

21 Ibid., pp. 35, 44–47. The case was *United States v. Rosen* (1896).

22 *Roth v. United States*, 354 U.S. 476.

23 Ernst and Schwartz, p. 13.

8 *The Sexual Revolution*

1   D. H. Lawrence, *Sex, Literature and Censorship* (New York: Viking Compass, 1973), p. 69.

2   Tocqueville, vol. 2, bk. 3, chs. 8–12.

3   Eberhard and Phyllis Kronhausen, *Pornography and the Law* (New York: Ballantine Books, 1959), p. 283.

4   Ibid., p. 283.

5   Ibid., pp. 273-74, 276. Justice Douglas makes the same point in his *Fanny Hill* concurrence: see p. 129 below.

6   Ibid., p. 268.

7   Ibid., pp. 282-89.

8   In Huxley, chs. 13, 3.

9   Kronhausen, p. 249.

10 Ibid., pp. 259-60, 28.

11 Ibid., pp. 286, 265.

12 This point is denied in Harry Clor's *Obscenity and Public Morality* (University of Chicago, 1969), p. 238. Clor counts only eight sensual passages, amounting to less than a tenth of the novel, and claims that "When physical acts are presented, they are always presented in their human context; their supra-biological meanings are never lost or depreciated." From the standpoint of political society, however, that part of the "supra-biological" involving marriage is *never* introduced—or, rather, is introduced only to be adulterously flouted. Moreover, even the lawyer defending Lawrence's book knew he was unable to say, as Judge Woolsey could say of James Joyce's *Ulysses*, that it was "emetic, not aphrodisiac."

    To be sure, Lawrence put a lot in his novel besides the sex. But sex was its theme, and the presentation of the theme involved the specific description of sexual experience. The "erotic passages" took much more of the book than those in *Ulysses*. Indeed, if impact as well as extent was considered, it was the nonsexual passages that might be deemed isolated. Nor could Lawrence's descriptions be said to make sex unattractive. What Mellors and Connie were up to sounded pretty good. Certainly, not emetic and to most people, probably aphrodisiac.

    See Charles Rembar, *The End of Obscenity* (New York: Bantam Books, 1969), p. 22, and also pp. 49, 94, 219.

13 Mill, *Utilitarianism*, ch. 2.

14 Mill, *On Liberty*, p. 61.

15 Ibid., p. 56.

16 Ibid., p. 76, also pp. 59-63.

17 Ibid., p. 78.

18 Ibid., p. 15.

19 Ibid., p. 55.

20 Ibid., p. 82.

21 Ibid., p. 107.

22 Gertrude Himmelfarb, *On Liberty and Liberalism* (New York: Knopf, 1974), p. 153 for both passages.

23 Ibid., p. 311.

9 *Extremism on the Court*

1 Rembar, p. 50, and also pp. 308, 333.
2 Ibid., p. 51; pp. 18, 50, 453, 465.
3 Ibid., pp. 484-86.
4 Ibid., p. 17, and also pp. 219, 263.
5 *Winters v. New York*, 333 U.S. 507 (1948).
6 Rembar, pp. 167, 464.
7 Ibid., pp. 4, 301-303, 437-39, 501-502.
8 Ibid., pp. 49, 128, 184; 175, 184, 186; 245, 482.
9 Ibid., pp. 429, 460, 450; 386-87.
10 *Memoirs* at 438.
11 Ibid., at 339.
12 Mill, *On Liberty*, p. 62.
13 *Memoirs*, at 428.
14 *Ginzburg v. United States*, at 489. The same dissent by Douglas also applies to *Mishkin v. New York*, decided at the same time.
15 Ibid. at 491.
16 Ibid. at 489.
17 In *Roth v. United States* at 514.
18 See Thomas Hobbes, *Leviathan*, ch. 13, on the state of nature as a state of war.

10 *Judicial Progress and Regress in 1973*

1 Justice Brennan, speaking for the Court majority in *Roth* at 193-95.
2 *Miller* at 25.
3 Ibid. at 27.
4 Ibid. at 35.
5 See pp. 99-107, *supra*.
6 This unfortunate subjectivistic language feeds into Justice Douglas's claim that obscenity is nothing but a matter of taste—offensive to some but not to others—and comes under the First Amendment's protection of "offensive ideas." See his views in *Miller* and *Paris* at 44-6 and 71-2 respectively.
7 *Paris* at 63.
8 See Clor, pp. 224-27.
9 This quotation from *Stanley v. Georgia* (1969) is also important to Justice Brennan's dissent, as we shall soon see.
10 The effort to link opposition to obscenity with religion is of course widespread: see Brennan's *Paris* dissent, at 109, and the view of the Kronhausens's above, pp. 112-116.

11 While obscenity implicitly contains and suggests "ideas" of the desirable and undesirable, right and wrong, it works directly on the passions and only indirectly on the intellect. Justice Douglas goes too far in likening it to tracts and treatises debating matters of public interest. See the passages at 44-46 and 71-72, and also Clor, pp. 96-102.

12 See pp. 99-120.

13 Brennan's dissent in *Paris* (at 97-99) contains this and other similar but less plausible criticisms of the imprecision of the test set forth in *Miller*.

14 Justice Douglas's main dissent appears in *Miller*, Justice Brennan's in *Paris*.

15 *Paris*, at 78, 112, 114.

16 Ibid., at 109.

17 Clor, pp. 95-102; Leonard W. Levy, pp. 266-67. In *Paris*, Douglas cites historical studies by "our leading colonial expert, Julius Goebel," published in 1946 and 1937, but seems unaware of Levy's book, published in 1960. Levy furnishes the historical origin, in the generation of the founders, for the view of obscenity (as unprotected by the First Amendment) that the Court has never abandoned.

18 These variations, changes and disagreements are cited by Burger in his majority opinion and in the dissent of Douglas and Brennan as well; at 80, 22, 37-9.

19 See the way Clor elaborates a definition, ch. 6.

11 *Regulating Obscenity: Why and How*

1 In *Burstyn v. Wilson*, 343 U.S. 495 (1952), and *Times Film Corp. v. City of Chicago*, 365 U.S. 43 (1961).

2 In *Burstyn*, *Kingsley* (1959), and *Freedman v. Maryland* (1965). The 1973 cases were *Paris Adult Theater* and *Miller*.

3 In *Mutual Film Corp. v. Ohio Industrial Commission*, 236 U.S. 230 (1952).

4 In *Burstyn*, and even four years earlier in *United States v. Paramount Pictures*, 334 U.S. 131 (1948).

5 Blackstone, vol. 4, p. 168.

6 Quoted in *Encyclopaedia Britannica*, 13th edition, vol. 26, under "Theater (Law)," p. 738 (left).

7 *Broadcasting and Government Regulation in a Free Society*, published by the Center for the Study of Democratic Institutions (New York: Fund for the Republic, 1959), pp. 5, 15, 20, 23.

8 Mary Lu Carnevale, "FCC Might Rescind Indecency Ruling After Court Throws Out 24-Hour Ban," *Wall Street Journal*, May 20, 1991.

9 Edmund L. Andrews, "Government Seeks to Extend Ban on Broadcast of Offensive Shows," *New York Times*, July 13, 1990.

10 Carnevale.

11 Paul M. Barrett, "High Court Lets Stand Reversal of FCC Ban on 'Indecent' Material," *Wall Street Journal*, March 3, 1992.

12 Ibid., p. 21.

13 Ibid., pp. 21, 29, where the problem of Congressional intent remains unresolved—in which case Congress should speak again on the matter. The station licensee, of course (as distinguished from the FCC), "is expected to censor."

14 *Areopagitica and Other Prose Works* (London: Dutton Everyman edition, 1950), pp. 37-8.

15 Blackstone, vol. IV, p. 152.

16 Quoted at the beginning of *Kingsley* (at 685-86).

17 Ibid. at 689.

18 Milton, *op.cit.*, pp. 36, 13. Milton condemns Plato's *Laws* for its political control over poetry and learning, yet also praises its "laws of virtuous education, religious and civil nurture." (p. 18).

19 *On Liberty*, p. 83.

20 The reader should consult Macaulay's *History of England* (London: J. M. Dent & Sons, Ltd., Everyman edition, 1910), vol. 3, pp. 374-77 (also 181-92 and 328) for his description of how the freest press in Europe became the "most prudish" through its very freedom—through "the opinion of the great body of educated English men, before whom good and evil were set, and who were left free to make their choice." This moral improvement occurred between 1695 and 1855, when Macaulay wrote. It continued into the twentieth century, when, somehow, freedom ceased being a sufficient guarantee of responsibility. Today, most of the intellectuals would ridicule Macaulay's assumption that a moral or prudish press is greatly preferable to an immoral press, or that there are essential connections between liberty and morality.

12 *The Meaning of the First Amendment*

1 *The Complete Jefferson*, pp. 518-519, dated 1802.

2 *Engel v. Vitale*, 370 U.S. 421, 445.

3 In *Schempp*, 374 U.S. 303, 304, Justice Brennan tries to save such ceremonies through a similar misinterpretation of their obvious meaning.

4 *Engel* at 437.

5 *Zorach v. Clausen*, 343 U.S. 306, (1952).

6 *Everson v. Board of Education*, 330 U.S. 1.

7 Jefferson, pp. 1097-98.

8 Ibid., p. 1076. Compare the improbable inference (that Jefferson was in fact calling for no use of the Bible) drawn by Levy in *Jefferson and Civil Liberties* (New York: Quadrangle, New York Times Book Co., 1963), p. 9.

9   Ibid., pp. 1104, 1112.

10   Ibid., pp. 957-58. Madison was one of the Visitors for whom Jefferson spoke here: see the *Writings of Thomas Jefferson* (Washington, D.C.: 1903), vol. 19, p. 408.

11   Ibid., pp. 1110, 958.

12   Ibid., p. 677 (Query XVIII of the Notes on Virginia, 1782).

13   Leonard Levy, "School Prayers and the Founding Fathers," in *Commentary*, Sept. 1962, pp. 228-29; Lynford Lardner, "How Far Does the Constitution Separate Church and State," in *American Political Science Review*, March 1951, pp. 112-15.Compare the overview supplied by Henry Abraham in *Freedom and the Court* (New York: Oxford University Press, 1967), pp. 175-76.

14   The *Oxford English Dictionary* traces the word to the second half of the sixteenth century, and the *Encyclopaedia Britannica* (13th edition, 1926) places its first full official use in the England of 1604.

15   In the section specifically devoted to religion in his *Notes on Virginia* (Query XVII), Jefferson uses the word in the same way: "But every State, says an inquisitor, has established some religion. No two, say I, have established the same. . . ."

     Leonard Levy's *The Establishment Clause* (New York: Macmillan, 1986) is an excellent test of this intepretation. Levy tries to prove that "an establishment of religion" covered non-preferential aid to all religions as well as aid to a particular religion. He does this by indentifying multiple establishments like Protestantism or Christianity with "all religions" on the grounds that there were few Catholics in Protestant states and few non-Christians in Christian states. Hence, "Congress shall make no law respecting an establishment of religion" would ban laws giving aid to all religions. But it is not the number of people actually excluded that makes multiple establishments in the preferential sense: it is the principle they employ, which singles out some religion (however multiple) by contrast to others. Otherwise, why speak of Protestantism or Christianity? Moreover, they did have an actual exclusionary effect, as Levy himself points out in the second sentence of his very first chapter. Thus, establishment always meant religious preference, as it did in the passage from Jefferson quoted above, and in everything Madison said throughout the House's consideration of this amendment. In Levy, see especially pp. 4, 9, 61-62, 71-74, 77-779, 82.

16   See the background Corwin provides in Congress's official commentary on the Constitution (1952), pp. 758-59. The legislative details supplied below are taken from Michael J. Malbin's *Religion and Politics: The Intention of the Authors of the First Amendment* (Washington, D.C.: American Enterprise Institute, 1978), pp. 1-17.

17   Justice Brennan adverts to this point in *Schempp* at 1588-89. It is discussed by Mark DeWolfe Howe in *The Garden in the Wilderness* (Chicago: University of Chicago Press, 1967), pp. 19-23. Citing the work of Joseph Snee and Wilbur Katz, Howe

says: "A respectable school of thought asserts that the First Amendment's prohibition against the enactment of laws 'respecting an establishment of religion' was intended to assure that existing religious establishments would not be interfered with by Congress." Howe finds this interpretation "grammatically persuasive" but "historically unconvincing." Yet his own "related but less radical view"—that the phrase was meant to give state religious arrangements protection in the federal courts— itself assumes, as a matter of course, that the Amendment kept Congress from interfering with these arrangements. More recently, Malbin's study of the First Amendment's use of "respecting" finds that history and grammar agree in compelling the conclusion reached here. Malbin also allows (without saying why) that "respecting" meant "tending toward," as liberal interpreters have claimed—a concession not repeated in his most recent account: see *Religion, Liberty and Law in the American Founding* (Washington, D.C.: American Enterprise Institute, 1981), p. 12.

18 Patrick Henry had proposed a bill in the Virginia legislature to assist Christian religion financially. For a moment it was changed to a bill for the support of *all* religions, and then to one "establishing a provision for teachers of the Christian religion." This elicited Madison's "Memorial and Remonstrance Against Religious Assessments" (1784), espousing religious liberty and the separation of church and state on the basis of natural right. Madison attacked establishments, with their supporting assessments, as violating the free exercise of religion. See Irving Brant, *James Madison, the Nationalist* (Indianapolis: Bobbs, Merrill and Co., 1948), pp. 343-48. A few years later (1786) Jefferson's Bill for Establishing Religious Freedom, introduced as early as 1779, was finally adopted, with some changes. Madison's text can be found in Meyers, pp. 7-16, and Jefferson's in Padover, p. 946.

19 See Malbin, *Religion and Politics*, pp. 6-9.

20 Ibid., pp. 9-10. This interpretation of Madison's motivation here is shared by Anson Phelps Stokes, *Church and State in the United States* (New York: Harper and Bros., 1950), I, p. 541, and accepted by Chief Justice Warren in *McGowan*, at 440.

21 Ibid., p. 13.

22 Malbin compares the views of Mason, Madison, and Jefferson: Malbin, pp. 21, 22, 27-28. He also places them against the background of Locke's philosophy (pp. 29-34). Such analyses can be most instructive, as they are here, but they run the risk (see pp. 36, 37) of substituting the thought of one or more of these men for the words and logic of the Constitution.

23 Jefferson, like Locke, seems to have used the words "church" and "religious society" interchangeably: see Padover, pp. 942, 518. The use of the phrase "church and state," and the idea of their separation (but with the superiority of the state at crucial points of conflict) comes directly from Locke's *Letter on Toleration*, pp. 28,

58. In his *Autobiography*, Jefferson speaks of Virginia's intending, through his bill for religious liberty, to "comprehend, within the mantle of its protection, the Jew and the Gentile, the Christian and Mohometan, the Hindoo, and the Infidel of every denomination" (p. 1147). Compare Locke, pp. 55, 56. See also ch. 14 below.

24   Article VI, sect. 3. The usual justification for this ban was not that it protected unbelievers but that it protected the variety of believers from being favored or disfavored by a particular religious test. Just before this provision is the requirement that all national and state officers "shall be bound by Oath or Affirmation to support this Constitution," and in the case of the president an oath or affirmation is actually spelled out (Article I, sect. 1, end). God is not mentioned in the president's oath, which, in a way, sets the model for the other oath. Nevertheless, oaths and affirmations were generally understood to be religious acts, an oath being a swearing by, to or in the presence of God, and an affirmation being the legal equivalent of an oath, allowed to those (like Quakers) who had *religious* scruples against oaths. It would ordinarily happen, therefore, that oaths or affirmations, publicly given, would in some way testify to God's existence, even though such testimony is not strictly required by the president's oath or the other oaths. Thus pledging by affirmation rather than by oath was not introduced into the Constitution to accommodate the non-believer. See Black's and Bouvier's legal dictionaries and the *Oxford Universal Dictionary*; also Joseph Story, *Commentaries on the U.S. Constitution* (Boston: Little, Brown, 1833), section 969.

25   Again the *locus classicus* for the combination of both appeals is Locke's *Letter on Toleration*, which makes religion a matter of personal conscience or choice from among a large number of religions, none known to be true, while preserving great dignity and even supervening importance for this choice, pp. 20, 30-32, 49.

26   Justice Rutledge's historical inquiry in *Everson* makes this error, which is rendered more egregious by attributing to Jefferson's "wall" an absoluteness he hardly observed in his educational views and practice. See Justice Brennan's text and note in *Schempp*, pp. 865-866, and Howe, "The Constitutional Question," in *Religion and Free Society* (New York: Fund for the Republic, 1958), pp. 50-51. While Madison seems to have shared most if not all of Jefferson's educational opinions, it is nonetheless true that in his actions as president he observed something approaching an absolute "wall of separation" on the national level. But we do not know precisely why he opposed chaplains in the armed services, tax exemptions to "Houses of Worship," and even presidential proclamations of days of Thanksgiving (though on this he acceded to popular demand). It might well be that Madison was guided in these matters more by Locke's view of separation and his own Memorial and Remonstrance—both to him embodying the greatest wisdom—than by the less demanding constitutional standards of the First Amendment, compare Berns, p. 59.

27   That the First Amendment does not incorporate the philosophy of Madison's
     Memorial and Remonstrance can also be deduced from its having two religious
     parts, not one. The adding together of a non-establishment and a free exercise
     part implies that neither one by itself would do what the framers intended. Non-
     establishment would not guarantee free exercise. But in Madison's Memorial free
     exercise does guarantee non-establishment: it detracts from one's freedom of re-
     ligion to be compelled to support one's own freely chosen religion, let alone the
     religion the state establishes. For Madison, in short, there is one central prin-
     ciple of religious liberty and separation of church and state from which all con-
     clusions flow. In his amendment proposals, and in his arguments in Congress,
     Madison forebore using the logic of his own Memorial, even when he pressed for
     limits on the states that were rejected. In other words, arguing in the Virginia
     legislature of 1783-86 and the United States Congress of 1789-90 were for him
     different things.

28   These innovations involve a paradox stated well by Berns: ". . . it is a peculiar First
     Amendment that subordinates religious belief to the point where it may not be
     encouraged by law, and, at the same time, exalts religious belief—and even 'reli-
     gious' belief—to a point where the believer need not obey law. Nothing in the
     original intention, and nothing in the requirements of sound public policy, justifies
     this" (p. 78).

29   In his commentary on the religious parts of the First Amendment, Joseph Story
     reads the First Amendment simply as preventing Congress from establishing any
     religion, and reduces the second to guaranteeing "the freedom of religious opin-
     ion and worship," not of religious practice generally. He supposes the promulga-
     tion of certain great doctrines of religion (having to do with God, our freedom
     and responsibility to him, a future state of rewards and punishments, the cultiva-
     tion of virtues) practically essential to any civilized society. Society and govern-
     ment therefore have an interest in strengthening religion. Of course, those who
     "believe in the truth of Christianity, as a divine revelation," also believe that gov-
     ernment must encourage it "among all the citizens and subjects." This latter was
     "the general, if not the universal, sentiment in America" when the First Amend-
     ment was passed. Thus, the First Amendment's ban on establishment was con-
     sidered consistent with encouraging religion generally and Christianity in par-
     ticular. Yet Story concludes his treatment of both religious parts (along with the
     ban on religious tests) by saying: "Thus, the whole power over the subject of re-
     ligion is left exclusively to the state governments, to be acted upon according to
     their own sense of justice, and the state constitutions; and the Catholic and the
     Protestant, the Calvinist and the Arminian, the Jew and the Infidel, may sit down
     at the common table of the national councils, without any inquisition into their

faith, or mode of worship." (*Commentaries*, sections 985-92). When Story speaks of "the whole power over the subject of religion" as belonging to the states alone, he must mean the power to compel, since he had already granted a compatibility between the power to encourage (even on the national level) and the First Amendment. We should also note the delicacy with which Story distinguishes between the kind of religion society generally requires and the particularities of Christianity, between what believers in Christian revelation demand and what would satisfy others.

13 *American Democracy's Need for Religion*

1　*Zorach v. Clauson,* 343 U.S. 306.
2　"Religion in America takes no direct part in the government of society, but it must be regarded as the first of their political institutions; for if it does not impart a taste for freedom, it facilitates the use of it.... I am certain that they hold it to be indispensable to the maintenance of republican institutions" (*Democracy in America,* I, 316).
3　The changes (additions and deletions) are noted by Carl Becker in *The Declaration of Independence* (New York: Vintage, 1958), pp. 183-84.
4　Locke, *Letter,* pp. 30-33, 37, 50-51; Padover, *Jefferson,* pp. 667, 675, 1036-37, 1058-59; Meyers, *Madison,* sects. 7, 8 of the Memorial, pp. 12, 13.
5　Jefferson, pp. 675-76, 1104.
6　"The Great Governor of the World," *American Historical Documents* (New York: P.F. Collier and Son, Harvard Classics (1910), vol. 43, p. 177.
7　While both men favored inculcating a "political creed" at the University of Virginia through well-chosen books and professors, they did not mean a set of trans-rational beliefs like those of revealed religion but of rational beliefs (like those in the Declaration) based on philosophy. See Jefferson's letter of Feb. 1, 1825, and Madison's response (described in Meyers, pp. 442-46). The point is discussed in Berns, p. 83.
8　*American Historical Documents,* p. 260. Washington took a position somewhere between Jefferson and Edmund Burke, who tried to offset the effects of all-out Enlightenment by defending not only the established Church of England but prejudice as such. See Burke's *Reflections on the Revolution in France* (New York: Liberal Arts Press, 1955), pp. 97-112. He said, "Prejudice renders a man's virtue his habit.... Through just prejudice, his duty becomes a part of his nature." (p. 99)
9　*Democracy in America,* I, 318.
10　Ibid., I, 315; II, 27, 135, 154-56.

11   Ibid., I, 328-30; also I, 54-55; II, 323.

12   *The Political Thought of Abraham Lincoln*, edited by Richard N. Current (Indianapolis: American Heritage paperback, 1967), pp. 16-17.

13.   Ibid., p. 12. In some ways this resembles Edmund Burke's famous description of the social contract as a "partnership not only between those who are living, but between those who are living, those who are dead, and those who are to be born." (*op.cit.*, p. 110). To the literal-minded Tom Paine this passage spoke nonsense, since a partnership between living and two sets of non-existent beings—ancestor and posterity—is physically impossible. Lincoln would not have fared better with Paine.

14   Ibid., pp. 15, 19.

15   Lincoln condemned John Brown's effort to free the slaves by force in his Cooper Institute address of 1860: Ibid., pp. 153-56. He treats him as a dangerous religious fanatic in the only action his admiring biographer, Lord Charnwood, could not understand (New York: Pocket Books, 1948), p. 164. For Lincoln's view of the dangers inherent in Christian virtue generally, see Harry Jaffa, *Crisis of the House Divided* (New York: Doubleday, 1959), ch. 10, especially pp. 244, 270.

16   For a somewhat tendentious version of Jefferson's "secularism," see Leonard Levy, *Jefferson and Civil Liberties*, pp. 7-15.

17   Criticizing the philosophers of the French Revolution, Burke said: "In the groves of *their* academy, at the end of every vista, you see nothing but the gallows. Nothing is left which engages the affections on the part of the commonwealth. On the principles of this mechanic philosophy, our institutions can never be embodied, if I may use the expression, in persons so as to create in us love, veneration, admiration or attachment. But that sort of reason which banishes the affections is incapable of filling their place. These public affections, combined with manners, are required sometimes as supplements, sometimes as correctives, always as aids to law." p. 88.

14   The Case against "Incorporation"

1   Between 1884 and 1908, Justice John Marshall Harlan had already become a lonely but insistent advocate of total incorporation. See Henry Abraham and Barbara Perry, *Freedom and the Court* (New York: Oxford University Press, 1994), pp. 49-51.

2   In 1949 Charles Fairman published a lengthy refutation of Black's position, later to be confirmed by Raoul Berger, who stressed the importance of the Civil Rights Bill of 1866 for understanding the Fourteenth Amendment. See Charles Fairman and Stanley Morrison, *The Fourteenth Amendment and the Bill of Rights* (New York: Da Capo Press, 1970), pp. 85-221, and Berger, *Government by Judiciary* (Cambridge,

Mass.: Harvard University Press, 1977), ch. 8. For their opponents in this still-boiling controversy, see the summary by Abraham and Perry, pp. 32-34.

3   See Christopher Wolfe's careful discussion of the meaning of the Fourteenth Amendment in *The Rise of Modern Judicial Review* (Rowman and Littlefield, 1994), pp. 123-31

4   Abraham and Perry, pp. 46-47.

5   See James McClellan, "Hand's Writing on the Wall of Separation: The Significance of *Jaffree* in Future Cases on Religious Establishment" in *How Does the Constitution Protect Religious Freedom?*, Goldwin and Kaufmann, eds. (Washington, D.C.: American Enterprise Institute, 1988), pp. 43-69.

6   Massachusetts was the last state to surrender its establishment—in 1833. See Evarts B. Greene, *Religion and the State* (Ithaca, N.Y.: Great Seal Books, 1959), p. 94.

7   This is why the only part of the Fourteenth Amendment that could possibly incorporate the Bill of Rights is the "privileges or immunities" clause, the language of which actually fails to do so.

15 The Establishment Clause

1   On pp. 900-901.

2   According to Montesquieu, "the Romans were the most religious people in the world when it came to an oath—which always formed the nerve of their military discipline." See his *Considerations of the Causes of the Greatness of the Romans and Their Decline* (New York: Free Press, 1965), p. 27.

3   See also the treatment of conscientious objectors below. Madison had included a provision for such exemptions among his proposed amendments, but it was removed by Congress on the ground that it should remain discretionary with Congress rather than a matter of right.

4   The position taken here is like that of the Rev. Robert Drinan with respect to national aid, though on different grounds. Father Drinan claims that parochial schools function semi-publicly in the area of secular education and therefore have a right to public support. In addition, support for the public schools alone, with their orthodoxy of secularism, would constitute an establishment of religion that the First Amendment forbids. The first of these arguments seems too nebulous as the foundation for such a rights; the second assumes, incorrectly, that "secularism" is a "religion" within the intendent meaning of the amendment.

An essay by Murray Gordon in the same volume adopts *Everson*'s "wall of separation" as strictly possible and therefore denies the constitutionality of aid to parochial schools as either a right or an option of public policy. See the essays by Drinan and Gordon in *The Wall Between Church and State*, edited by Dallin M. Oaks (Chicago: University of Chicago Press, 1963).

5 *Walz v. Tax Commission of the City of New York*, 397 U.S. 664. The vote was 7 to 1.

6 This is also the conclusion of Paul G. Kauper in "The Constitutionality of Tax Exemptions for Religious Activities" in the volume edited by Oaks (see note 4 above).

7 On the views of Horace Mann, stressing civic education, broadly conceived, and Bible-reading as a nonsectarian instrument of moral education at the same time, see Corwin, p. 761; Donald E. Boles, *The Bible, Religion and the Public Schools* (New York: Collier Books, 1963), pp. 32-36, 153; Newton Edwards and Herman Richey, *The School in the American Social Order* (Boston: Houghton Mifflin, 1947), p. 346.

8 See pp. 87-93, 185-91, and 203-15, *supra*.

9 At pp. 891-92.

10 A problem with using the Lord's Prayer, for example, is its Biblical link to Christ, from whom it originated.

11 Representatives of several religions were asked to frame the prayer itself.

12 See pp. 179-85, *supra*.

13 What has disappeared from the schools is not only Bible readings, prayers, and civics courses, but a moral and political tone that gave public meaning to the subjects studied and the educational experience as a whole. With the slackening and disappearance of this tone, the schools have become training grounds in vague universalistic sentiment and blatant egoism rather than civic responsibility. A reminder of the great change from yesterday to today can still be seen in the famous McGuffey's Readers, republished with an excellent introduction by Henry Steele Commager.

14 They may, however, be specifically barred from receiving such assistance by other provisions in state constitutions.

16 *"Free Exercise" and "Religion" in the Modern Court*

1 In *Reynolds v. United States*, 98 U.S. 145 (1878), *Davis v. Beason*, 133 U.S. 333 (1890), and *Late Corporation of the Church of Jesus Christ of Latter-day Saints v. United States*, 136 U.S. 1 (1890).

2 *Davis v. Beason* at 342.

3 *Cantwell v. Connecticut*, 310 U.S. 296, 303.

4 Ibid. at 303-04

5 Ibid. at 308, 309.

6 Ibid. at 310.

7 Ibid.

8 *Minersville School District v. Gobitis*, 310 U.S. 586, 604.

9 *West Virginia Board of Education v. Barnette*, 319 U.S. 624, 642.

10 Ibid. at 625-26.

11 *Davis v. Beason* (1890) found that a Mormon falsified an oath abjuring bigamy and polygamy that was required of all voters: see Abraham, *loc.cit.*, p. 252. Pritchett summarizes some of the modern Court's findings on loyalty oaths, pp. 462-63.

12 *West Virginia*, etc., at 642.

13 *Torcaso v. Watkins*, 367 U.S. 488, 495.

14 Locke, *Letter*, p. 52; *Second Treatise*, sect. 4, 6.

15 Abraham, p. 247.

16 *Sherbert v. Verner*, 374 U.S. 398, 406.

17 Ibid. at 423.

18 *Wisconsin v. Yoder*, 406 U.S. 205.

19 Fortunately, in 1990, the Court took an important step toward reviving its earlier tradition. In *Employment Division, etc., of Oregon v. Smith*, 494 U.S. 827, Justice Scalia maintained for a majority of five that the free exercise clause did not entail making religious exceptions from valid criminal laws and did not require the Court to balance state interests against the free exercise claim to see whether the state interests are "compelling." But three members of the majority, while concurring in the result, still held to the need for a Court finding of compelling state interest to overcome a free exercise claim, joining in this with the three dissenters.

20 Quoted in *United States v. Seeger*, 380 U.S. 163, 165.

21 Ibid. at 166.

22 Ibid. at 165-66.

23 *Welsh v. United States*, 398 U.S. 333.

Index

David Lowenthal, a native of Brooklyn, New York, has taught political science at Boston College since 1966, where his teaching and writing have focused on the philosophy and problems of liberalism. From 2000 to 2002 he was the D'Alzon Professor of Political Science at Assumption College.

He taught previously at Harvard University, Wheaton College, and North Carolina State College. He holds undergraduate degrees from Brooklyn College and New York University and a Ph.D. from the New School for Social Research, where he studied under Leo Strauss.

Professor Lowenthal served on the National Council for the Humanities and is a past president of the New England Political Science Association. An editor of *Interpretation*, he has translated Montesquieu's *Considerations on the Causes of the Greatness of the Romans and their Decline* and is the author of *Shakespeare and the Good Life: Ethics and Politics in Dramatic Form*. He lives in Princeton, Massachusetts, with his wife and children.

This book was designed and set into type
by Mitchell S. Muncy,
with cover art by Stephen J. Ott,
and printed and bound
by Edwards Brothers, Inc.,
Ann Arbor, Michigan.

The text face is Adobe Caslon,
designed by Carol Twombly,
based on faces cut by William Caslon, London, in the 1730s,
and issued in digital form by Adobe Systems,
Mountain View, California, in 1989.

The index is by IndExpert,
Fort Worth, Texas.

The paper is acid-free and is of archival quality.

3